D1393909

The Illustrated
Book of
Pistols

WITHDRAWN
FROM STOCK

Frederick Wilkinson

The Illustrated Book of Pistols

Optimum Books

Acknowledgments

Colour

Bodleian Library, Oxford 15; Christies, London 43; Mary Evans Picture Library, London 35; Gunshots, London 19, 23, 26, 31, 55, 59, 66–7, 70, 71, 83, 95, 99, 107, 115, 118, 119, 122, 126, 127, 130, 131, 138, 143, 147, 155 bottom, 158, 159, 183, 186; Hamlyn Group Picture Library 18, 47, 51, 62–3, 87 top and bottom, 94, 102–3, 103, 111, 123, 134, 139, 146, 151, 154, 155 top, 171, 179; National Army Museum, London 167, 174–5, 187; W. Keith Neal 26–7, 91, 163; Ann Ronan Picture Library, Loughton 7, 79, 135.

Black and white

Christies, London 28 top and bottom; Crown Copyright 68 bottom, 86 bottom, 113, 116; Mary Evans Picture Library, London 49, 136; Glasgow Museum and Art Gallery 114; Gunshots, London 8, 10 top, 16, 20 top, 21, 24 centre and bottom, 30 top, 32, 33, 36 top, 41 top and bottom, 42, 44, 45, 48 top and bottom, 50, 52, 53, 56, 57 left and right, 58 top, centre and bottom, 61, 62, 65 left, 66, 68 top, 69, 70, 72, 73, 74, 75, 80 top and bottom, 81, 82, 84, 86 top, 88 left and right, 89 top and bottom, 90, 92, 93, 96, 97, 98, 100, 101 left and right, 104, 105 top, 108 top, 109, 120, 121 top and centre right, 124, 125 top left, bottom left and right, 128, 129 top and bottom, 133 top, 140, 141 top, centre and bottom, 142, 144–5, 145 top and bottom, 148 top and bottom, 149, 150, 152 top, centre and bottom, 153, 156 top and bottom, 157 top and bottom, 160 top, centre and bottom, 165, 166 top, centre and right, 168 top and bottom, 170 left, 173 top, bottom left and bottom right, 176 bottom, 177, 181 top and bottom, 182 bottom, 185 top, centre and bottom, 186 bottom, 188 top and bottom; Hamlyn Group Picture Library 30 centre and bottom, 37, 38 top, centre and bottom, 60 top and bottom, 64, 65 right, 77 top and bottom, 78, 85, 105 bottom, 108 bottom, 169, 170 right, 172 right; Library of Congress, Washington 180; Livrustkammeren, Stockholm 25; MacClancy Press, London 184, 189 top and bottom; Musée de l'Armée, Paris 29 top; W. Keith Neal 10 bottom, 13 right, 17, 20 bottom, 29 bottom, 162, 164; Palazzo Ducale, Venice 13 left; Radio Times Hulton Picture Library, London 24 top, 46, 137 bottom, 178; Ann Ronan Picture Library, Loughton 9, 112, 121 centre left and bottom, 132, 133 bottom, 161, 176 top; Western Americana Picture Library, Brentwood 137 top, 182 top; West Point Museum, Virginia 172 left; Fred Wilkinson, London 34; Winchester Gun Museum, Connecticut 36 bottom, 117 top and bottom.

Note: All the metric conversions used in this volume are the direct equivalents of the imperial units and, in the case of calibres, many vary slightly from conventional usage.

This edition published by Optimum Books in 1979
Second Impression 1981
© Copyright The Hamlyn Publishing Group Limited 1979
ISBN 0 600 37204 9

All rights reserved. No part of this publication may be reproduced, stored in a retrieval system, or transmitted, in any form or by any means, electronic, mechanical, photocopying, recording or otherwise, without the permission of The Hamlyn Publishing Group.

Printed in Spain

Contents

Introduction

The development of pistols created a fear of assassination among rulers and leaders. The fears were justified on many occasions, exemplified here by the killing in 1891 of Mr Beltchef, the Bulgarian Finance Minister, in Sofia.

Man, unfortunately, has always been an aggressive animal. In the beginning he had to fight against other animals in order to survive. Later, as men began to live in communities, much of their time and effort was spent in fighting their neighbours. The ancient empires of Egypt, Assyria, Ur, Athens and Rome were created by men who risked their lives in battle. Their weapons were simple and, with the exception of the javelin and arrow, committed them to hand-to-hand combat.

For centuries the military planners and designers sought weapons which would enable them to attack an enemy from a distance. The bow was developed and probably reached its peak in the sixteenth century when the English longbow could drive an arrow over 150 yards and still penetrate armour. The crossbow was even more powerful and had greater range and penetrative power, but it was slow to load and discharge. Although these long-range weapons had their place, most battles were still decided by hand-to-hand combat.

Military engineers designed and built great fortresses which could resist all the attacks of a besieging force. Behind their thick walls and cunningly placed towers, the defenders could usually fend off the enemy until either relief arrived or starvation and illness forced them to surrender.

In distant China a discovery, probably made around 1000 AD, was to change the whole situation. The product of this discovery was a coarse black powder, described by some as the powder of the devil, but usually referred to as gunpowder. Gunpowder was to change the whole system and style of both war and hunting. It was to place in the hands of men unskilled in the use of weapons the means of killing trained knights wearing the most expensive, best-quality armour. It gave the engineer the ability to strike an enemy from a great distance and to demolish the strongest fortification. Firearms were to enable technically advanced nations to impose their will on more backward lands, for small bodies of troops armed with firearms could defeat more numerous opponents armed only with simple hand weapons. The officers and cavalry of most of these armies were armed with a small, portable, hand-held firearm. Today the modern infantry officer and the crew of a tank or other armoured fighting vehicle still carry handguns.

The story of handguns is a fascinating one, tracing their development from a crude, iron barrel to a gleaming, stainless-steel piece of modern engineering. The story includes details of the men and women who carried them: some were brave and selfless people, and others were assassins and thugs – but no less fascinating for that.

In today's violent world most of the publicity that the handgun receives is bad, and the average person sees such weapons as instruments of death and injury; nor could anyone claim that

The pistol as a work of art in miniature.
Top German ball-butted wheellock pistol, the stock elaborately inlaid with horn.
Centre Similar pistol from the last quarter of the sixteenth century, with blued barrel and lockplate.
Bottom Fine priming powder was carried in this silver-mounted flask with spring-operated cut-off and inlaid pattern and caricature head.

they are not so used. However, to many thousands of ordinary people they are inoffensive instruments which allow their owners to test themselves and their equipment to the utmost, for competitive shooting is a growing and popular worldwide pastime.

The handgun has been produced in a far greater variety of shapes, sizes and designs than almost any other firearm. Some are no longer than two or three inches, a few even smaller types weigh only a few ounces, whilst there have been giants like the Montenegrin Gasser revolver which weighed four or five pounds. Most of the early handguns were single-shot, but later others were made to fire as many as 28 or 30 rounds before they needed reloading. Some, like those turned out in quantity in Birmingham and Liège in the latter part of the

nineteenth century, were cheap and rather nasty. Others, especially the wheellocks of the sixteenth century, were works of art in miniature, involving the efforts of many different craftsmen and artists. The duelling pistols produced in the late eighteenth and early nineteenth centuries were instruments of great accuracy and severe classic beauty. Their purpose may have been terrible and cold-blooded, but the weapons themselves still have an aesthetic appeal. The names of other weapons, like Colt, Luger and Mauser, have become household words and legends in their own rights.

Whether one sees them as deadly, horrible, murderous items or as fascinating works of art and mechanical ingenuity, handguns have a fascinating history full of excitement and colour. This book tells their story.

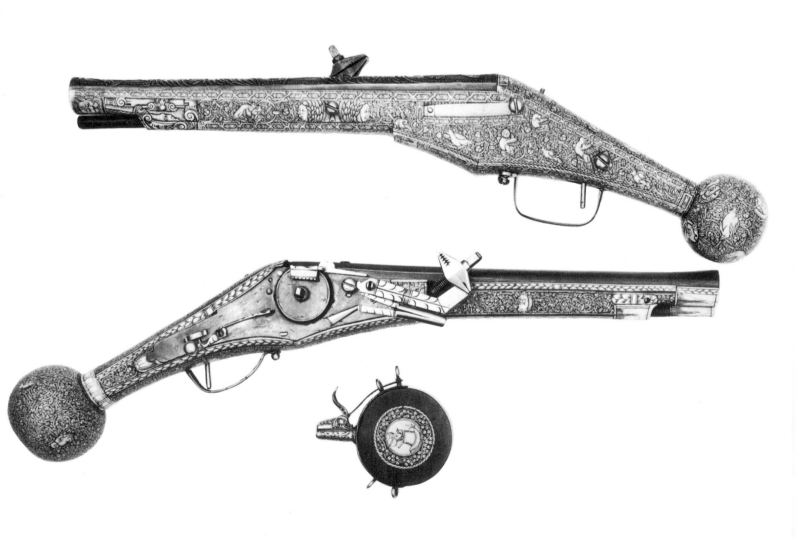

Gunpowder and Early Firearms

Tradition states that it was a monk who made the first gun in Europe. One day in his laboratory – he was a scientific monk – he was pounding away at a mixture of chemicals in a container. A spark ignited the mixture and the resulting explosion hurled from his hand the pestle with which he was hammering the mixture. In a moment of genius the monk, Black Berthold, also referred to as Berthold Schwartz, appreciated the significance of this event and the concept of guns and shooting was born. Berthold lived in the German town of Freiburg, and a statue there commemorates the event. There is, however, one weakness in this very plausible tale: unfortunately, no solid proof can be found that he ever existed!

If there is no proof of this monk and his accidental discovery, where did the first guns originate? The question has exercised historians for many years. Many theories were advanced by early scholars to show that the Hindus and Chinese were using gunpowder in ancient times. All these early theories were based on very shaky evidence, and relied on suspect manuscripts and the interpretation of terms which could well refer to weapons other than firearms.

The country which has the strongest, most acceptable claim to being the home of gunpowder is China. There is good evidence to suggest that the Chinese certainly knew of its composition by the beginning of the eleventh century. The occasion on

This woodcut by Jost Amman shows the shop of a sixteenth-century gunmaker. Samples of his wares hang from a rack while the master discusses a weapon with one of his customers.

which the three component parts were first mixed together, and the circumstances leading to it, are of course unknown. Charcoal, *i.e.* charred wood, could have been found or made anywhere in the world. Saltpetre or potassium nitrate is a naturally occurring mineral which is found near the surface of the earth in both India and China. At the beginning of the nineteenth century saltpetre was still imported into Britain from India and used to make gunpowder at the Waltham Abbey gunpowder mill. Sulphur, the third component, is also found in various parts of the world although, strangely enough, China is not a country noted as being especially rich in the chemical. Although the original proportions are not known, they later became more or less standardized at about 75% saltpetre, 15% charcoal and 10% sulphur.

The mixture was apparently first used as an explosive or incendiary mixture, and probably served as a deterrent that produced a great flash, clouds of smoke and a loud detonation – enough, in those days, to frighten any enemy. The step to using this powder as a propellant to discharge a missile seems to have taken some time. Reliable evidence suggests that by the twelfth century, certainly by about 1130, the powder was being poured into a simple barrel formed by a bamboo tube. By the thirteenth century this tube had been strengthened by external binding, and one end was blocked by a plug of clay and a metal plate. The *huo ch'iang*, as it was called, seems to have fired not a single bullet but a number of small missiles, and contemporary descriptions speak of 'fragments' and 'pellets'. Although the earliest form of gun appears to have been a simple tube, possibly held in the hand, there is evidence that later on copper tubes were fitted at the ends of wooden rods, but these were used to fire arrows rather than bullets.

Although the Chinese obviously possessed the ability to make hand firearms, they do not seem to have taken the next logical step, of producing a cannon, until much later. There is no evidence to suggest that they were casting metal cannons prior to the fourteenth century.

How and when the knowledge of

Above
Two *Landsknechte* of the early sixteenth century with simple matchlock arquebuses. One soldier fires his from the shoulder while the other loads the charge.

Left
Early form of gun mounted on a long wooden stock and steadied on a rest. The charge was fired by ignition with, possibly, a pre-heated iron. The engraving is taken from a German manuscript of about 1400.

Right
Page from the Milemete Manuscript of 1326 showing the vase gun being fired by a mail-clad knight. Christ Church, Oxford.

10

gunpowder, this mysterious black powder of the devil, reached Europe is not at all clear. Formulae for gunpowder are to be found in books which apparently date from the twelfth and thirteenth centuries, but original copies of these books are non-existent. The earliest surviving copies are usually of a later date and it is extremely difficult to be certain that the formulae and other details were not added when the copies were made.

One of the most commonly quoted sources of this early knowledge of gunpowder is the works of Roger Bacon, a famous English scholar who lived in the thirteenth century. One of his books about the 'secrets of nature' was written about 1260, and the last chapter contains an anagram which has been resolved and rearranged to show that it was indeed a formula for gunpowder. This would seem to argue conclusively that Roger Bacon

knew of it. Unfortunately, the earliest copy extant of his work which contains this anagram is dated 1618, some 350 years after he wrote it! The position is even more confused by the fact that the only copy of Bacon's work which dates from the thirteenth century does not include this chapter at all, while in another fifteenth-century copy there is a different version of the anagram which has yet to be solved. Although there may be doubt as to whether Bacon knew the exact formula and composition of gunpowder, there is far less uncertainty about the fact that he knew of its existence. At least one passage in his works refers to the explosive effect of the mixture if confined in a parchment tube.

Despite the rather sketchy evidence, it is not unreasonable to assume that the secret of gunpowder was carried west by the principal traders of the period, the Arabs. At least one Arab manuscript dating from the early fourteenth century shows soldiers using crude firearms or incendiary devices, and the men certainly have a Chinese or Mongol appearance.

When the first European guns were developed has yet to be decided, but there is little dispute that they were certainly in use by the second quarter of the fourteenth century. There are references, some pictorial and some written, which would seem to prove this beyond doubt. The records of the Republic of Florence, in Italy, refer in 1326 to the employment of two men to make cannon balls and arrows that were to be fired from the cannon, and to the cannon themselves. This date is confirmed from English sources, for Walter de Milemete, the chaplain to the young Edward III, produced two illuminated manuscripts as part of his educational scheme for the young king. Although they are not mentioned in the text, in the margins of both manuscripts are the first European representations of a gun. Both show a vase-shaped receptacle, presumably of metal, lying on a table. One of them, if it bears any relation in scale to the men who are handling the weapon, must have been some 5–6 ft (1.5–1.8 m) long. The other, fired by one man, seems to be smaller, prob-

ably around 3 ft (90 cm). Neither appears to be secured in any way to the base on which it rests, and both are fired by mailed knights. The larger gun apparently needed the attention of three knights, who hold a long, metal rod with an angled tip which they are touching to the side of the metal vase. From the open end of each vase protrudes the point of an arrow. Although the use of arrows as projectiles may seem surprising, they were evidently regarded as being quite satisfactory. Records of the fifteenth, sixteenth and seventeenth centuries all have references to feathered arrows for use in cannon. The Tower of London records of 1600 refer to arrows which were apparently fitted with a round leather base that rested on the charge of gunpowder.

Examples of these vase-shaped guns are extremely rare. The earliest known example was excavated at Loshult in Sweden. It is only about 12 in (30 cm) long, is made of bronze and has a cylindrical bore. Drilled through the side at the base, at right-angles to the bore, is a small hole, the touch-hole, with a countersunk depression on the outside. From the size of the weapon it can be reasonably deduced that the missile was a small bullet. Gunpowder would have been poured down the barrel and then a ball of some sort was pushed down on top of the powder. A pinch of powder, the priming, was then placed over the touch-hole and if this were ignited the flash would pass through to ignite the main charge. Since it was compressed, the powder would explode and the gases generated would force the small projectile out with some considerable force and great inaccuracy.

The method of igniting the priming is not at all clear. The earliest illustrations show a rod which might have been used in one of a number of ways. It could have been heated in a fire and then touched into the powder. This method would have been very inconvenient since the firer would either have had to carry some source of heat with him or he would have had to stay near some brazier or other fire. More likely, although it cannot be proved, he used an ember or piece of smouldering moss or rag,

which he somehow fastened to the tip of the metal rod. This method would have given the firer much greater independence and freedom of movement.

The next problem is: how was the weapon held? The Swedish gun shows no obvious sign of a means of attachment. There are references in British accounts of 1346 which refer to guns with 'tillers'. This term was used for the wooden stock of a crossbow, so it is reasonable to assume that some of these early guns were fixed to a form of wooden handle. The size of these stocks, indeed of the guns themselves, is uncertain; not until 1388 is there reference to a 'handgun'. This does not necessarily mean that the weapon was small enough to be held in the hand. It may well mean only that the tiller, or stock, was held in the hand. The weapon itself may still have been 2–3 ft (60–90 cm) long. The barrel may have been secured to the tiller or stock by any one of several methods; probably the simplest was to anchor the bronze or wrought-iron barrel by means of bands of iron or leather. Later, improvements were introduced and a socket was fashioned into the base of the barrel, into which the wooden stock was inserted. In what was possibly the most sophisticated method, the breech block was hammered out to form a metal rod which served as the stock, making it an integral part of the gun.

The majority of these handguns appear to have had fairly short barrels; the few surviving examples are around 6–7 in (15–18 cm) long. Some of the guns were intended to be supported on a wall or the side of a ship. A small hook projected below the barrel and this was hooked over the wall to reduce the recoil or kick-back of the explosion. The weapon was known as a 'hook gun' or, in German, *Hackenbüchse*; the French equivalent was *Harquebus*, whence the English 'arquebus'. Some guns with an integral metal stock had a loop at the tip, and this could be fastened to a thong around the neck. The weapon was thus secure from loss, and this fitting enabled horsemen to use them: they could support the weapon with one hand and fire it with the other.

These early hand guns were ex-

tremely awkward to manage, whether on horseback or on foot. The difficulties of holding the weapon, trying to aim it and touching some means of ignition into the priming powder can well be imagined. The source of fire, already mentioned, was another serious problem, but the solution which was to gain general acceptance was that of the slow match. A piece of cord or twine was soaked in a very strong solution of potassium nitrate and then allowed to dry. If the end was now lit the cord slowly smouldered and spluttered with a bright glowing tip. A length of this cord could be carried curled around the hand or even looped across the saddle ready for immediate use. There were difficulties, since it was exposed to the effects of wind and weather; nevertheless the match represented a distinct improvement. Despite its obvious advantages, however, the match still required one hand for its management which meant that only one hand could be used to support the gun. What was wanted was some mechanical means of applying this glowing match to the touch-hole.

The first recorded illustration of such a device, known as a serpentine, appears in a manuscript dated 1411. It consisted of a long, Z-shaped lever, pivoted at the centre and fastened to the side of the stock. A length of match was secured to the fore-end of the angled arm, and when the rear arm, situated below the stock of the weapon, was pressed, the upper arm swung forward and down. If the lever was correctly positioned, this movement pressed the glowing end of the match into the touch-hole to fire the charge. Later the serpentine was replaced by a simple mechanical arrangement known as the match-lock. The great advantage of this system was that now both hands could be used to grip the stock and so steady the weapon and even permit some kind of aim to be taken.

The gunner had by now achieved some skill in his trade, and there are references in contemporary accounts to some of the extras which he needed. Among these were bullet moulds in which to cast his bullets, ladles for scooping out molten lead, and iron

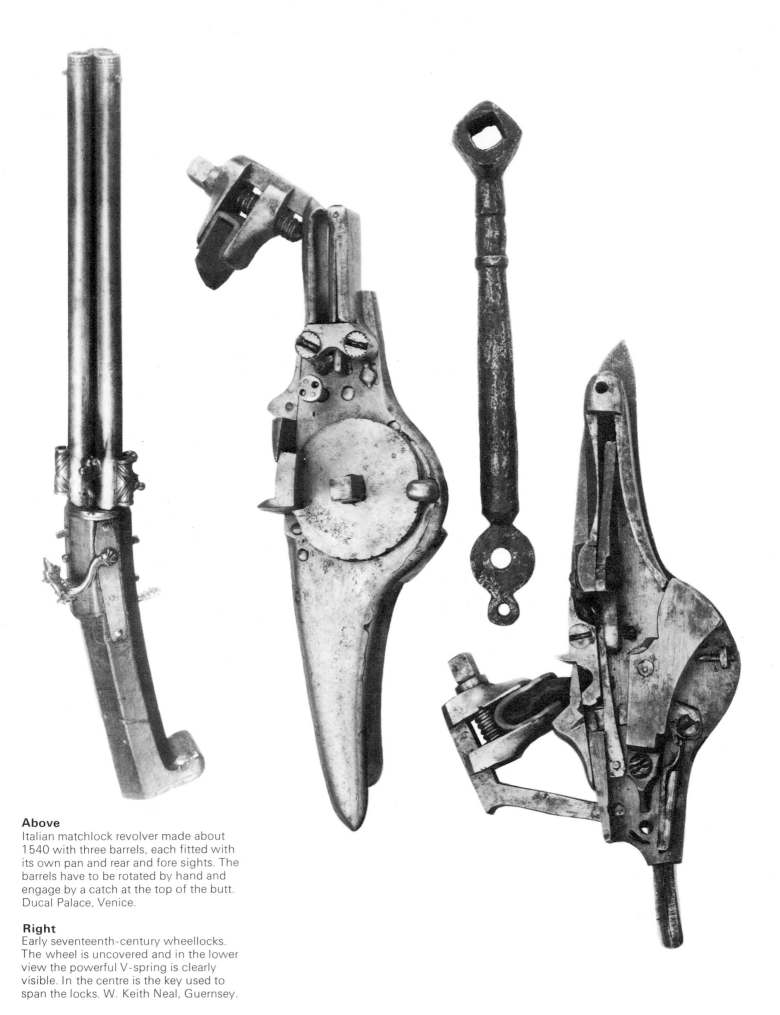

Above
Italian matchlock revolver made about
1540 with three barrels, each fitted with
its own pan and rear and fore sights. The
barrels have to be rotated by hand and
engage by a catch at the top of the butt.
Ducal Palace, Venice.

Right
Early seventeenth-century wheellocks.
The wheel is uncovered and in the lower
view the powerful V-spring is clearly
visible. In the centre is the key used to
span the locks. W. Keith Neal, Guernsey.

ramrods used to push the lead ball down the barrel so that it was seated firmly on top of the gunpowder. Bitter experience, no doubt, would have demonstrated to the gunners that any gap left between the top of the powder charge and the base of the bullet usually meant, at worst, a disastrous explosion, and at best a bulged barrel which made the weapon virtually useless.

Although some of the early matchlocks appear to be small, they were certainly not what today we would call a pistol. They were essentially small shoulder or long arms; in many the stock was shaped to fit more comfortably against the shoulder, and so permit a better aim to be taken.

The origin of the name 'pistol' is in itself something of a mystery. The term did not come into general use in documents until late in the sixteenth century. Prior to this they were generally described as 'small arquebusses'. In England, until about the last quarter of the sixteenth century, they were known as 'dags'. One of the earliest known uses of the word 'pistol' is in a French document of 1544, and it is likely that because of the long-standing connection arising from the 'Old Alliance' between Scotland and France, the word passed to Scotland and thence to England where, by the middle of the century, it seems to have been in common use.

What, then, is the origin of the word 'pistol', meaning a hand-held

Above
Crossbows, poleaxes, sword and buckler, bow and arrow, fire pot and an example of an early firearm all figure in this battle picture of 1473. In the right-hand corner are three simple artillery pieces. British Museum, London.

Right
The searspring (1) presses down on the sear (2), ensuring that the serpentine (3) is held away from the pan. Pressure on the bar or trigger (4) activates the sear (2), which turns on the pivot (5), making the lug press down in the slot and forcing the serpentine to rotate. This forward movement brings the glowing tip of the match (6) into the pan. When the trigger is released, the sear is returned to the first position by the pressure of the searspring (1).

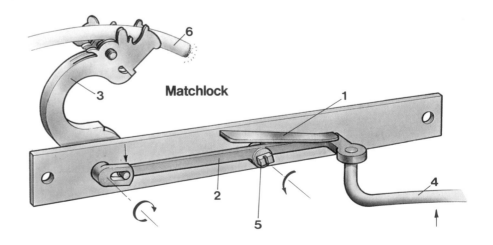

Matchlock

firearm? Various suggestions have been made. One proposes that it was derived from a Bohemian word meaning a pipe or whistle, but the evidence for this is somewhat suspect. A stronger claim for its origin would appear to come from the town of Pistoia in Italy. As early as 1565 one writer stated that the word 'pistolet' was derived from the town of Pistoia, which had made a speciality of producing small daggers known as 'pistoyes'. The same craftsmen with their tradition of working in miniature also produced small arquebusses, and the name 'pistolet' was applied to both dagger and firearm. Certainly 'pistolet' is used in contemporary English sources indiscriminately to describe a coin, a dagger, and a firearm.

When the first true pistol, that is, one designed to be carried and used in the hand, appeared is uncertain. By the middle of the fourteenth century there are references to 'hand bombards' which were a span in length, or about 9 in (23 cm). In the fifteenth century an attempt was made to incorporate small barrels of this type into the design of other weapons. Maces, and war hammers, in effect small axes, were made with the haft in the form of a metal tube which could serve as a barrel. Although a foot soldier could manage a musket fitted with a serpentine, it was no easy task for a horseman, and although some early illustrations show mounted men firing them, it seems unlikely that they were ever more than a novelty on the battlefield. Surviving examples of small handguns or pistols fitted with matchlocks are extremely rare, and this would seem to argue that they were never in general use.

Although the European matchlock pistol is virtually unknown, it was not uncommon in Japan. Portuguese traders were the first to introduce the firearm to Japan; this happened in about 1542, when the first known contact was made by the Portuguese with the Japanese islands. Owing to the self-imposed isolation of the Japanese, the matchlock, which was soon abandoned in Europe, continued in Japan until the middle of the nineteenth century. The Japanese pistol is really a scaled-down version

of the more conventional longarm. The stock, often of ebony, is fitted with a short, rather thick-walled, chunky barrel, and the firing mechanism, the so-called matchlock, is fitted to the side of the stock. Most of the fittings are of brass.

The Japanese adopted a rather dangerous form of matchlock known as the snap lock. In the conventional European pattern the arm holding the match was usually in the up-position, away from the pan; pressure on the trigger then forced down the arm. In the Japanese version the normal position was with the arm of the serpentine pressing down into the pan. To set the mechanism the serpentine arm was raised until it engaged with another small arm, known as a sear. Pressure on the trigger, usually a brass ball mounted beneath the stock, caused the sear to slide back so allowing the serpentine, impelled by a weak, coiled spring, to fall forward and press the match into the powder. The dangers of accidental discharge are obvious!

In every trade and profession there are always a few people who are constantly seeking to improve their product. They see the problems involved, and experiment to overcome them. This was just as true of the early gunmakers as it is, for example, of today's aviation experts; they sought ways to make their weapons easier to handle, to load, to hold and, above all, to shoot. Some ideas were, to say the least, unusual, and some were totally impractical, but one or two were to change the whole design of firearms. However, any new idea, no matter how good, does not immediately relegate all old weapons to the scrap heap. New and old flourish side by side. This was true of the old matchlock, for although it was rendered obsolete in the sixteenth century it continued in use well into the eighteenth.

The matchlock was simple, easy to make and repair, cheap and, within its limits, reliable. Although the infantryman was well able to cope with his long matchlock musket, the cavalryman was not. He, no doubt, demanded a firearm that he could use on horseback, and the gunmaker soon

Portrait of Sir Martin Frobisher (1535–94), the noted navigator who sought a north-west passage to the north of America. In his hand is a small wheellock dag. Bodleian Library, Oxford.

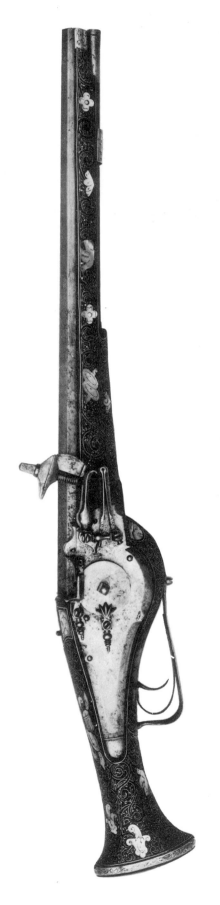

French wheellock with straight stock decorated with mother-of-pearl inlay, brass and silver wire. It was made at the end of the sixteenth century.

came up with an answer. In addition to the problem of size, the cavalryman wanted to ignite his powder without using the dangerous, constantly glowing match. What was wanted was a device to produce fire on demand. The answer was the so-called wheellock. The basic principle was simple, and was based on the old idea of striking sparks between flint and steel, a system of firemaking almost as old as man himself. The gunmaker's task was to convert the manual process of striking flint and steel into a mechanical one which did not require the use of both hands.

The solution was to use a rotating steel wheel and a piece of a common mineral called pyrites. The wheel was a thick, flat, steel disc, its edge roughened by a series of grooves. This wheel was connected by means of a short linked chain to a strong V-spring. The wheel was turned by placing a key over its squared axle and this movement compressed the spring. When the V-spring was fully compressed, a small spring-activated arm or sear moved forward to engage with a recess cut into the flat side of the wheel. The action of pressing the trigger withdrew the sear and the V-spring then rotated the wheel. The edge of the wheel was so positioned that its rim formed part of the floor of a small pan situated next to the touch-hole.

Fitted to the plate which also held the wheel was an angled metal arm, the doghead. At the tip of the arm were two adjustable jaws which held the piece of pyrites. This arm was pivoted so that it could be moved forward to press the pyrites into the pan and against the rim of the wheel. A charge of powder was poured down the barrel and was usually held in place by a wad of felt, thick card or other material. A lead ball of appropriate diameter was pushed down the barrel until it sat on top of the wad. The wheel was now rotated or spanned by means of the key until the sear locked it in position, and then a pinch of priming powder was placed in the pan. The doghead was swung forward so that the pyrites pressed against the rim of the wheel and the weapon was now ready for firing. When the trigger was pressed the sear

was withdrawn, the wheel, impelled by the spring, rotated and the friction between the roughened edge of the wheel and the tip of the pyrites produced small, incandescent sparks of steel which fell into the priming powder. The priming flashed and the flame passed through the touch-hole to ignite the main charge. To keep the priming in position, a sliding cover was fitted over the pan. On some weapons this had to be pushed away manually before firing; on others the pan cover was automatically pushed clear by an internal collection of levers.

This system of ignition offered many advantages: not least, it did away with the inconvenient length of glowing match. Provided the doghead was pushed clear of the pan, there was no danger of an accidental discharge when the weapon was loaded. Even if the trigger was pressed and the wheel turned it could not strike sparks since it was not in contact with the pyrites. Another great advantage was that the weapon could be loaded and made ready to fire and then left until it was needed, something it was impossible to do with a matchlock. Perhaps the most important advantage was that the gunsmith now had a practical firing mechanism which he could use to make fire-arms small enough to be used in one hand. The pistol had arrived.

The earliest surviving examples of wheellocks all date from about the 1530s but it is not clear when the system was first developed. There is reasonably good evidence to indicate that men were exploring the idea around the turn of the century. One pioneer developing this system was the great scholar and Renaissance man, Leonardo da Vinci (1452–1519). His military drawings in the *Codex Atlanticus* include sketches of a similar mechanism. The exact date of these drawings is in dispute but they were certainly done either at the end of the fifteenth century or in the first decade of the sixteenth century. Several sketches are of details but two show complete mechanisms that are very clearly basic wheellocks. Modern reconstructions of the lock have shown that it works and does produce a spark. Whether Leonardo's

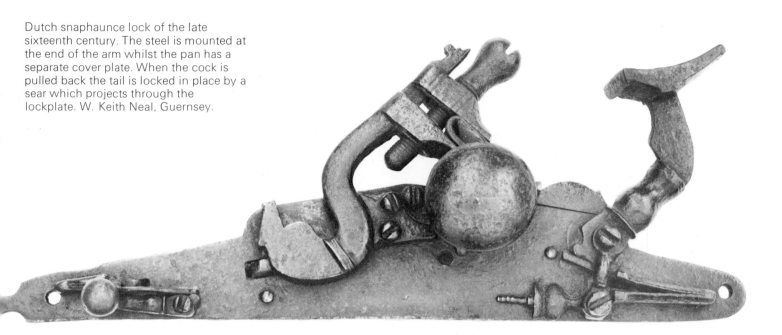

Dutch snaphaunce lock of the late sixteenth century. The steel is mounted at the end of the arm whilst the pan has a separate cover plate. When the cock is pulled back the tail is locked in place by a sear which projects through the lockplate. W. Keith Neal, Guernsey.

plans for the mechanism were his own, or whether he was merely noting down the design of a mechanism he had seen, is of course impossible to say.

Further evidence for the appearance of the wheellock about this time was provided by the Löffelholz Manuscript, whose present location is unknown but which was at one time in Berlin. The manuscript had two drawings which were quite explicit and showed a wheel and a doghead with a split top to hold the pyrites. One wheel was activated by pulling a leather thong which was wound around the axle. The second drawing showed another wheellock mechanism which was far more complex and, in some details, was very similar to the one in the sketch by Leonardo. Motive power was provided, as with the da Vinci lock, by means of a U-shaped spring.

During the first decades of the sixteenth century there are several references which could well refer to a wheellock. In 1507 the Bishop of Zagreb ordered a gun which is 'kindled by a stone'. In 1515 a young man of Augsburg accidentally injured a lady of the town with a gun which 'ignited itself'. In 1517 Maximilian I, Emperor of Austria, forbade the use of guns 'which ignite themselves'. His edict highlighted a realization that these new weapons represented a new and previously unsuspected threat to authority. Prior to the sixteenth century an assassin had to get close to

his victim. The new pistol gave him the chance to strike from a distance using a weapon which he could easily conceal. The edict of Maximilian was to be repeated later by many rulers in many countries. This evidence suggests that the wheellock was probably first introduced at the end of the fifteenth century or at the beginning of the sixteenth, possibly in Italy although Germany also has a good claim. The wheellock mechanism was to remain in use for a century or more, and during this period it underwent a number of changes.

Most of the early examples were fitted with some sort of safety catch which locked either the trigger or the sear; but it was soon realized that it was superfluous since the weapon could be carried in perfect safety simply by lifting the doghead clear of the wheel. Spring-operated pan covers were a common feature on these early wheellocks and pressure on a button allowed a small plate to move forward over the pan, so holding the priming safely in place as well as protecting it from the weather. On the pistols the wheel was almost invariably fitted on the outside of the lock plate, sometimes with a decorative cover. On wheellock rifles, from about 1625, the wheel was often fitted on the inside of the lockplate.

Despite the many and obvious advantages of the wheellock, it was not devoid of problems. The mechanism, although fairly simple by

modern standards, presented at the time quite considerable problems of manufacture which called for skill on the part of the gunmaker, and on the part of the person who had to maintain it. A broken link on the chain, for example, a not uncommon occurrence, could so easily render the weapon totally useless. The matchlock could be repaired by any competent blacksmith, but the wheellock called for finer skills.

The lock first of all had to be spanned by placing a key over the squared end of the axle and turning it to tension the mainspring; loss of the key rendered the weapon virtually useless. Some wheellocks were fitted with self-spanning mechanisms which meant that as the doghead was pulled down into the firing position, coupling cogs rotated the wheel. These were even more complex and far less common than the standard form. In addition to problems caused by breakages and loss of the key, the mechanism could easily become jammed by accumulated deposits of burnt powder. Moreover, the difficulty of manufacture made the wheellocks expensive weapons, and consequently they were only issued to troops on a very limited scale.

The idea of a 'self-igniting' mechanism was now firmly established, and during the sixteenth century gunmakers in various parts of Europe were experimenting with other systems. The idea was to generate a

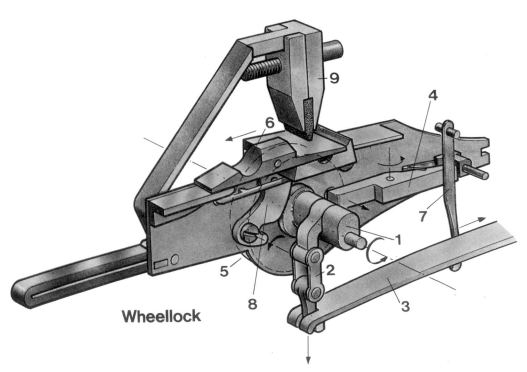

Wheellock

Above
Pair of short-barrelled wheellock pistols with small pommels, made about 1590. The stocks are inlaid with horn.

Above right
Queen Anne pistol of characteristic shape with silver butt cap. There is no ramrod since the barrel unscrews for loading. There is a silver escutcheon on the butt. The frizzen spring is specially shaped and the trigger guard operates as a safety catch. Made by Clarkson of London.

Left
A key or spanner is placed over the square-ended spindle (1) and rotated. This forces the transmission chain (2) to lift the arm of the mainspring (3). Spring-pressure causes the tip of the sear (4) to lock into a hole cut in the wheel (5). The pan cover (6) is pushed manually to the rear to cover the priming. When the trigger (7) is pressed, it releases the tip of the sear (4), and the wheel (5), under the impetus of the spring, turns in the direction indicated. As the spindle turns, it knocks a cam, the pan-cover arm (8), and this pushes the cover (6) forward, clear of the priming. The pyrites, held in the cock (9), press against the wheel's edge and produce the sparks.

spark using mechanisms that were simpler, less liable to faults and cheaper to manufacture. The system which was to gain general acceptance and to remain more or less standard until the mid-nineteenth century was the so-called flintlock. This system substituted a piece of flint, a far commoner substance, for the pyrites, and in place of the rather complex wheel there was a plain, flat steel plate.

Like the wheellock it is very difficult to be precise about the origin of the flintlock. When contemporary documents refer to 'self-igniting' weapons the term could equally well apply to a wheellock or a flintlock. However, the evidence indicates that the wheellock was the earlier invention – certainly the earliest known wheellocks pre-date the earliest surviving flintlocks. So far the first known reference to the flintlock appears in a Florentine document of 1547, at least 40 years after the first reference to wheellocks.

Although there were variations on the basic mechanism, the flintlock generally consisted of a V-shaped spring which powered a cock, the equivalent of the doghead, which held a wedge-shaped piece of flint. In place of the intricate linked chain, the tip of the V-spring pressed directly on a shaped block of metal coupled to the cock. Situated above the pan which held the priming was a vertical steel plate on a pivoted arm. When the cock swung forward and down the flint was so positioned that it scraped along the steel plate. Friction produced tiny flakes of incandescent steel which dropped into the priming and so ignited the charge. At the same time as the flint and steel struck sparks, the impact pushed this steel plate clear of the pan. The forward and downward swing of the cock presumably suggested to the early gunsmiths a movement similar to the pecking of a hen. The Dutch named the lock the *snaphaan*, the 'snapping hen', and in English this became the snaphaunce or snaphance. Originally the name was applied to all forms of

flintlock, but by common usage it has now come to mean just one particular kind in which the steel and the pan cover are separate.

One of the earliest forms of this flintlock was popular in the countries bordering the Baltic Sea. It cannot be assumed that the lock evolved in this area for it is known that German gunmakers were working at Arboga in Sweden. The lock could therefore have been of German origin. Augsburg and Nuremberg had by now become centres for the production of firearms, and from those cities they were exported all over Europe.

The Baltic lock has a gracefully curving cock similar in shape to that on Leonardo da Vinci's early wheellock. The bottom or heel of this cock is in direct contact with a V-shaped mainspring mounted on the outside of the lock plate. As the cock is pulled back a small arm, or sear, pokes through the lock plate and locks the heel in place. At the front of the lockplate is another curved arm terminating in a small rectangular

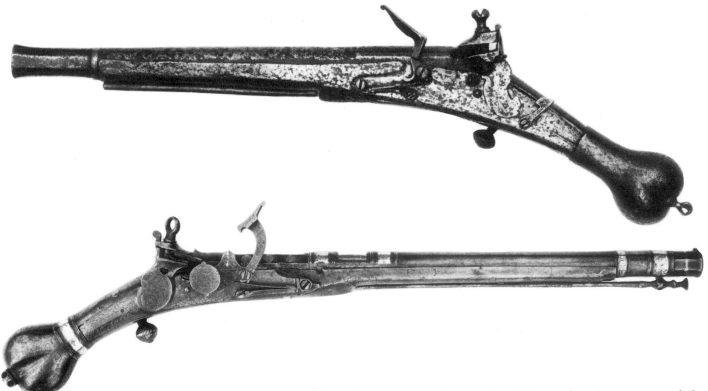

All-metal Scottish pistol from the second half of the seventeenth century. This example is unusual in having a left-hand lock. The butt shape and ball trigger are typical of this type of weapon.

Above
Fine, all-metal Scottish pistol with snaphaunce lock, made by John Stuart c. 1675. These pistols formed a distinct group and retained certain features throughout the centuries, including the ball trigger and thin metal ramrod. W. Keith Neal, Guernsey.

steel plate. When this is pulled down it rests directly above and in front of the pan. Once the trigger is pressed the sear is withdrawn and releases the cock which, under the pressure of the V-spring, swings forward and down, striking sparks from the steel and, at the same time, pushing it clear of the priming pan. This simple lock was certainly in use by the middle of the sixteenth century and was to remain in use throughout the Baltic area until well into the eighteenth century, when it was replaced by slightly more sophisticated mechanisms.

To protect the priming the Baltic lock had, like the wheellock, a small pan cover. Many of the early weapons were fitted with an interlocking device which pushed the pan cover clear as the cock swung forward. At first the connecting lever was situated on the outside of the lock but it soon became common practice to fit it on the inside. This coupling lever, linking cock and pan cover, was a complicated device, and gunmakers experimented with ideas which would overcome the problem. Probably during the second part of the sixteenth century the idea was developed of uniting the pan cover and the steel to form an L-shaped piece of metal known today as the frizzen. As the flint struck the steel it was knocked clear and the L-shaped piece of metal, pivoted at the end of the short arm,

tipped forward and so uncovered the priming to receive the sparks.

As so often happens, the solution to one problem raised another. With the separate pan cover and steel the weapon could be loaded and primed and the cock drawn back ready for firing, and until the steel was brought down into position there was no possibility of an accidental discharge. When the combined L-shaped pan cover and steel was closed, the steel was automatically in position and the chances of an accidental firing were obviously much increased. One solution to the problem was to make the steel section so that it could be pivoted away from the firing position, and some locks were made with such an arrangement. Another, more positive, idea was to have a safety catch fitted to the lock plate. When the cock was pulled back to the firing position a small hooked arm, known as a dog, situated behind the cock, was swung forward to lock into the back of the cock. Even if the trigger was pressed, this safety device held the cock in the upright position.

Gunmakers were also examining the release mechanism of the flintlock. The early examples were similar to the wheellock with a lateral sear which operated through the lockplate. A small hole was drilled through the plate and the sear protruded through to engage with a notch or recess on the rear of the cock. This was another feature which could be simplified, for the sear was liable to breakage and jamming.

Early in the seventeenth century, probably around 1610, another step forward was made, this time by a French gunsmith, Marin le Bourgeoys. He removed the lateral sear passing through the lock plate and substituted an internal, vertical sear. He fitted the cock to a spindle which passed through the lock plate and which was part of a shaped block of metal, the tumbler. A projecting toe on the tumbler engaged with the tip of the V-mainspring. This would afford the power to move the cock forward. Further round the edge of the tumbler two more slots were cut and, resting against the edge, held there by a small spring, was a flat bar or sear. As the cock was pulled back the tumbler rotated and the sear engaged with the first slot. If the cock was now released it was held in this position, known as the half-cock. Pressure on the trigger

could not withdraw the sear and this meant that the pistol could now be loaded, primed and the frizzen closed, but the weapon could be carried with reasonable safety. To make ready for firing, the cock was now pulled back a little further and, as the tumbler turned, the sear disengaged from the first notch and slipped into the second slot. Pressure on the trigger would now release the sear so allowing the mainspring, pressing on the other side of the tumbler, to swing the cock forward to discharge the weapon.

Despite the obvious advantages of this system it did not immediately receive general acceptance, and for the first half of the seventeenth century there were locks with a whole range of combinations of the old and new systems. By the middle of the century the French-style lock gradually established itself and by the end of the century was more or less standard. The working life of the French lock was to continue well into the nineteenth century, and during that

A typical late eighteenth-century flintlock stripped to its component parts. Each piece was made and assembled by hand.

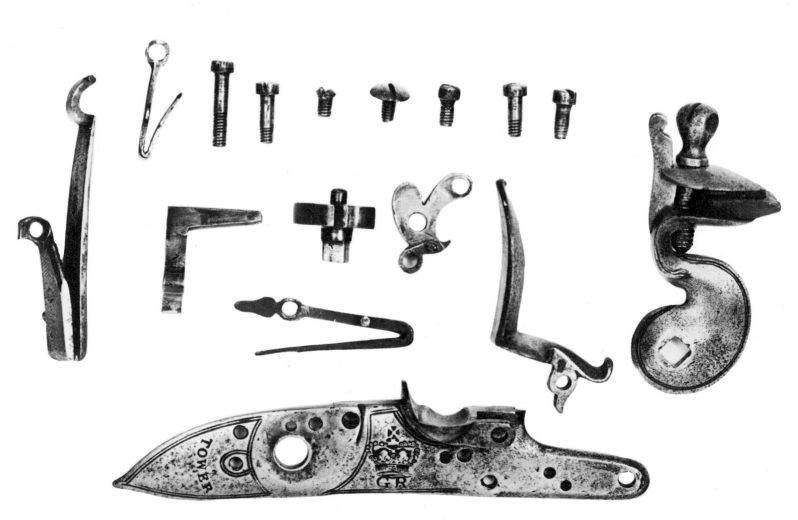

Below

The cock (1) is pulled back, causing the tumbler (2) to rotate. Simultaneously, the nose of the combined sear and trigger lever (3), which passes through a hole (4) in the lockplate, engages with the heel of the cock (1) and locks it in position. The steel (5) is placed vertically in front of the pan (6), and the pan cover (7) is pushed back to cover the priming. When the trigger is pressed, the sear (3) pivots backwards, disengaging the nose from the cock. The mainspring (8), compressed via the tumbler by the movement of the cock, now presses down on the tip of the tumbler, forcing the cock forward. The flint scrapes down the steel making sparks and knocking it clear. The arm (9) moves forward, causing the pan cover to be displaced, and the sparks ignite the priming.

Bottom

The cock (1) is pulled back, automatically rotating the tumbler (2). The tip of the sear (3) is pressed against the tumbler and engages with the first notch (4). In this half-cock notch the trigger (5) cannot disengage the sear. If the cock is pulled further back, the sear engages with the second notch (6), the full cock. Pressure on the trigger (5) can now disengage the sear, allowing the mainspring (7), compressed by the tumbler's rotation, to press down on the tip of the tumbler, thus swinging the cock (1) forward. The combined steel and pan cover, the frizzen (8), is struck by the flint, producing sparks and tilting to uncover the pan (9) so that the priming is ignited. The tumbler is secured by the bridle (10), which is screwed to the lockplate (11).

period the only changes were comparatively minor and designed to improve its efficiency and reliability. Various safety catches were fitted: one was a small bolt which, in the half-cock position, could be pushed forward to lock the cock, so making doubly sure that there would be no accident. Some makers reverted to the English dog with a small hook which, in the half-cock position, could lock into the rear of the cock. The shape of the lock changed slightly over the years: it tended to become smoother and flatter, and the earlier, slightly down-curving, banana shape of the lock plate was gradually replaced by a straighter, simpler form.

Although the flintlock was used by most European countries, not all of them adopted the French design. Many of the Mediterranean countries, Italy, Spain, Portugal and Sicily, used a form of flintlock known as the miquelet. There are several forms of this lock but most have the mainspring mounted on the outside of the lock plate. Spanish versions of the miquelet became characterized by certain easily recognizable features. The frizzen was rather squat and often had a grooved face, and the cock was also rather squat and square in general appearance. The mainspring on the miquelet was very strong and there was often either a ring or a V-shaped bar at the top of the cock to afford a firmer grip when cocking the action.

The flintlock, though for most purposes quite satisfactory and adequate, was not without its limitations. The flint was an essential part of the lock and each piece was usually reckoned to be good for some 30 strikes, although some would fail after four or five and others were still good after 40 or 50. The best flints were reckoned to be the black variety and it was not unknown for flint knappers – the men who shaped the flints – to apply blacking to cover up any white spots which might suggest that the flint was not of the best quality. The fact that it wore out meant that soldiers and travellers had, of necessity, to carry spare flints with them. Even with a good-quality flint there was always the possibility of a misfire

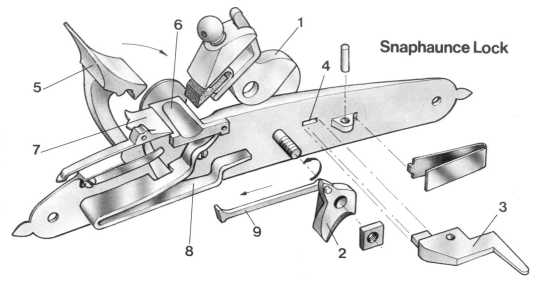

Snaphaunce Lock

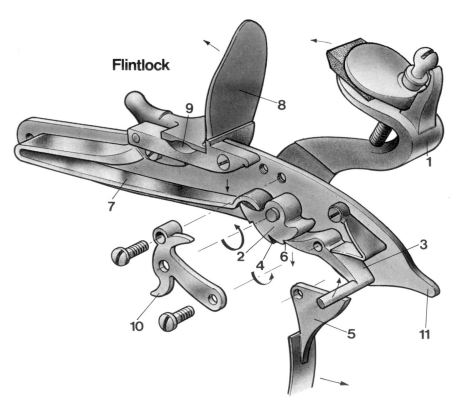

Flintlock

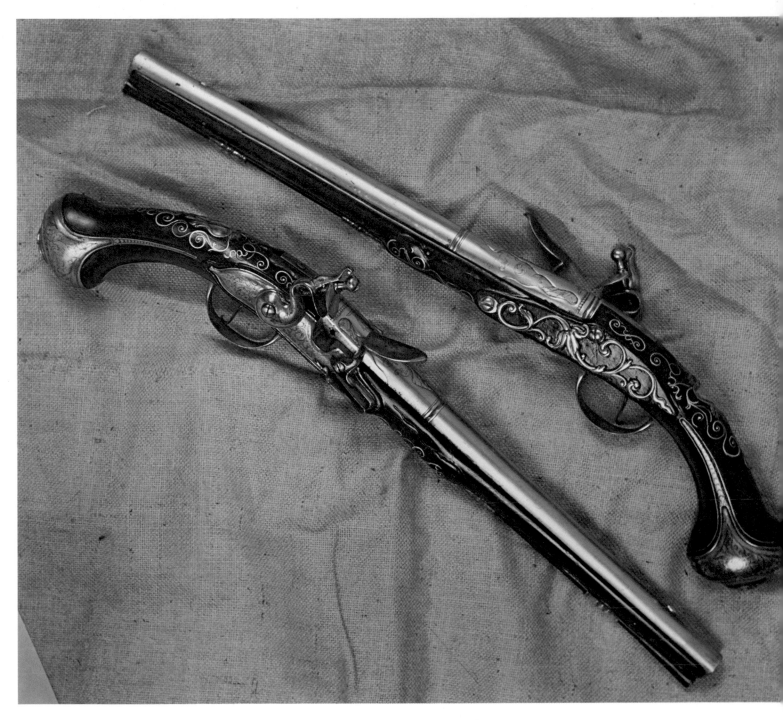

Above
Pair of fine holster pistols by Barbar of London, *c* 1720. The stocks have silver decoration and the steel butt cap bears a chiselled grotesque head. K. Mathers, Stockport, Greater Manchester.

when, for some reason or other, the sparks did not fall directly into the pan or the flint did not strike sparks. For the hunter a misfire was of no great importance, merely an annoyance, but for one who depended upon the pistol for his life the results could be fatal.

For the hunter the greatest drawback of the flintlock was unquestionably the phenomenon known as the hangfire. This was the accumulation of the small periods of time required for each operation of the flintlock, the total of which was still short but, nevertheless, appreciable. When the trigger was pressed the cock moved forward, which took a certain time; it then had to strike down the face of the steel, and again a certain time elapsed. The sparks then fell into the priming which flashed, the flash passed through the touch-hole to ignite the main charge which, despite the speed of ignition, still took time. The result of all these delays meant that after the trigger was pulled and the sequences set in motion, there was a brief delay before the weapon fired. Because of this hangfire, the sportsman or the target shooter had to allow for a lapse of time when taking aim –

Right
Anne Bonney, left, and Mary Reed, two women who gained notoriety as pirates in the early eighteenth century. Here they wear crossbelts with their flintlock pistols attached, a common method of carrying them.

Below
Ornate pair of flintlock pistols made in England for export to the East. They are decorated with gold damascening and inlay on the stock and marked 'Richards' on the lockplate. The silver carries Birmingham hallmarks for 1790.

Bottom
A flintlock holster pistol from one of a pair made at Brescia, Northern Italy. The stocks are of burr walnut and the lock and furniture are of gilt bronze. The lock is signed 'F. Bigoni'.

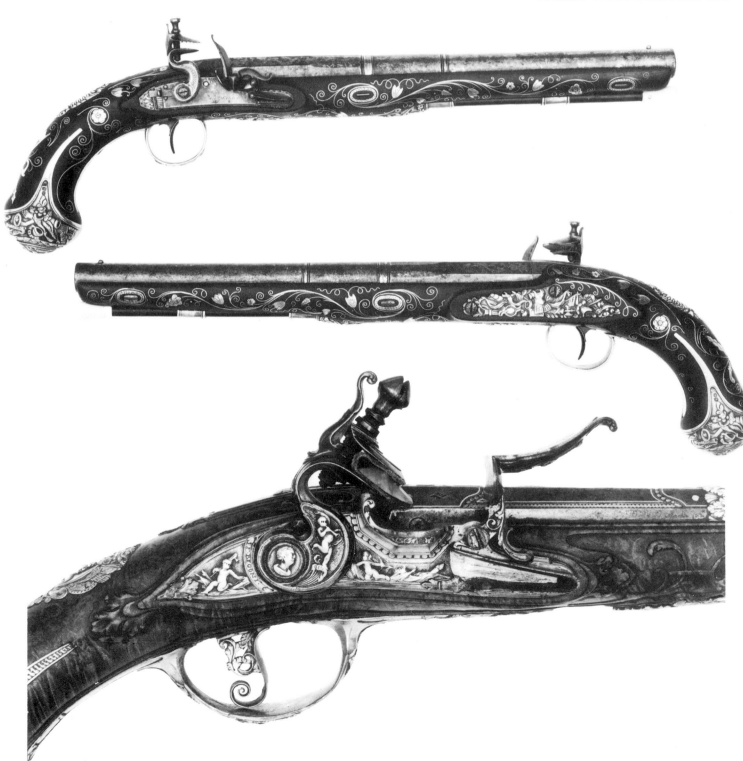

not always easy to do. Another drawback for the hunter was the puff of priming smoke which occurred fractionally before the main charge. A wary quarry saw the smoke and the flash of the priming and this was sufficient to give it warning and start it moving.

The solution to all these problems came as a result of the efforts of a Scottish clergyman of Belhelvie in Aberdeenshire. As he was an amateur chemist one might draw a parallel with Black Berthold, always remembering the essential distinction that there is no doubt at all of the existence of Alexander Forsyth. Forsyth's interest in science meant that he knew of a group of chemicals known as fulminates which were so unstable that any knock was sufficient to cause them to explode. Over the centuries several people had experimented with various fulminates in the hope that they could either be mixed with or replace ordinary gunpowder. The instability of the chemicals had resulted in several unfortunate accidents and on the whole the outcome did not look good. Forsyth knew of these experiments and had carried out some of his own. In 1799 he had published a paper on the properties of mercury fulminate. He, unlike previous experimenters, turned his attention from using the fulminates as a substitute for gunpowder to using them as an alternative form of priming.

He devised a system whereby minute quantities, a few grains, could be deposited above the touch-hole in place of the old priming powder. To do this he designed an ingenious little device known as the 'scent bottle', not because of its perfume but because of its shape. It consisted of a tiny metal bottle, one end of which contained a

A selection of designs for flintlock pistols by Jean Berain, a French gunmaker. His book of designs was published in Paris in 1659.

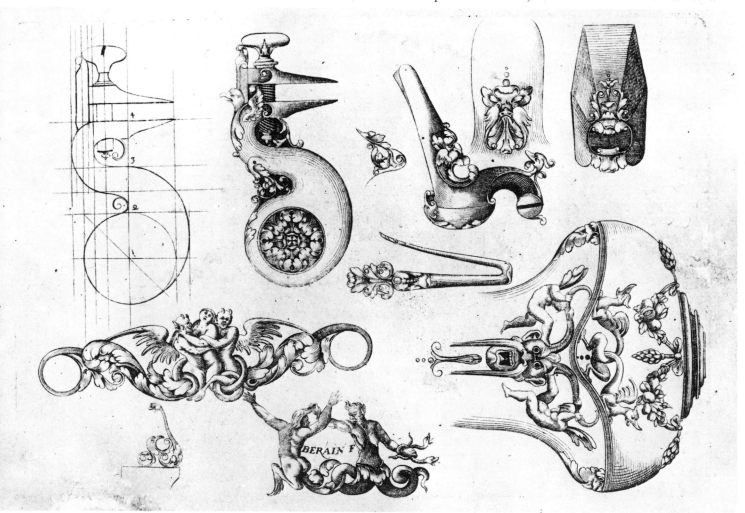

small amount of the fulminates or chlorates. The bottle pivoted about a central axle which was drilled through it. When the scent bottle was upended a few grains of powder fell into a small depression at the end of this tunnel which, in effect, replaced the old touch-hole. The scent bottle was then returned to its original position, and this brought into place above those few grains of fulminate a small, spring-loaded plunger. When this plunger was struck it was driven down on to the fulminate which exploded, and the flash passed through the touch-hole to ignite the main charge. Although the scent bottle was rather complex and potentially dangerous, since an accidental discharge of the reservoir of fulminate could have disastrous results, one great virtue of the system was that any existing flintlock could be easily converted to the new system. Pan, frizzen and springs were removed from the outside of the lock plate, the scent bottle was fixed to the barrel at the touch-hole, and the flint-

holding cock was replaced by a solid hammer. These were the only changes that were required since the internal mechanism of the flintlock remained unchanged.

The system worked beautifully, there was no tell-tale flash of priming smoke, there were fewer misfires and the hangfire was very considerably reduced. Forsyth was so encouraged with the results of his experiments that he came down to London to see the Master General of the Ordnance in an attempt to persuade him to adopt this system for the British armed forces, at that time heavily involved in the Napoleonic Wars. The Master, Lord Moira, saw some value in the invention and offered Forsyth facilities at the Tower of London to carry on with his experiments. Unfortunately for Forsyth, the experimental locks for carronade and carbine did not prove as satisfactory as he had hoped, probably because they were too complicated to function well in the conditions of military service. Forsyth's facilities at the

Above left
Detail of one of the Barbar pistols (see page 23) showing the steel butt cap. K. Mathers, Stockport, Greater Manchester.

Above
Pair of flintlock pistols covered with elaborate silver decoration with hallmarks for 1815. These were made by Brunn of Charing Cross, probably for the Prince Regent. W. Keith Neal, Guernsey.

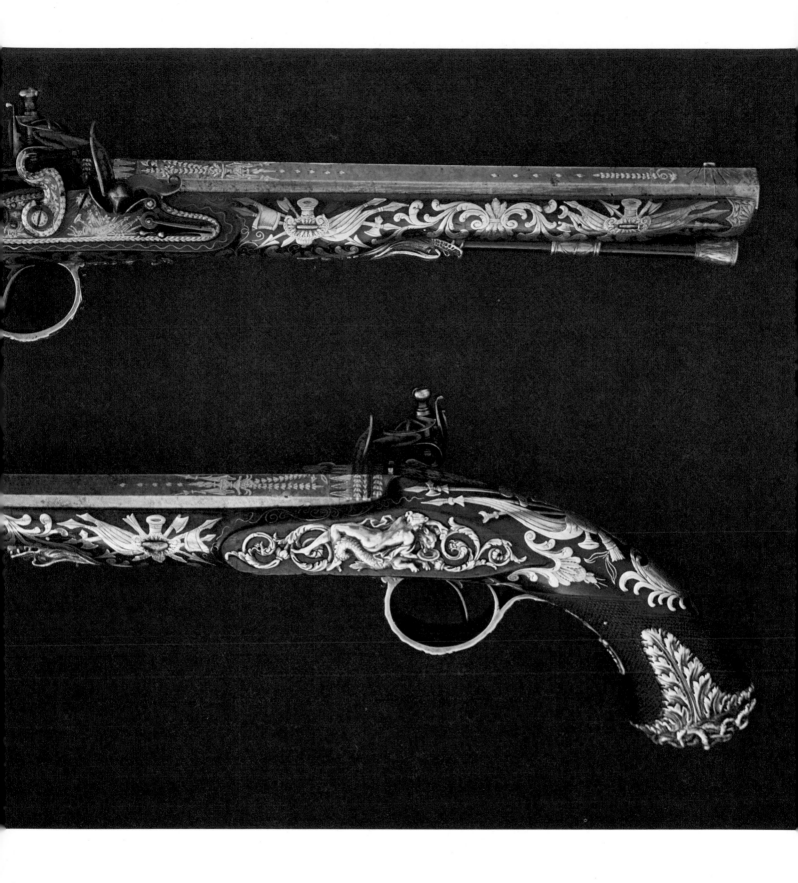

Tower were withdrawn and the authorities lost all interest in his revolutionary device. Forsyth, however, patented it in April 1807, and opened a shop in Piccadilly, London, where he sold guns fitted with his patent lock.

Forsyth's patent was valid for 14 years, and during that time he successfully prevented English gunmakers from copying his lock. On the Continent, where the patent was not recognized, there were many copies of his scent-bottle type of lock. Nevertheless it was complicated and a little unsafe, and gunmakers, including those who were prevented from making the Forsyth lock because of his patent, sought ways in which they could improve on his basic design.

One problem was that the chlorates or fulminates were available only in powder form, which made them inconvenient to handle. There were numerous attempts to overcome this problem by mixing the powder with wax, but the resulting small pellets were difficult to handle and in hot weather they tended to mass together. A London gunmaker, Joseph Manton, patented this idea in 1816 and a few weapons were produced which used these pills or pellets. In America Samuel Guthrie, one of the discoverers of chloroform, mixed chlorate with gum arabic to form pills. These and other pills and pellets were still very small and, under military conditions or on the hunting field, were difficult to handle. In 1825 an English artist, Joshua Shaw, improved their handling qualities by fixing the small pellet of detonating compound in the centre of a small cardboard disc. A well-known American gunmaker, Christian Sharps, made his small discs from copper, and although they represented an improvement on the old pellet, they were still small and inconvenient.

Yet another attempt to solve the problem was by the use of tubes. Small copper tubes, about an inch long, held the fulminate and were pushed into the touch-hole leaving just one end exposed. The hammer struck down against an anvil beneath the tube to achieve detonation. All these devices offered some advantage, but they remained difficult to store and were certainly inconvenient to use. The search for better, safer and simpler methods continued. The answer which was finally developed and became almost universally accepted was the percussion cap.

Like many other facets of firearms history the invention of the cap is surrounded by controversy and uncertainty. Many famous gunmakers and shooters of the period claimed the distinction of being the inventor, but in no case is there absolute and

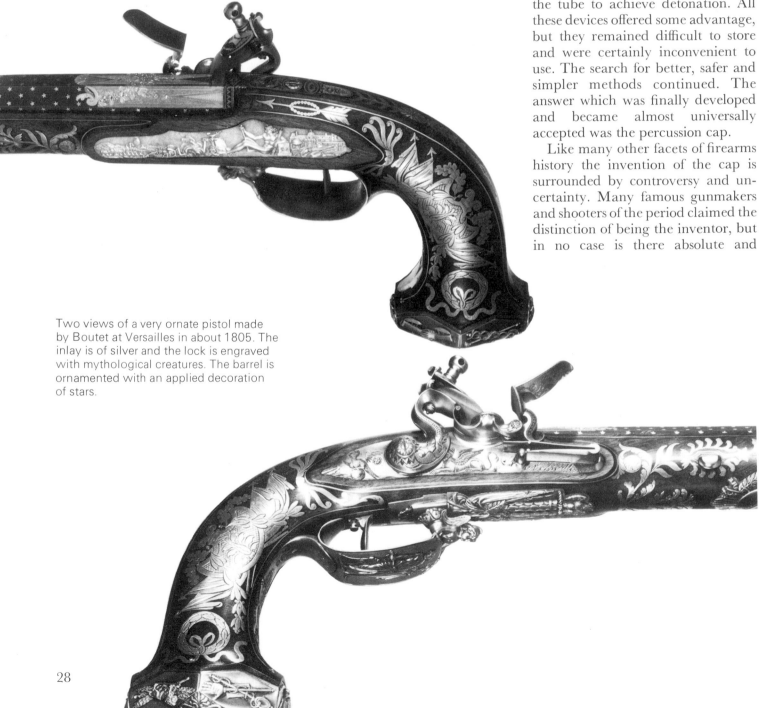

Two views of a very ornate pistol made by Boutet at Versailles in about 1805. The inlay is of silver and the lock is engraved with mythological creatures. The barrel is ornamented with an applied decoration of stars.

Russian Cossacks in the Napoleonic
Wars carried their ball-butted pistols
pushed under their belts ready for use
when the lance was too inconvenient.
Print by Peter Hess Musée de l'Armée,
Paris.

An example of Forsyth's 'scent-bottle'
lock. The spring-loaded plunger can be
seen protruding at the top, just beneath
the hammer. W. Keith Neal, Guernsey.

Loading the percussion revolver: the powder has been poured into the chamber and the bullet is now being forced home by means of the loading lever.

conclusive proof. On the whole the claim of Joshua Shaw seems to be the strongest. He claimed to have been working on the idea as early as 1815; in 1819 he emigrated from Britain to America, and patented his percussion cap there three years later, in 1822. In 1847 he was awarded the very large sum of $18,000 for his part in introducing the percussion cap to the American authorities.

The small cap was shaped rather like a top hat or a thimble, and on the inside of the crown was deposited a small quantity of the fulminate. The sides of the cap were usually grooved and it was pushed over a small rod, the nipple, through which was drilled a tiny passage connected to the touch-hole. The cap was held in place by friction and the hammer crushed the cap against the top of the nipple to produce an explosion and a flash. The detonation split the cap, and at first there were problems caused by flying splinters of metal. Later the hammer was made with a hollow nose which encircled the cap and nipple and held the pieces in place. When the hammer was recocked the pieces of the old cap were easily dislodged. Although other metals were tried, copper was the most satisfactory.

The introduction of the percussion cap certainly made loading easier and firing more certain. However, the vast majority of pistols were still muzzle-loading, and powder and shot had to be poured down from the muzzle and rammed home, a slow business.

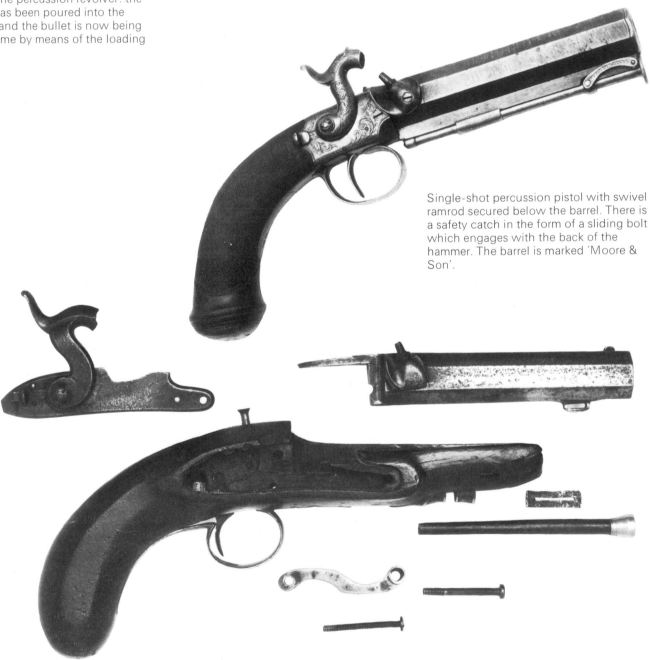

Single-shot percussion pistol with swivel ramrod secured below the barrel. There is a safety catch in the form of a sliding bolt which engages with the back of the hammer. The barrel is marked 'Moore & Son'.

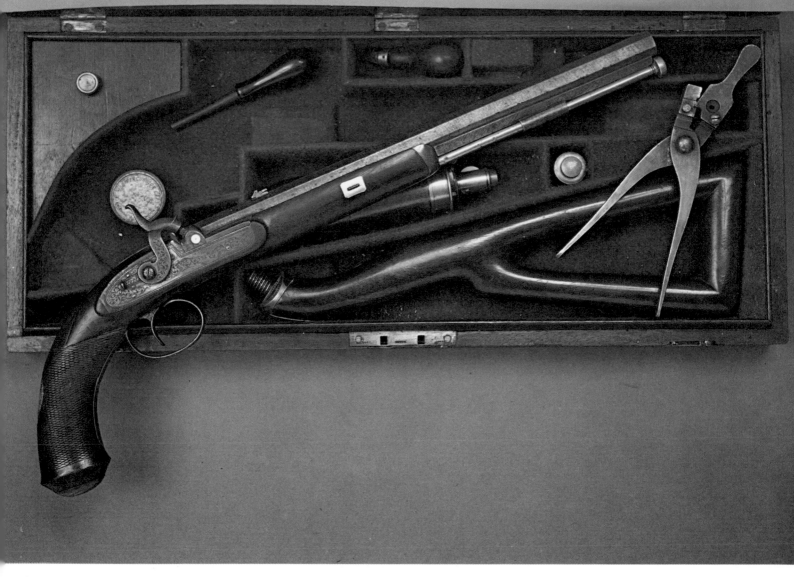

Unusual cased set incorporating a long-barrelled percussion pistol with shoulder stock. The 14-in (35.6-cm) octagonal barrel is rifled and of .32-in (8.1-mm) calibre. The skeleton stock screws to the butt to convert the weapon into a useful carbine. It is marked on the lock 'Jackson'.

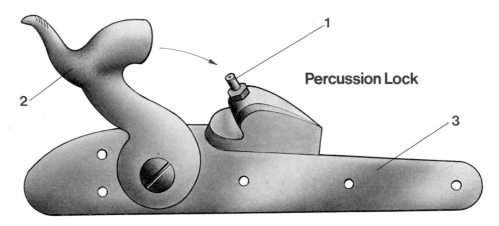

Percussion Lock

Left
Dismantled percussion pistol. The stock is of walnut and the short, octagonal barrel is secured by the tang screw and the bar which engages with the lug beneath the barrel. The lock is secured by means of the long screws and the brass side-plate.

Above
A percussion cap is placed over the small metal pillar, the nipple (1). The hammer (2) is pulled back to the full-cock position and the internal mechanism operates in exactly the same manner as on the flintlock. When the trigger is pressed, the hammer (2) falls forward to strike the cap on the nipple so achieving detonation. The nipple is attached to the barrel and not the lockplate (3).

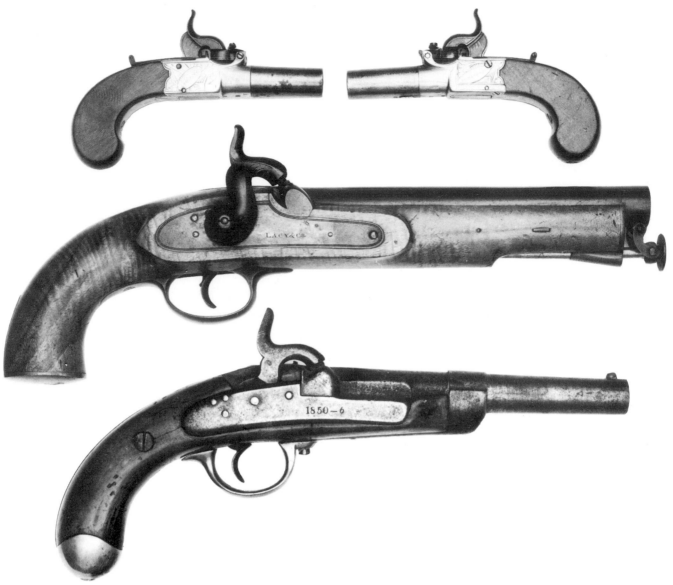

Above

Top Pair of percussion pistols with concealed triggers, made in about 1825 by Tomlinson Thame.
Centre Percussion pistol with London-proved barrel and lock marked 'Lacey & Co'. It is typical of cavalry pistols in the mid-nineteenth century.
Bottom Danish military percussion pistol with lock marked '1850–6'.

Right

Pair of percussion pocket pistols in a contoured travelling case with all accessories. As the barrels are rifled there is a mallet for forcing home the tight-fitting bullets. The pistols were made in Prague by A. V. Lebeda, who exhibited them at the Great Exhibition of 1851 in London.

Although the hunter often used a powder flask, the military normally used paper cartridges. These were hollow tubes of thick cartridge paper which contained one charge of powder, plus a little extra for priming, and a lead ball. To load, the end of the cartridge was bitten or torn off, and, if the weapon used a flintlock, a pinch of powder was placed in the pan (on a percussion weapon this step was unnecessary). The rest of the powder, the ball and the paper were rammed down the barrel, making the whole process of loading rather messy, slow and inconvenient.

From the very beginning of fire-arms, many attempts were made to design a weapon which could be loaded directly into the breech, so doing away with the pouring and ramming. All the early systems suffered from severe problems but the search went on. In 1812 a Swiss inventor, Samuel Pauly, designed a breech-loading sporting gun which employed an astonishingly modern type of cartridge. It had a base of wood or metal, the centre of which held a small charge of detonating compound. This base was secured by glue to a paper case holding the main charge and the shot. The shotgun breech could be opened, and one of these composite cartridges inserted. As the cartridge base was bevelled, it was held in the chamber; the breech was then closed and when the trigger was pressed the detonating pellet at the centre of the base was struck by a pin to fire the charge. The gun was then opened and the used base extracted; it could then be used again. Despite its superiority, few contemporaries appreciated the virtues of Pauly's system and it was not developed.

Work in this field continued, and in 1835 a Frenchman, Casimir Lefaucheux, patented a pin-fire cartridge which, in some ways, resembled that of Pauly; it also permitted the weapon to be loaded at the breech. The cartridge had a metal base and a paper body and the fulminate was

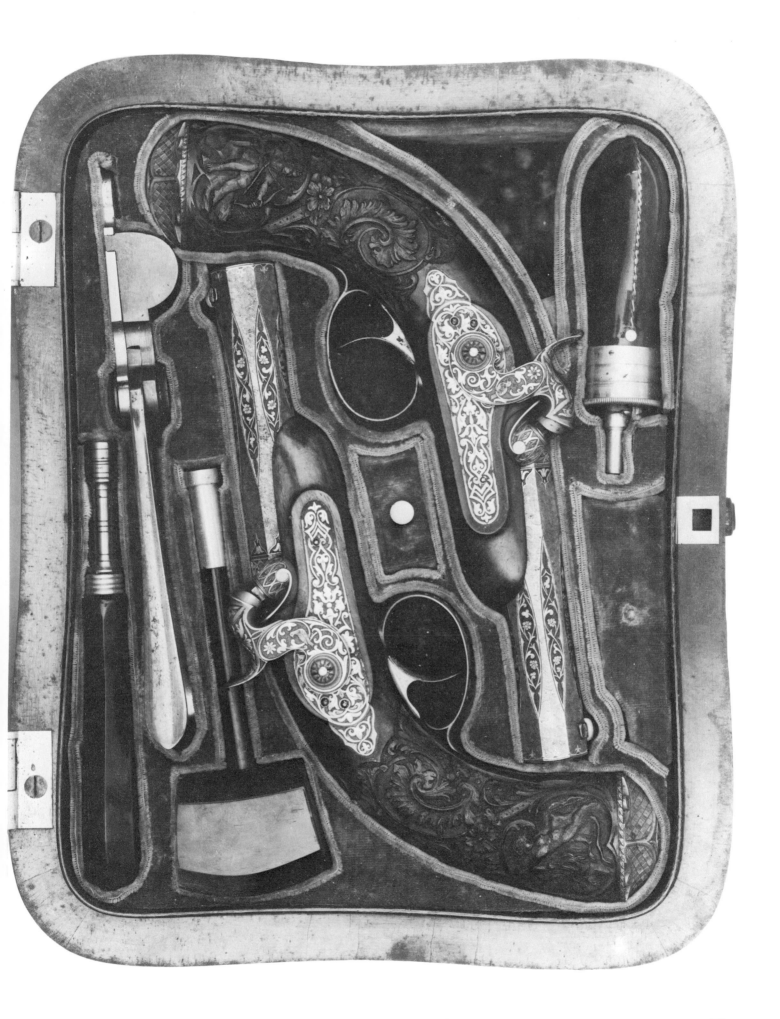

contained in the metal base, but it was detonated by a small metal pin which projected through the side of the metal base and was struck by the hammer of the pistol. In 1855 a Frenchman, Clément Pottet, patented the first really successful centre-fire cartridge. This had a small percussion cap, or primer, set at the centre of a metal base. In 1866 Colonel Edward Boxer, Superintend-ent of the Royal Laboratory at Woolwich in London, patented a centre-fire cartridge which had a metal base and a coiled brass body. Further work improved the design and construction of the metal cased cartridge, and by the third quarter of the nineteenth century the modern firearm had arrived. Future developments were merely improvements on the basic system.

The Continental style of decoration was always a little more florid than the British and American taste. These examples were exhibited by French makers at the Great Exhibition in London in 1851.

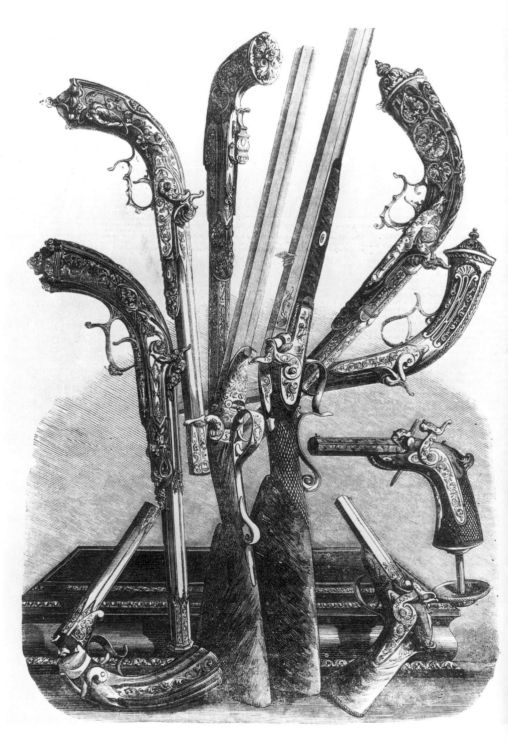

Duelling Pistols

The unknown author of *The British Code of Duel*, writing in 1829, tried hard to justify the barbarous practice of duelling. He argued that when all else had failed, war was an accepted means of settling an international dispute, and the same credibility had to be given to the duel. He claimed that duelling could be called 'the last reasoning of men'. There is some superficial justification for his argument that if it is acceptable for a nation to go to war it should be acceptable for an individual to duel since each was, in a manner of speaking, backing their position with their lives. The same writer goes on at length to justify the crude practice and explains all by saying that *honour* is the reason for the very existence of the duel. He equates this quality of honour as being the requisite of a gentleman. The eighteenth and early nineteenth-century conception of honour seems to have been extremely flexible. There was at least one duel which arose over a fight between two dogs, and resulted in the death of one of the (human) contenders.

Our unknown writer was at pains to point out that although the duel might result in death, it should be

A famous French duel recorded in 1893 by *Le Petit Journal* between the eminent politicians Paul Déroulède and Georges Clemenceau. Despite his great reputation with, as Déroulède put it, 'his sword, his pistol, his tongue', Clemenceau missed his opponent three times; he in turn was not hit.

conducted in a gentlemanly, re-strained manner. Once the insult had been offered the only requirement for the injured party was to ascertain the address of the offender and pass this on to a friend, who became his second and henceforward was solely respon-sible for the arrangements leading up to the cold-blooded climax of the dispute. It was the second who actually delivered the challenge; it was then up to him to agree the weapons, the site, the time and all other pertinent arrangements with the opponent's second.

This settling of a quarrel by personal combat has a long history. The sagas of the Greeks and Vikings all make great play of the individual combat. The duel, however, seems to have become a speciality of the French, indeed so much so that in 1679 Louis XIV made duelling a capital offence. Certainly there were duels in other countries but France seems to have been particularly afflicted by this inane and vicious practice. Britain and America seem to have avoided its worst excesses.

Until the eighteenth century, cert-ainly in Britain and America, the majority of these so-called affairs of honour were decided with the sword. Since no gentleman's education was considered complete without some tuition in the art of swordsmanship, each man's chances were, in theory at least, more or less equal. Soon after the introduction of firearms people began to use them for fighting duels, but this did not become general practice until much later in the eighteenth century. The reason was probably that the sword was still considered to be the only weapon of the gentleman, and it was no doubt thought to be a little vulgar to use such a commonplace thing as a pistol. Pistols were used occasionally, how-ever, at a quite early date, and there were one or two combats which were unusual in that they were fought on horseback and there was at least one in which a musket was used.

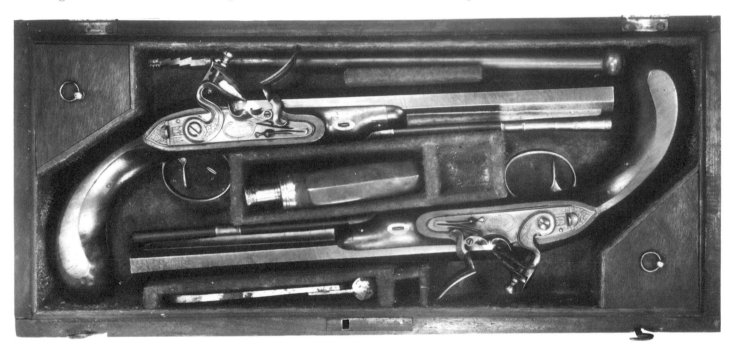

Above
American flintlock pistol made by Jacob Grubb *c* 1770-80, fitted with a brass barrel 6¾ in (17.14 mm) long and firing a .45-in (11.4-mm) bullet. The barrel is octagonal at the breech but converts to round. Winchester Gun Museum, New Haven, Connecticut.

Top
Cased pair of duelling pistols by Wogdon & Barton, made about 1780 but later modified by the addition of the steel holders for the ramrod. The locks are signed in gold.

In all duels it was very important that each of the opponents should be seen to have exactly the same chance, or, put another way, exactly the same opportunity to survive. In the days of swords this had meant seeing that both weapons were the same length, that neither duellist was wearing any form of protective clothing, and that the ground gave no advantage to either contestant. When pistols were used, it was equally important to see that the weapons were identical.

Until the mid-nineteenth century it was common practice to sell pistols in pairs, so there was no great problem to acquire two similar pistols. While, however, until the 1770s any pistol of reasonable quality met the requirements of the duellist, from this period on it became increasingly common to make weapons solely and specifically for use in the duel. In Britain and America the manufacture of duelling pistols did not dwindle until after the mid-nineteenth century. On the Continent they were more gradually transformed from a weapon of death to a weapon of pleasure, until what had originally been a duelling pistol became a target or saloon pistol.

From the 1770s until the early 1800s the duelling pistol was, of course, a flintlock weapon, and the writer of 1829 gives some valuable advice to the would-be duellist on what he should look for when examining the weapons. He writes, 'In the use of pistols their examination requires care, it is obviously proper that those of the same degree of excellence should be used by both parties.' He then goes on to list what the seconds should look for: they should examine the pistol 'and see that they are perfect, even to the flint to preclude mis-fire; and then to load them equally in the presence of each other'. After this they should see that 'the ground on which the combatants are to stand affords no direction to their fire; such as highways, footpaths, walls, hedges, ridges or even the line formed by an horizon apparent'.

The next advice that he gives is on the distance between the two shooters, and it is interesting that he says 'nice calculators have found, that from the parabola described by a ball on its projection, twelve or fourteen

paces are, at times, more dangerous than eight. The distance nevertheless is entirely in the discretion of the seconds, ten paces of not less than 30 inches being, however, always the minimum.' This means a minimum distance of 25 ft (7.6 m). When the two duellists were in their positions and were correctly sited according to the seconds' commands, the signal to fire was given. This varied: sometimes

Pair of flintlock duelling pistols made *c* 1790 by one of the best-known British makers of such weapons, Messrs Wogdon & Barton. The 9.6-in (24.1-cm) barrels are round and fitted with sights. The locks are fitted with bolt safety catches. There is a variation in the ramrods, one being fitted with a worm to pull out a bullet and the other with a powder measure. S. Durrant, London.

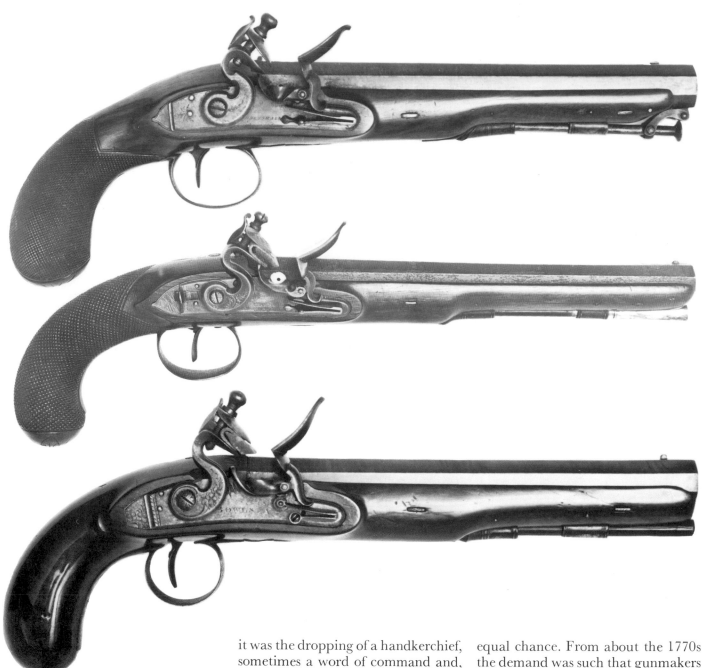

From top to bottom.
Officer's pistol, made by the British
gunmaker Henshall in about 1810.
It could well have served as a duelling
pistol. It has a swivel ramrod and a patent
waterproof pan. S. Durrant, London.
Single duelling pistol by John Richards
of London, *c* 1800. The butt is cross-
hatched and the lock has a bolt safety
catch. The octagonal barrel has sights
and the touch-hole is fitted with a
platinum plug to reduce fouling and
corrosion. G. Kellam, Broadstairs, Kent.
Duelling pistol made by Bowls of Cork in
Ireland. It has no safety catch but the
frizzen spring is fitted with a small roller
to reduce friction and ensure crisp action.
S. Durrant, London.

it was the dropping of a handkerchief, sometimes a word of command and, occasionally, some naturally occurring event was used as the signal.

In the most usual form of duel, on the command to fire each opponent was expected to raise his pistol and fire without delay. Obviously in this situation it was imperative that the pistol should be reliable. There should be no risk of a misfire or excessive hangfire, but rather a quick, sharp, single, accurate shot. If the first requirement of such a weapon was reliability, the second had to be accuracy, and what was wanted was a pistol that would come naturally and easily into the aiming position. Prior to the 1770s it seems that virtually any pair of pistols could be used in a duel; obviously a pair, rather than just any two pistols, had to be used since each opponent had to be accorded an equal chance. From about the 1770s the demand was such that gunmakers felt that they could concentrate on producing a weapon which was designed specifically for the duel, seeking to achieve reliability and ease of aiming.

In a very short time the stock most appropriate for a duelling pistol had been devised. All superfluous decoration was removed, leaving the stock very plain and simple. The butt was curved and slightly more hooked than most pistols of the period. It was usually, but not invariably, cross-hatched; that is, the surface was roughened by a series of criss-crossed, incised lines producing a diamond shaped pattern which gave a slightly firmer grip to a hand that might well be made slippery by the sweat of fear. Another way of improving the grip was to flatten the sides of the butt. The

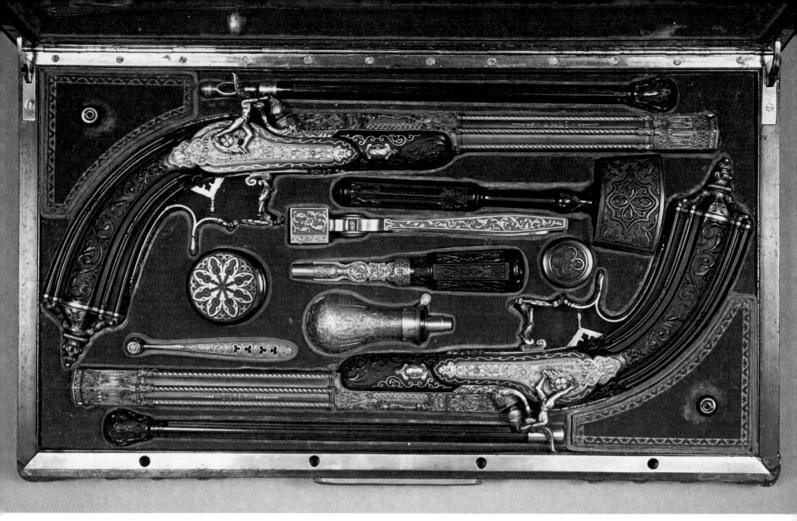

Although typical in shape and style, these pistols are far more elaborate than usual. The hammers are fashioned into figures and the barrels are elaborately chiselled and gilded. All accessories are chiselled or inlaid, and the entire set is held in a velvet-lined case. It was made by Renette and Gastinne of Paris in about 1850.

walnut stock normally extended the full length of the barrel; half-stocked duelling pistols were far more typical of the late Continental style. For the dedicated enthusiast, writers of the period recommended that they should go to their gunmakers and have their duelling pistol stocks made to measure! The butt should be of just the right thickness, and should sit comfortably in the hand, and the stock should be of just the right length and weight to balance in this position.

The next important point was that, when in the aiming position, there should be nothing at all about the weapon that should distract the eye of the duellist from his target. All the furniture, the name given to the metal parts of the pistol such as the trigger guard and lock plate, were normally blued. This means that during manufacture they were treated by heat to produce a rather pleasant deep blue which would not reflect the light and so could not dazzle the duellist when taking aim.

Having a weapon which came naturally to the aim was the first step on the road to a first-class duelling pistol. Next, and of scarcely less vital

importance, was the barrel. In general, eighteenth-century pistols were fitted with barrels round in section and usually 10–12 in (25–30 cm) long. From the late eighteenth century to the early nineteenth century there was a tendency to reduce the length of the barrel and also to make them considerably heavier; in addition, many of the later barrels were octagonal in section. The bore was very carefully polished and smoothed, and all the authorities writing on the subject insisted that this must be kept scrupulously clean. The bullets were designed to fit closely so that they were delivered with maximum power and maximum accuracy. A loose-fitting ball tended to wander from side to side on its journey along the bore, and accuracy suffered.

The majority of British duelling pistols were smooth-bored but there was a tendency, particularly on the Continent, to rifle the barrels. A rifled barrel gives a far more accurate shot but British practice was to eschew this although certain gunmakers did produce barrels which had half, scratch or secret rifling. These were so designed that, viewed from the muzzle, there were no indications of rifling at all. The barrel was rifled from the breech to approximately half way along its length leaving the muzzle end smooth-bored. Another anonymous writer, using the pseudonym 'A Traveller', in 1836 condemned these rifled pistols as being 'an unfair weapon to duel with' and he claimed, after having made many trials, that the difference in accuracy between a half-rifled and a smooth-bore barrel at the normal distance at which a duel was fought, 12–15 paces, was so small as to be pointless.

The barrels of duelling pistols were normally fitted with sights and 'A Traveller' recommends that silver fore-sights, fitted on some pistols, should be avoided. He feared that they might catch the light of early dawn and possibly throw the shooter off-target.

Gunmakers sought to improve the accuracy of their pistols by adjusting the angle of the bore. Most pistols of the period shot high, and makers of quality pistols tried to compensate for this in various ways. Some gave the bore a slight curve whilst others made the barrel very heavy. The Rigby brothers, John and William, of Dublin, produced a barrel in which the bore was not central in the barrel but sloped down, and they claimed that this made the weapon shoot dead straight. They claimed that their pistols were so accurate that the number of duels fell markedly since people felt their chances of survival were greatly reduced. Quite what difference this accuracy made, whether one struck the man in the third rib or the second rib, is difficult to judge, and most of those who suffered the consequences were in no position to comment.

Next, but by no means of less importance, was the lock and the means of ignition. In a top-quality duelling pistol a great deal of time and effort was given to the individual components of the lock. Surfaces which bore on one another were made small in area and honed and polished so as to be as smooth as possible and to reduce friction and any possible chance of a slight snag or snatch during the functioning of the

lock. 'A Traveller' disapproves of the back-action locks developed in the 1830s in which the main spring was set behind the hammer. With flintlocks, and indeed the majority of pistols, the pressure required to operate the mechanism by squeezing the trigger is quite considerable. This could affect the point of aim since the pressure might swing the pistol to one side or the other, or raise or lower the muzzle. To overcome this, the gunmakers fitted a little device which had been used as far back as the sixteenth century and then largely forgotten.

This was the set, or hair trigger, which consisted of a small, internal set of levers and springs activated by the trigger. The mechanism could be adjusted so that only the slightest pressure on the trigger was necessary to activate it and cause an arm to push clear the sear which was holding the tumbler in the full-cock position. On earlier weapons this device had been operated by a separate trigger, but on most duelling pistols it was made ready to act by pushing the trigger forward. So finely set were some of these hair mechanisms that a jolt was sufficient to activate them. That connoisseur of duelling, 'A Traveller', recommends that they should be treated with the greatest of caution. He stresses that the hair trigger mechanism should not be set too finely and that the firer should at all times practise constantly so that he knew instinctively how much pressure was required. It was so easy to discharge the weapon as the arm was coming up to the aiming position just by touching the trigger. It was considered unwise, furthermore, to set the hair trigger until the weapon was loaded and the duellist was in position, with the pistol pointing to the ground.

This plain, somewhat hook-butted weapon was the basic duelling pistol at the turn of the eighteenth century. However, various other refinements were added later and some pistol stocks were made with a pointed extension at the top of the butt which projected back over the joint of thumb and forefinger. Such pistols were known as saw-handled, because of their resemblance to the tool. They do not seem to have been very

Above right
Although made by a London gunmaker, Clarke of Holborn, these duelling pistols have a rather Continental-shaped butt. The locks are fitted with anti-friction rollers on the tips of the frizzen springs. Their date is *c* 1800.

Right
While very similar in style to Clarke's pistols, these were probably made as a pair of officer's pistols rather than for duelling. The barrels are round and the pistols would probably have been less accurate than a pair of duellers. Made by H. W. Mortimer of London in about 1825, they are in an oak case with cleaning rods, bullet mould, spare flints and powder flask.

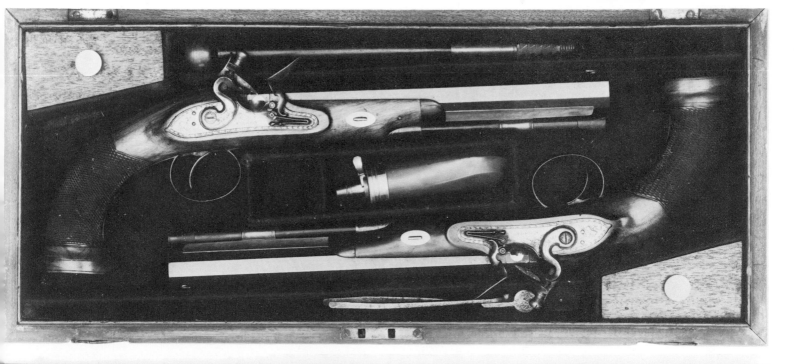

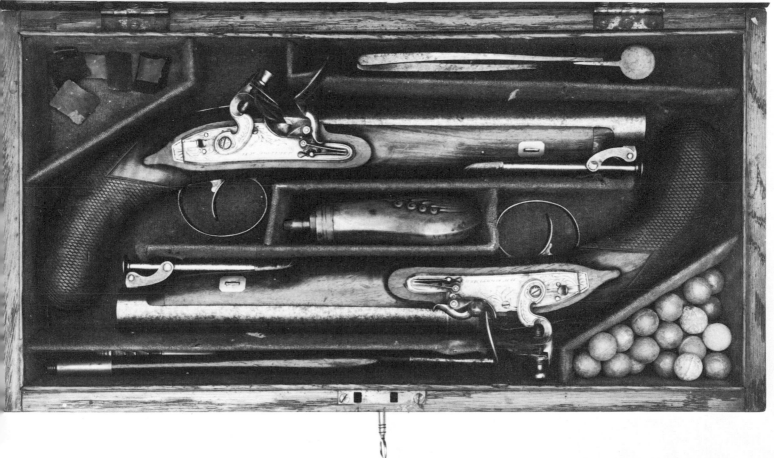

popular since the number of examples which have survived is comparatively small in comparison with the standard pattern. 'A Traveller' describes them as being clumsy and does not recommend them. He does, on the other hand, recommend another refinement which appeared at the turn of the century. This was a slightly curved metal bar set beneath the trigger guard so that the pistol butt was now gripped with the index finger through the trigger guard, the second finger gripping the spur below the trigger guard, the third and fourth fingers firmly gripping the main body of the butt.

Duelling pistols were supplied in pairs, and no true-born gentleman of honour would have considered his possessions complete without his own cased set. The cases, usually of oak, were partitioned by a number of fences and lined with velvet or baize,

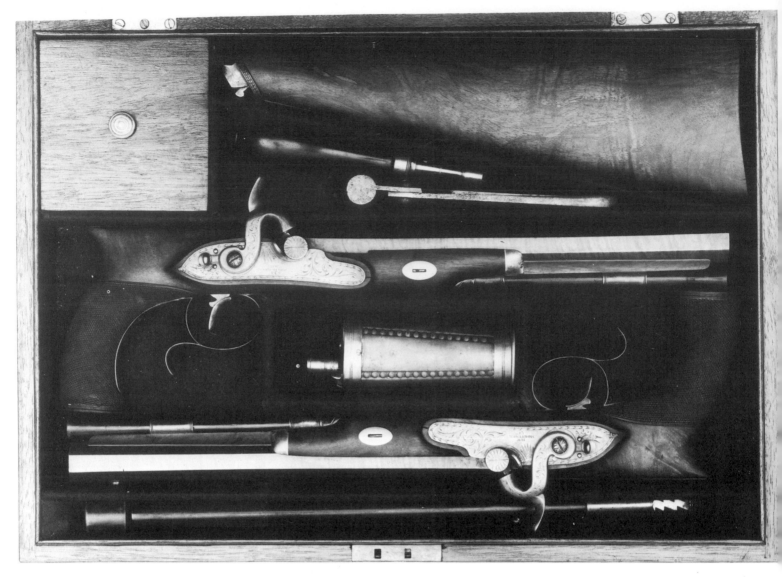

and held the two pistols and accompanying accessories. These varied slightly but, in general, consisted of a bullet mould, a cleaning rod and a powder flask. The cases were fitted with a lock, and on the outside of the lid was a small metal plate, the escutcheon, on which were engraved the initials or arms of the owner. Inside the lid the gunmaker stuck his trade label which was often quite elaborate and decorative.

On arrival at the field of honour, with duellists, seconds and doctor in attendance, the case was opened and inspected by the seconds. The loading was closely supervised and every effort was made to see that each was given exactly identical charges. It was recommended that before the pistol was loaded one should blow gently down the barrel to remove any dust and to ensure that the touch-hole was clear of any obstruction. Most powder flasks were fitted with a graduated nozzle which could be adjusted to give the correct charge required. On some pistols the ramrod, normally housed beneath the barrel, had a brass tip which could be unscrewed to reveal a small, tubular container which held just the requisite charge of powder. This was filled with powder and held vertically, the barrel was lowered over the ramrod until the section holding the powder touched the breech. Barrel and ramrod were then inverted so that the powder was deposited directly into the breech with no possibility of any grains adhering to the bore which could have reduced the power or impeded the smooth movement of the bullet. A small amount of powder was then placed in the pan, the frizzen closed and the weapon was then ready.

Each time the pistol was fired the exploding black powder produced a certain amount of corrosion and deposit, and it was important to keep this to a minimum. Many of the better-quality pistols had their pans

Above
These pistols are by H. W. Mortimer, a London gunmaker famed for the quality of his work, who made them as flintlocks; they were later converted to percussion *c* 1810. They have saw-handled butts and spurred trigger guards. Included in the set is a detachable butt to convert either into a carbine. Overall length $15\frac{3}{8}$ in (39 cm).

Right
Nicholas Noel Boutet was made responsible for the artistic direction of the Manufacture de Versailles in August 1792. A special workshop was formed to produce *armes de luxe* such as this pair of fine flintlock duelling pistols. The butt shape is typical of many French pistols.

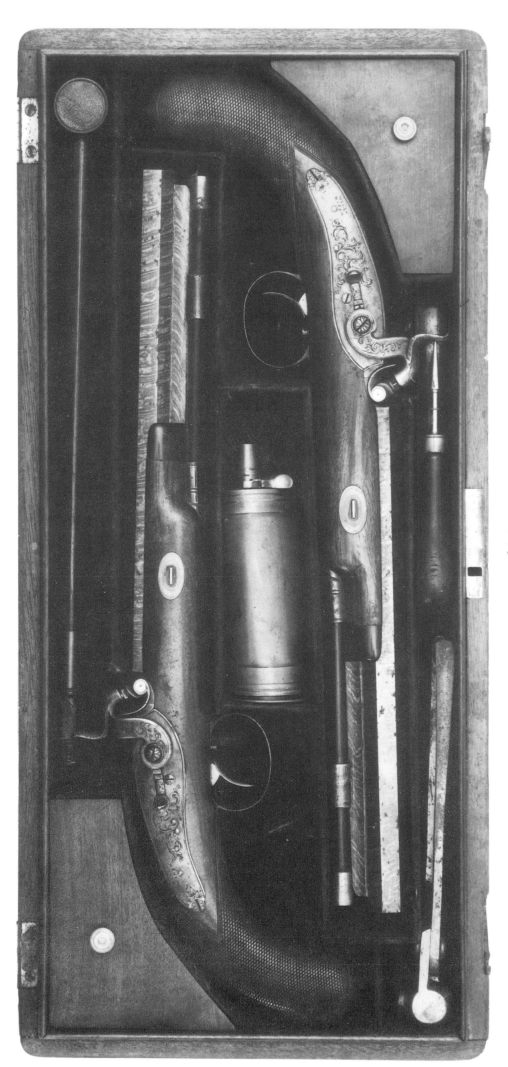

Back-action locks are fitted on these percussion pistols. They also have bolt safety catches and good-quality octagonal barrels. They were made by William Mills of Holborn, London *c* 1840.

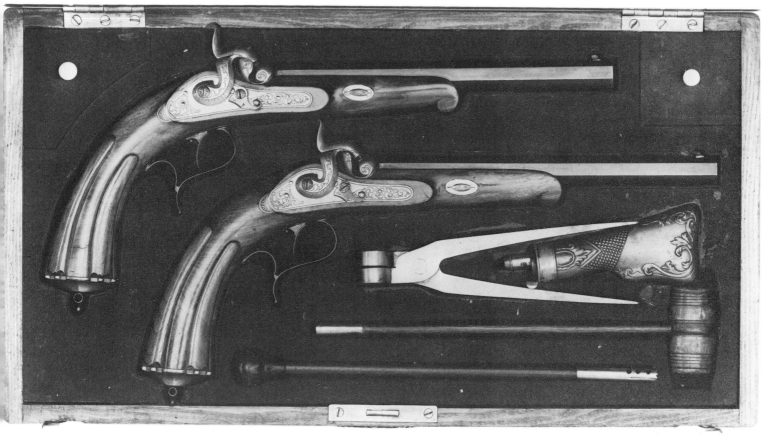

Mid-nineteenth-century German duelling or target pistols made by O. Ulbricht of Döbeln in about 1850. The barrels are rifled, a practice not favoured in British weapons. An unusual style of safety catch is fitted to the lock plate. Overall length 15 in (38.1 cm).

and touch-holes lined with gold or platinum since these metals were better able to resist the effects of burning and corrosion, so reducing wear around these two places. Writers of this period stress that a flash in the pan – when the priming fired but not the main charge – counted as a shot, so it was obviously essential to make sure that this did not happen. When the percussion system was established, gunmakers naturally used it when making duelling pistols; the case then included a small tin or horn box to hold the percussion caps.

Despite all the effort that was devoted to the production of a good-quality, straight-shooting, reliable pistol, the effort seems, according to 'A Traveller', to have been rather pointless. In one of his chapters he considers the possibility of death or injury in a duel. He argues, on statistical evidence gained from the study of a number of cases, that the chances of a man being killed are about 14 to 1, and of being hit about 6 to 1. He then goes on to point out that even if hit the chances of death or serious injury are not excessive and he writes quite happily of a friend, 'an officer in the Hanoverian service', who had been twice shot through the

head and 'although minus many of his teeth, and part of his jaw he still survives and enjoys good health'. He lists other friends who have been shot through the lungs and other vulnerable parts of the body. He does admit that 'Recovery, however, in such cases, depends much on the sufferer's habit of body and strength of constitution.'

He then goes on to a detailed survey of the consequences of wounds. He divides a man's body into nine parts and claims that only in three of these would a wound prove mortal. He argues that, on this basis, if a man is hit the chances are 3 to 1 against the wound being fatal, and then contradicts his previous figure by saying that the odds against being hit are 5 to 1. However, recognizing that he has fallen into something of a trap, for his book is designed to improve the duellists' chances, he adds 'that is, however, provided his antagonist has not read my work of followed any of my practical rules, if he has the case may be different'. Despite all his optimistic predictions the writer insists 'that upon the previous day he [the duellist] should have been careful to secure the services of his medical attendant who will provide himself

The Duel

Left
This engraving of 1846 shows the fatal outcome of a duel. The detail is good, showing both the smoke of the priming and the main charge. It was unusual for a duel to be held before such an audience.

Right
Characteristic of the French and Belgian style of pistols, these were made by Verney in Lyons, France c 1850. The screwdriver has a reversible head which converts it to a nipple key.

with all the necessary apparatus for tying up wounds or arteries and extracting balls'.

In Britain the duelling habit was never quite as prevalent as on the Continent although there were a number of quite important duels. Duels were not unknown in America and it was there that the practice of 'posting' is said to have developed. The author of *The British Code of Duel* (1829) disapproves strongly of this as being unworthy of a gentleman. According to tradition a Virginian Congressman once issued a challenge which was refused; he then stuck up notices in all the taverns and on street corners, drawing everyone's attention to the fact that his opponent, another member of Congress, was 'a prevaricating, base, calumniating scoundrel, a poltroon and a coward'.

Neither in Britain nor America was the practice of duelling limited to any particular social group; certainly, some very important people indulged. In America there was a duel between Alexander Hamilton, a close friend of George Washington, and Aaron Burr, the Vice-President of the United States. The quarrel was basically political in origin and resulted in Burr challenging for a duel which took place in New Jersey on 11 July 1804. The outcome was that Hamilton fell dead and Burr was charged with his murder, as a result of which he died almost in obscurity in 1836.

Despite the tragic example of this event another duel between two great leaders was fought in May 1806, by General Andrew Jackson and Charles Dickinson. Both contestants were good shots, and on the command to fire Jackson was hit in the breast by a ball which broke two ribs and gave a very painful wound, but this did not prevent him from taking careful aim and firing. Unfortunately the pistol jammed at the half-cock position, but calmly and with deliberation Jackson re-cocked, took aim again, and killed his man. Jackson did not suffer the fate of Burr for he was later elected to the Presidency of the United States. Duelling in the Northern parts of the United States was never as widespread as it was in the South, and New Orleans in particular might almost have earned the name of Duelling Capital of the New World. By the

Top
Percussion duelling pistol made by
W. Parker *c* 1840. It has the typical spur
trigger guard, octagonal barrel and swivel
ramrod of the later pistols. The trigger can
be adjusted for a light pull by means of
the screw just visible in front of the
trigger.

Above
Pair of fine-quality pistols intended
primarily for target shooting rather than
duelling. The pistols are fitted with back-
action locks and the octagonal barrels
have clear sights fitted. These pistols,
made by Dickson & Co, are numbered
4070 and 4071 and were made in about
1850–60.

1860s, however, even in the hot-
blooded South, duelling was on the
decline although it had persisted
there longer than in Britain.

The United States were not alone
in seeing their leaders indulge in duels
for in Britain, in September 1809, at
Putney Heath, just outside London,
Lord Castlereagh, the Secretary of
War, challenged George Canning,
the Secretary of State for Foreign
Affairs. The first exchange of shots
was inconclusive so a second was
fired, and this time Canning was
wounded in the left thigh. In 1829 one

of the most famous of British duels
took place between the Duke of
Wellington and the Earl of Winchelsea. The quarrel was partly political, partly religious. The Duke of
Wellington was accused by Lord
Winchelsea, a fanatical Protestant, of
introducing Catholicism into all
government departments. After
efforts to obtain satisfaction the
matter was pressed by the Duke of
Wellington to the point of a challenge. There seems to be some
uncertainty as to the actual progress
of the duel. Some accounts say that

The duel remained a strong tradition on the Continent, especially in France. Shown here is an engraving of a duel held in 1878. The two contestants are apparently using single-shot percussion pistols. On the left are the seconds.

the Duke fired his pistol at Winchelsea, others say that he merely fired at random with no intention of hitting him; and the Earl of Winchelsea is said to have 'deloped', the duellists' term for firing into the air.

No doubt encouraged by the example of the highest in the land, the number of duels increased. As a result of several very unpleasant incidents British public opinion swung rapidly to the view that duelling was contrary to the law and the feelings of people as a whole. In 1843 the Anti-Duelling Association was formed with the sole intention of discouraging and, if possible, stopping the practice of duelling throughout Britain.

In 1844 Queen Victoria and her government decided that they would amend the Articles of War which set out the regulations for the behaviour of officers in the Army. They accordingly deleted the section which had stated that officers who did not redeem their honour by duel should be cashiered. Later that year the War Office issued an order that any officer who issued a challenge, took part in a duel, knew of a duel and did nothing to stop it, would be court-martialled; if found guilty, he would be cashiered or punished in some other way. Any officer who took part as a second was also liable to be punished, and all officers were encouraged to explain and, if necessary, apologise for conduct which gave rise to a challenge. After this directive to the armed forces duelling, which to a very large extent had been limited during this period to officers in the Army and Navy, declined and virtually ceased in Britain. By the late 1840s, although there were a few exceptions, British duelling was finished. With the abandonment of duelling, the need for duelling pistols also ended, and they were no longer made by the gunmakers of Britain or America.

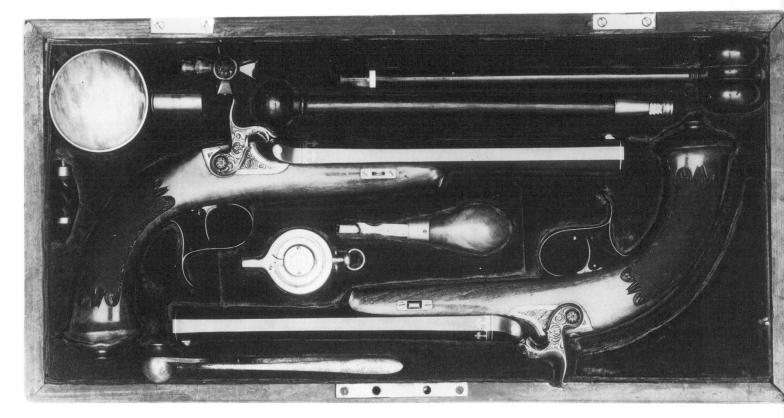

On the Continent the position was somewhat different. In France the desire to duel seems to have been particularly strong, and although in Britain the demand for duelling pistols ceased from about the 1840s, this certainly did not happen to French gunsmiths. They continued to produce beautifully cased sets of pistols which, while normally described as duelling pistols, more often than not were intended for target practice and only occasionally were put to their original, deadly use. A typical mid or late nineteenth-century duelling set from a French or Belgian gunmaker consisted of a very handsome case, quite possibly of mahogany, lined throughout with purple or red velvet, and each compartment contoured to hold a specific item. In the case were the usual accessories together with a number of extras, including a mallet. The majority of these pistols were rifled; it is very difficult to push the bullet down a rifled barrel because it has to bite into the rifling, and sometimes the fit was so tight that the ramrod had to be tapped with a wooden mallet; hence its presence in the case. Ramrods were normally separate, for the pistols were half-stocked and made without any facility for the ramrod. The pistol itself usually had a stock and butt of ebony, fluted and exquisitely chiselled and blued.

The furniture, the lock, the trigger guard and the barrel itself were frequently blued. The barrel was fluted and the lock carefully chiselled with various floral and geometric patterns. A bullet mould was included and the powder measure was often of a quite complicated design. A screwdriver is also usually supplied.

In 1849, at about the same time as the quality duelling pistol was falling from popularity, L. N. A. Flobert patented a breech-loading system. This used a very small, copper cartridge which held a charge of powder; the fulminate in the base was in the form of a disc. The cartridge was loaded into the breech and was struck by a very solid hammer with a raised, central rib. The strong spring and the weight of the hammer were sufficient to hold the cartridge in place even when the charge was exploding. This system was very simple indeed, for it consisted only of a bored-through barrel with a slightly recessed section at the end to receive the cartridge. Its simplicity made the pistol easy to manufacture and consequently very cheap, and it achieved great popularity particularly for target practice.

Above
Decorative German percussion duelling pistols with octagonal rifled barrels, decorated in gold, silver and platinum. The velvet-lined mahogany case has all the usual accessories as well as a cap dispenser, a circular container which held a number of caps and fed them out one by one as required.

Right
These ornate pistols were made in Austria in about 1860, and although they resemble percussion weapons they are actually breech-loading cartridge weapons. They were probably made as target weapons rather than for the duel. Victoria and Albert Museum, London.

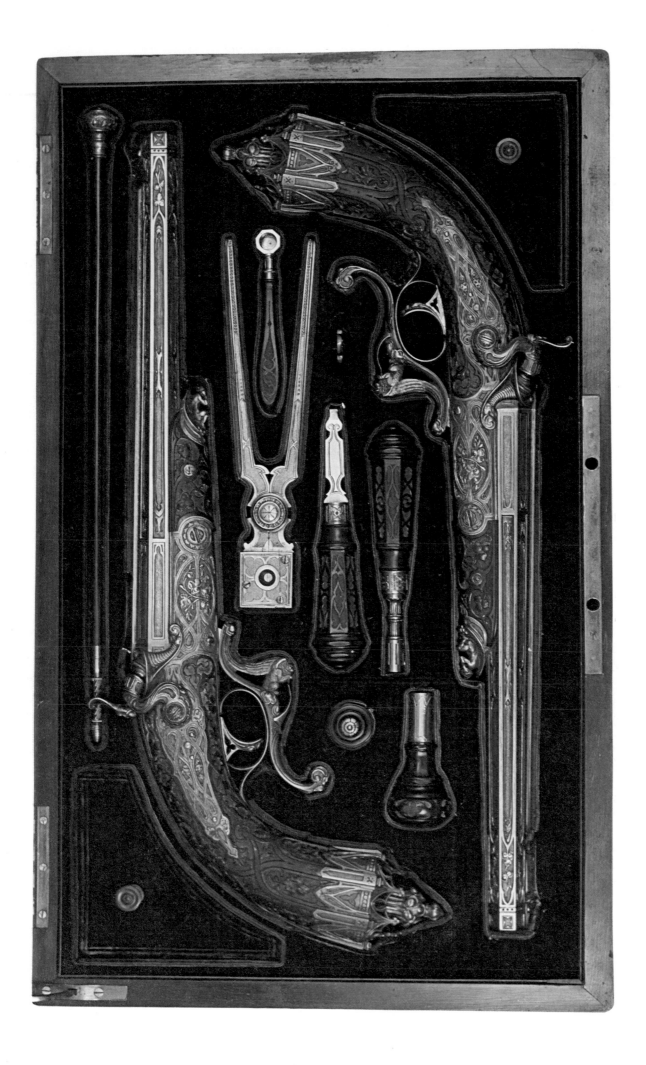

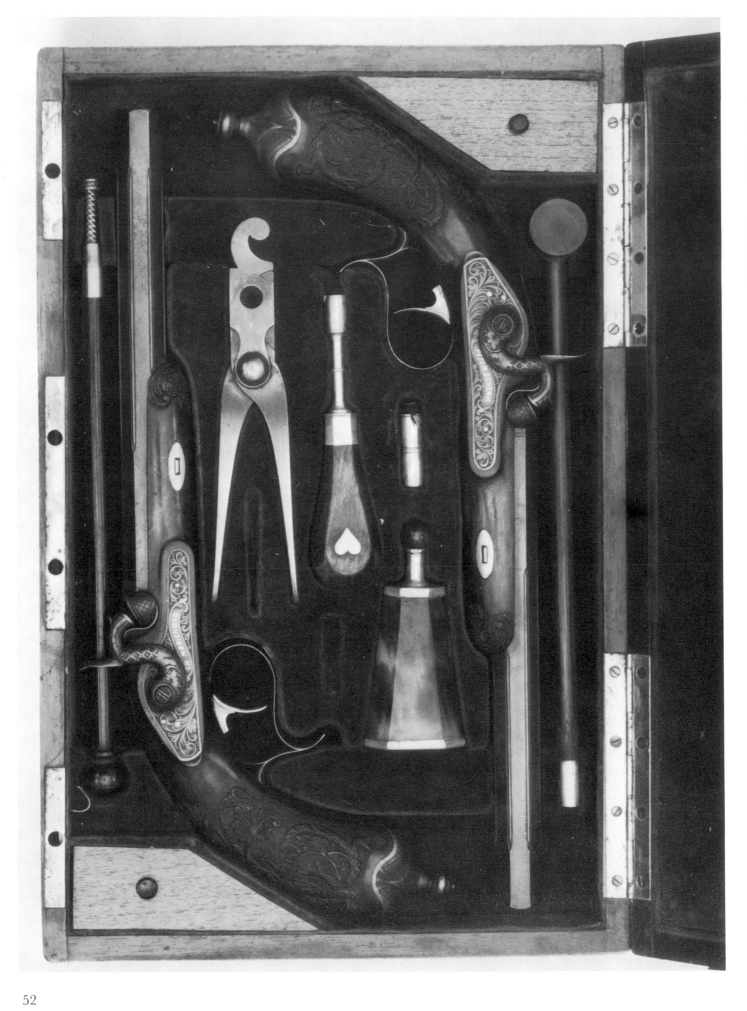

Above
Fine, saw-handled flintlock duelling
pistols by the London gunmaker Thomas
Hewson. They have platinum-lined
touch-holes and there are gold lines at
the breech. The butts are cut square and
the trigger guard has the finger spur.

Left
Elaborate German target/duelling pistol
by Peter Schenk of Marienbad, with
accessories including bullet mould,
powder flask, ramrod and cleaning rods.

The Flobert pistol became one of
the most popular saloon or indoor
target weapons replacing the older,
expensive, duelling-type pistols.
Later examples differ somewhat from
the original Flobert which had an
extractor for removing the empty
cartridge. This worked by two small
hooks on the face of the hammer
which slipped over the end and
gripped the case so that when the
hammer was re-cocked, it automatically withdrew the cartridge
case. The later weapons had a simple
half-gate at the face of the breech
which was tipped back to extract the
cartridge case. They were fairly
crude, with a very simple butt and
normally a sleeved trigger, and
remained in continuous production –
in quantity – until 1935.

In the late nineteenth century
there was a vogue for what might be
called 'artificial' duelling, using this
type of weapon. The participants
covered themselves with a heavy
canvas cloak, a glass-visored helmet
and used a pistol patented by a Dr
Devillier. It fired wax bullets which, it
was claimed, were accurate up to a
range of 15–20 yards. The pistol had a
special guard to protect the firer's
hand.

On modern ranges duelling is the
name given to a system of shooting in
which a turning target is used. The
shooter faces a target turned side-on
to him or her; after a certain time
lapse, it turns to face the shooter and
stays exposed for a short time, usually
three seconds, and then turns side-on
again. During this exposure time the
shooter must aim and fire.

Although the function of the
duelling pistol was particularly unpleasant, a good-quality example
represented a peak of the gunmaker's
skill. Totally functional, with all
superfluous furniture removed and
fitted with a smoothly efficient lock
and a well-made barrel, it was the
result of a great deal of technical skill
and craftsmanship. Some gunmakers
such as Mortimer, Manton and
Wogden helped build up their repu-
tations on the quality of their duelling
pistols. However, knowing the history
of duelling in Britain, and looking at
the considerable quantity of surviving
weapons, one is driven to the con-
clusion that a very large number of
cased duellers were probably owned
by men who had them largely as a
status symbol, and who secretly
prayed that they might never be
called upon to use them!

Multishot Weapons

One of the problems with the majority of firearms from their beginnings until the mid-nineteenth century was that for part of their cycle of operation they were virtually useless as weapons. This, moreover, occurred at the time when they were most needed. A sword, axe, spear or club was ready for continuous use once it was in the hand until it was either broken or lost. These weapons were always potentially effective, needing only the user's skill to make them so. The longbow was available for immediate use at any time and required only a second or so to be drawn ready to discharge an arrow. Provided he was supplied with arrows, the archer could maintain a barrage of missiles limited only by his physical endurance. Crossbows more closely resembled the firearm for both were useless for part of the time. Once the gun had been fired or the bolt discharged from the crossbow, they were totally ineffective until they had been reloaded. During the time it took to do this the soldier was a liability to others since he was almost defenceless and might well need to be protected against attack.

There was yet another aspect to this problem: when the shooter had fired his weapon, he had used up his only chance of scoring a hit. For the soldier in battle a target missed could well cost him his life; if the hunter missed he probably lost only his quarry. The problem affected battle tactics in various ways. For example, when the cavalry first acquired pistols

the only way in which they could be used effectively was for the horsemen to charge the enemy, fire their pistols, and then turn and ride back so that they could reload.

The problem was obvious to the gunmakers from the very beginning, and one easy solution was to equip each soldier with a pair of pistols. Most firearms were sold in pairs and this practice continued until well into the nineteenth century. As an answer, however, it could only be a stopgap, for if both pistols were fired one after the other the chances of a hit were not necessarily greater. Almost every pistol shooter has a strong and a weak hand: with right-handed people their left hand is usually the weaker, and vice versa. Shots fired with the weak hand are almost invariably less accurate so that if the first shot, fired with the strong hand, missed, then the second was even less likely to hit the target. If the shooter used only his strong hand for firing, he had the added difficulty of swapping the empty pistol for the loaded one. The chances of fumbling or dropping the weapon were considerable, especially in the stress of combat. It was also not such a simple matter to carry two pistols. On horseback they could be pushed into the holsters at the front of the saddle, but on foot they were much more of an encumbrance. With the eighteenth-century pocket pistols, which were much smaller and simpler, there was no great difficulty, but long-barrelled, military holster pistols were a very different matter.

The lock mechanism of a double-barrelled wheellock carbine made in Nuremberg in the late sixteenth century. The twin locks each had to be spanned; the rear one fires the top barrel. Overall length $34\frac{1}{2}$ in (87.63 cm).

54

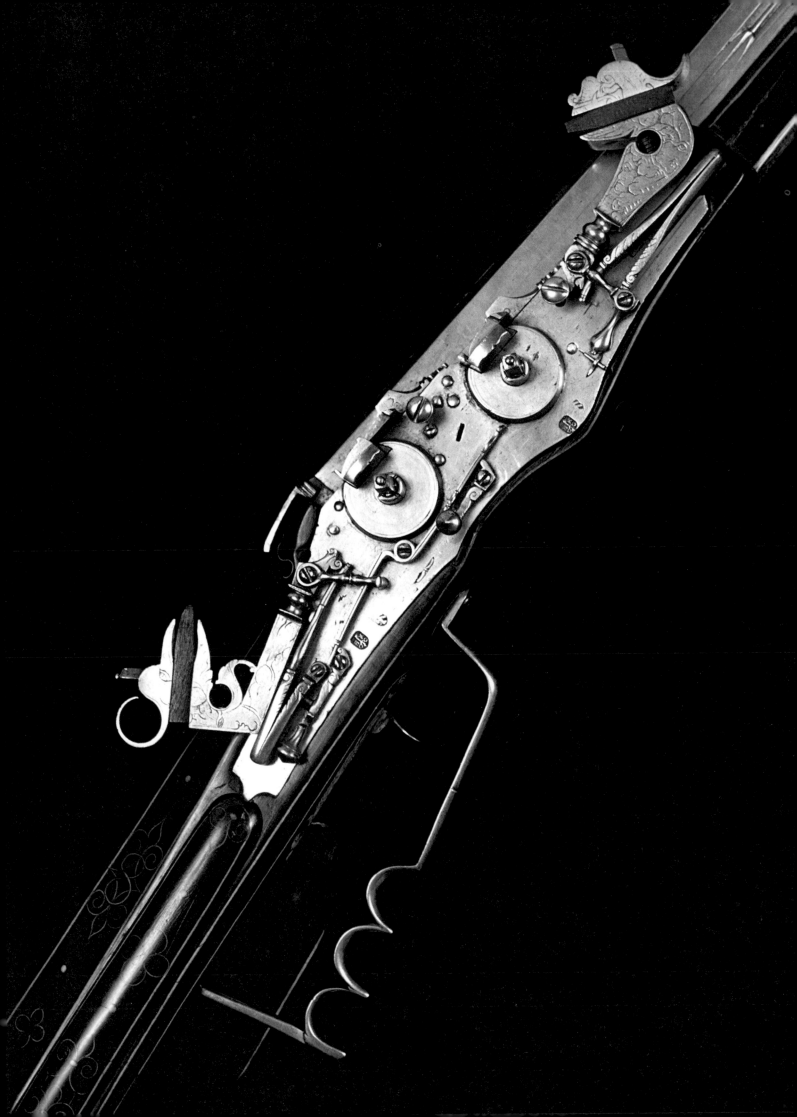

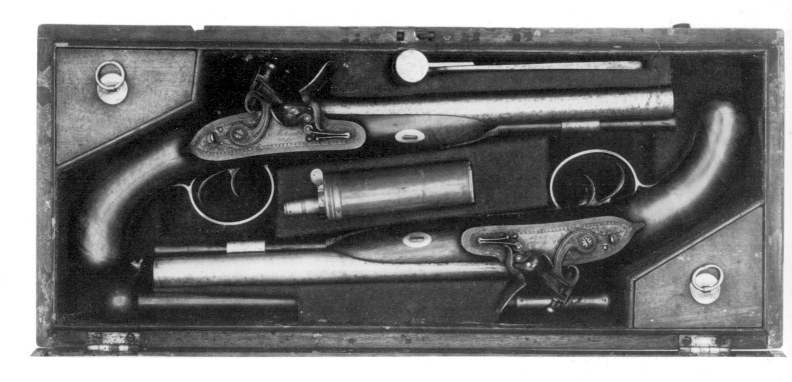

It was unusual to have a pair of double-barrelled pistols cased, as shown here. They are silver-mounted and carry the hallmarks for 1811 and the maker's mark of the famous London silversmiths Moses Brent. The pistols are by H. W. Mortimer & Son of London, Gunmaker to His Majesty.

It was obvious that a better solution would be to supply the soldier with a single weapon that could be loaded and would then fire a number of shots as and when required. The first attempts to achieve this were based on the idea of fitting one pistol with several barrels; this idea was tried out from an early date, and the modern, double-barrelled shotgun is simply a contemporary application of this very old concept. As early as the beginning of the fifteenth century, crude forms of double-barrelled weapons were being made. The Emperor Maximilian I of Austria (1493–1519) had some in his armoury which consisted of two separate barrels mounted on a single baseboard. The barrels were loaded and could be fired independently by means of a slow match. The first genuine, double-barrelled pistols appeared around the 1530s and a number of wheellock examples have survived.

The big problem with double-barrelled pistols is to find one simple means of ignition to operate both barrels. Generally, double-barrelled wheellocks had two separate locks mounted either on opposite sides of the stock or one in front of the other. Most of these pistols had separate triggers for each lock, since it was simpler to make duplicate triggers rather than to design a complex single-trigger mechanism – although

this was done occasionally. The two barrels were normally mounted one above the other, a design known to shooters as an 'over and under'. This arrangement makes the weapon rather less bulky than the alternative side-by-side arrangement. A few seventeenth-century pistols were of the side-by-side variety but the fashion only became common in the second half of the eighteenth century.

The development of the centrally mounted boxlock in the eighteenth century made it simpler to design systems which could operate both barrels in turn. There were two common methods of achieving this result. The first, and in many ways the simpler, method was fitted to pistols with side-by-side barrels, each with its own pan and touch-hole. There was a single, wide frizzen which, when closed, covered both pans and touch-holes. The barrels were charged and the pans primed in the usual fashion, and then a sliding plate was pushed forward, generally by means of a catch at the side of the breech. This plate covered one of the pans so that when the frizzen was closed and the lock activated, the sparks fell only into the uncovered pan and fired just one barrel. The catch was then pushed again to uncover the second pan; the frizzen was closed and the mechanism re-cocked, and the weapon was ready to fire the second shot.

Far right
View of the underside of one of the pair of Mortimer pistols showing decoration typical of the period.

Right
Side view of one of the Mortimer pistols: the touch-hole is platinum-lined and the frizzen spring is fitted with anti-friction rollers; the pans are the rainproof type.

The second and slightly more complex system used the tap action. A pair of over-and-under barrels was fitted to a large block, on one side of which was a bar or raised loop. This bar, the tap, was connected to a vertically mounted, flat disc set inside the metal block and just to the rear of the breeches of the barrels. A small, V-shaped section was cut out of the disc, and from this slot a small hole connected directly to the touch-hole of the lower barrel. In the first position of the side tap, the V-notch was directly under an opening at the top of the block, and if priming were poured in, the V-notch was filled. Turning the tap through 90° moved the powder-filled notch away from beneath the opening which was now blocked at the bottom by the edge of the disc so that it made a pan for the top barrel. A small hole in the wall of the pan formed the touch-hole for the top barrel. This pan was now primed and the frizzen closed over the top.

The sequence of events was then as follows: the trigger was pressed, the flint struck sparks which fell into the pan and fired the top barrel; the tap was turned back through 90° which meant that the powder-filled V-notch was now in line with the opening of the pan. If the frizzen was then closed and the pistol fired, the sparks fell into the lower notch to fire the bottom barrel.

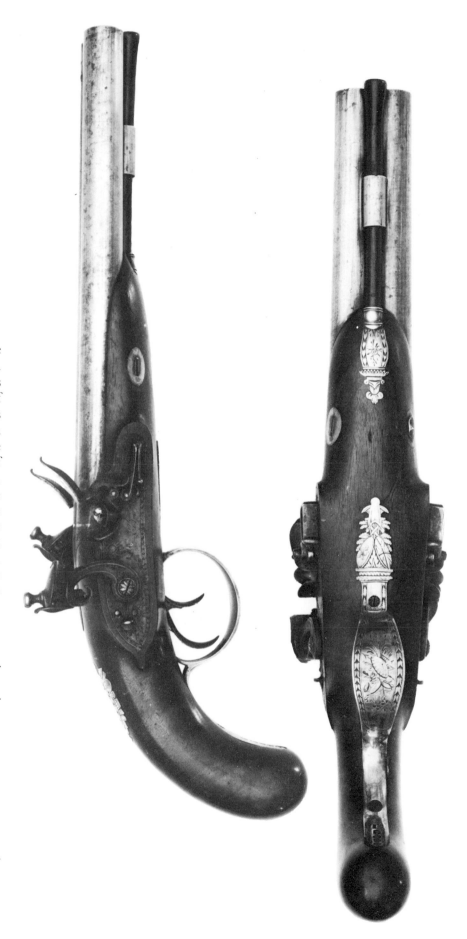

Tap-action flintlock by Geo. Jones, *circa* 1790. The top barrel is unscrewed for reloading. The selection of barrel was made by the tap at the side.

The tap action was modified to operate in a few pistols which had three barrels, and in these the disc had two V-notches cut in the edge. The system was also used in some four-barrelled pistols. These were, in effect, two double-barrelled weapons mounted with a common breech section which had two taps, one for each pair of barrels. The quadruple barrel arrangement made the weapon rather heavy and cumbersome, but it was capable of discharging four independent shots with only a minimum of mechanical adjustment.

In place of fixed barrels and an adjustable lock, gunmakers experimented with an alternative system in which the lock was conventional but the barrels were moveable. There are examples of this system dating back to the early sixteenth century, and in the Armoury at Venice there is a matchlock weapon of about 1540 which has a single lock and three barrels. The trigger causes the serpentine to swing forward and discharge the top barrel; the barrel assembly was then unlocked and turned through 120°. This brought the second barrel into the firing position where it was locked in place by a small spring catch. When required, the barrel assembly could again be unlocked and the third barrel turned into position. In the Turin Museum is a three-barrelled wheellock pistol: this is a little more

Above

Side-by-side, double-barrelled flintlock pistol fitted with a single frizzen serving both pans. One pan can be covered by a sliding cut-off.

Above left and left

The business end of a three-barrelled, flintlock pistol made *c* 1780. The muzzle ridges are to receive a square-cut key used to unscrew the barrel. Below is a close-up of the pistol's tap. As the first shot was fired, the tap was turned to select the second barrel, and then the third barrel. The maker's name, Gill, is enclosed in a military motif — a style common at this period.

sophisticated, for the barrels are rotated by turning a butterfly nut situated at the tip of the butt. This example is rather interesting for it was designed to fire steel darts rather than bullets, recalling the very earliest of firearms which discharged arrows.

Rotating barrels seem to have fallen from favour for the next century or so, and there are few weapons to be seen using this system until the mid-seventeenth century. The majority of surviving examples are of French workmanship and have a conventional flintlock action and cock mounted on the butt section. Each of the barrels has its own pan and frizzen, and both are mounted on a block which can be locked in position or rotated to bring each into the firing position. The lock had to be re-cocked between shots, and prior to firing both barrels and pans had to be charged. A few examples were fitted with three or four barrels, but they were rather unwieldy because of the projecting pans and frizzens.

Yet another approach to the problem of limited capability was to improve the chances of hitting the target first time. Increasing the size of the bullet would not help but splitting or dividing the missile would, and several types of pistol were built with this object in view. When they fired they sent out a number of bullets scattering over a wide area.

One such weapon, the 'duck's foot' pistol, had four slightly diverging barrels which were fitted to a common breech-block with a single touch-hole and pan. When this curious weapon was fired, the four shots spread out over an angle of approximately 45°. No doubt gunsmiths sold them to army, naval or prison officers who might conceivably be faced with the need to hold off a mob of determined men, for they were also known as 'mob' or 'boarding' pistols. The odds on scoring a hit with such a pistol were much greater than from a single weapon or even a pair of pistols. They are scarce today, how-

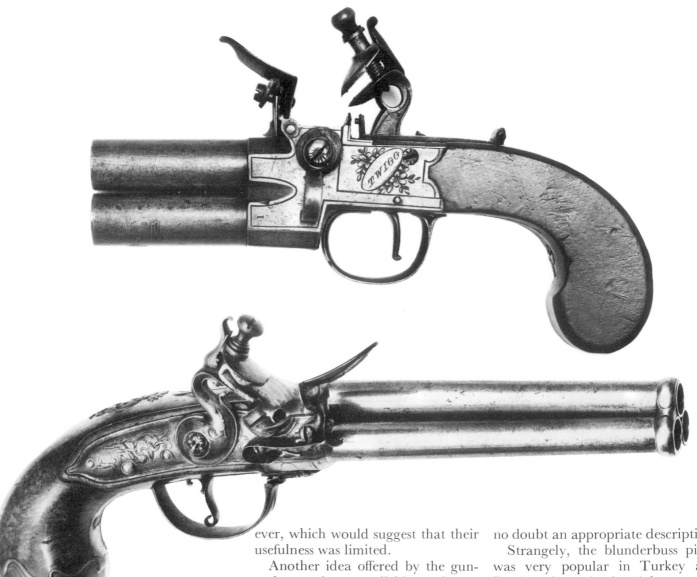

Top
Typical double-barrelled tap-action pocket pistol by Twigg, a London gunmaker. G. Kellam, Broadstairs, Kent.

Above
Michele Lorenzoni of Florence made this flintlock pistol with three barrels, each fired in turn by a single lock. The barrel assembly had to be rotated by hand. The weapon was made c 1680. Victoria and Albert Museum, London.

ever, which would suggest that their usefulness was limited.

Another idea offered by the gunmaker anxious to sell his goods was that if, instead of one bullet, the pistol could discharge a number of smaller bullets, then the chances of scoring a hit were better. If the muzzle was made wider, then the shot could spread even further; or so it was thought. However, despite the apparent logic of this idea, it just is not true. Muzzle diameter has very little effect on the spread of shot; the main spread occurs after the missiles have left the barrel. The idea was taken up in the seventeenth century, but pistols with these flaring barrels enjoyed their greatest popularity during the latter part of the eighteenth century. They were loaded with a number of small balls held in place with a wad. Although the wide, flaring muzzle might have had little effect on the spread of shot, it acted as a megaphone to magnify the roar of the explosion. The name given to these pistols was blunderbuss, a corruption of the German *Dunderbusche* and the Dutch *Donderbuss*, or 'thunder gun' –

no doubt an appropriate description!

Strangely, the blunderbuss pistol was very popular in Turkey and Persia and remained so right up to the beginning of this century. The Asiatic weapon was a miniature version of the large, musket type of blunderbuss although it was intended to be fired in the hand and not from the shoulder.

There was an unusual variation on the blunderbuss pistol which was patented by the Marquis of Clanricarde in 1832 and manufactured by James Wilkinson. It was a percussion pistol with a hinged chamber which pivoted at the breech. A paper cartridge contained the cap, powder charge and a multi-missile. The bullet was a lead cylinder which was made up of three lead discs, each divided into four equal segments. The barrel was flattened laterally to give it an oval muzzle, and the idea was that the segmented cylinder was discharged and split into 12 separate projectiles. A special bullet mould was necessary to cast the segmented bullet and the rarity of pistols of this type is an indication that it was not really a practical idea.

Yet another way to fire a volley of shots was to arrange a number of barrels in a cluster around a central axis. In 1779 the gunmaker James Wilson patented his idea for a seven-barrelled volley gun, and quantities were ordered for the Royal Navy. These were supplied by Henry Nock, a well known London gunmaker, who also produced a pistol version. The barrels had a common touch-hole so that all seven shots were discharged simultaneously. The bullets were quite small, .18 in (4.6 mm) in diameter, but even so the effect of seven shots all at once must have been disconcerting.

Most of the multishot weapons so far discussed have had more than one barrel, but one system was devised which used only one barrel: the superimposed load. On paper the idea looks very straightforward, but making it work was not quite so simple, for into the single barrel went several charges which were then fired, one at a time, in sequence. The first charge of powder was poured down the barrel, to be followed by the ball which was then covered by a fairly thick wad. Another charge of powder and a ball were inserted and covered by a second wad. By one means or another the first charge was fired, but the rear charge was isolated and so was unaffected until this too was detonated. There was always the risk of a flash penetrating the separating wad, in which case the result was spectacular. The big problem was to detonate each in the correct order.

Many gunmakers devised systems, some of which were ingenious, some were optimistic and some were downright impractical. One obvious way of igniting the charges was to fit each with its own touch-hole, and this method was adopted by several gunmakers. Some superimposed wheel-locks of the mid-sixteenth century held three charges and had two locks on one side of the stock, and the third on the opposite side. The objections to this arrangement were its expense, and also the inconvenience of having the three locks projecting around the pistol, making it heavy and awkward. There was also a risk that the locks might not be operated in the correct sequence, with disastrous results.

Pair of magazine flintlock pistols made by Michele Lorenzoni in the early eighteenth century. The lever, visible on the bottom pistol, operates the loading action of powder and ball held in reservoirs in the butt. The decoration is silver-wire inlay.

Blunderbuss pistol with lock dated 1760, made by Galton. Since the lockplate bears the royal cypher 'GR', this was evidently an 'official' weapon passed by the Tower inspectors.

Right
Four-barrelled, duck's foot pistol designed to discharge its shots over a wide area. Marked 'Bass & Co.', it dates from the late eighteenth century.

With sufficient skill and disregard of expense it was possible to make a neat, efficient, superimposed wheel-lock. In 1635 Pierre Bergier presented a wheellock pistol to King Louis XIII of France which was a four-shot, superimposed weapon. Using the fine skills and techniques that had made him a superb watchmaker, Bergier used coiled springs and other means to produce compact miniature locks which gave the weapon a graceful appearance.

Another method evolved to cope with these spaced loads was to drill the appropriate touch-holes and fit a lock which could be moved physically along the stock to ignite each charge in turn. A pair of such pistols, made by Jover and Belton of London, *circa* 1786, have an ingenious lock fitted with an automatic priming system. It slides along a rail on the stock and is operated by a pair of triggers inset in the stock. Another variation was to fix the lock and move the barrel along, but the mechanical problems were considerable. Some gunmakers modified another technique and fitted a lock with two touch-holes communicating with the charges. One touch-hole was cut off by a sliding plate until required.

An unusual form of superimposed load weapon was the so-called Roman candle gun, which took its name from the firework which spat out a series of burning balls. The basic idea was an old one dating back to the early fifteenth century in Germany, but pistols using the system were briefly popular during the middle of the seventeenth century. There were four barrels, each fashioned separately in a long block of metal, with the four blocks joined into one large assembly. One barrel was perfectly conventional except for a touch-hole situated near the muzzle. This hole communicated with one of the other barrels which was loaded only with powder. The other two barrels each contained a number of superimposed loads connected by touch-holes to the powder-filled barrel.

The firing sequence was complicated and began with the first barrel which fired a single shot. The burning charge ignited the powder in the second barrel. As the column of

powder burnt down, the flame ignited charges in each of the adjacent barrels and the result was a sequence of 15 shots. Just how long it took is a matter for conjecture, and modern experiments have not been conclusive, giving times as diverse as $1\frac{1}{2}$–70 seconds. The shortest time would produce a volley which would have been rather spectacular but probably ineffective. The longest time at least would have made it possible to aim at different targets, but again the weapon's effectiveness must be in question.

Other guns of a similar nature used bullets drilled with a hole which permitted a flash from one charge to pass through the bullet to another. However, the loading of such projectiles must have been fiddly and time-consuming, and longer than for the more conventional types.

Despite the inherent difficulties of superimposed-load weapons the US Government decided to experiment with them, and in February 1814 planned to issue them to a number of troops. The model chosen was one patented in March 1813 by Joseph Chambers, but the details of his weapon were destroyed in a fire. It seems likely from some evidence that this weapon used the drilled-bullet method of passing on ignition. It is of interest to note that the order for them states that these weapons 'will discharge six or eight loads in succession with a space between each to take aim'.

The advent of the percussion cap simplified the task of gunmakers trying to design multishot weapons, for the awkward frizzen and pan were no longer required, permitting smoother outlines to the weapon and less complicated mechanisms. Superimposed ignition was simplified and many weapons had locks with two hammers, each of which fell in turn on a capped nipple to fire one of the charges. Even the 'moving-lock' type of ignition was simpler when using percussion caps, and some such weapons were manufactured. The main point, however, was that superimposed firearms had been relegated largely to the status of a novelty rather than a serious, practical weapon. A careless loading, a defective wad, and the result might well be a rather spectacular display of useless firepower as the flame ignited a whole sequence of shots.

There were alternative methods available of making multishot weapons. A number of percussion and, later, cartridge pistols were made with a special type of hammer which had a nose that could be rotated. This special hammer was fitted to pistols which had, perhaps, four barrels, and the nipples were arranged in a small group on top of the breech. The hammer was cocked and, when released by the trigger, fell forward and the nose struck one nipple to fire the first shot. If the hammer was now re-cocked the nose was rotated and the pistol was ready to fire a second

Right
Wheellock pistol with three superimposed loads, made *c* 1550. Each was discharged by its own lock, the front one first. Superimposed loads were used in various weapons right up to the invention of cartridge revolvers.

Far right
Made by Pierre Bergier in 1636, this pair of French wheellock pistols is designed to fire superimposed loads of two shots each. The pistols have cleverly constructed locks which are compact and waterproof. The furniture is of gilt bronze to ensure resistance to corrosion. Musée de l'Armée, Paris.

Brass-barrelled blunderbuss pistol designed to spread the shot. These weapons enjoyed a certain popularity in the second half of the eighteenth century; this example was made by Trulock of Dublin. G. Kellam, Broadstairs, Kent.

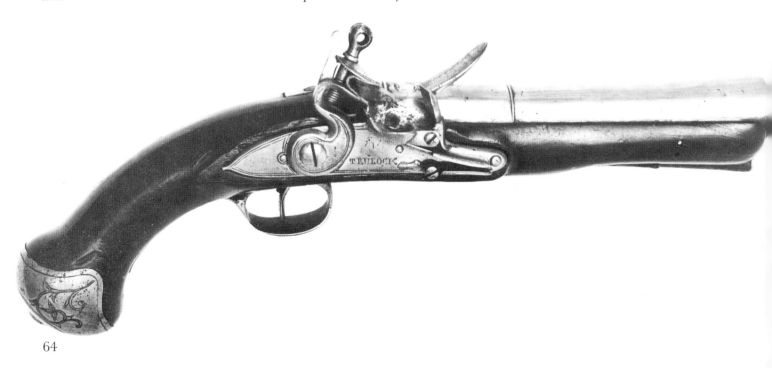

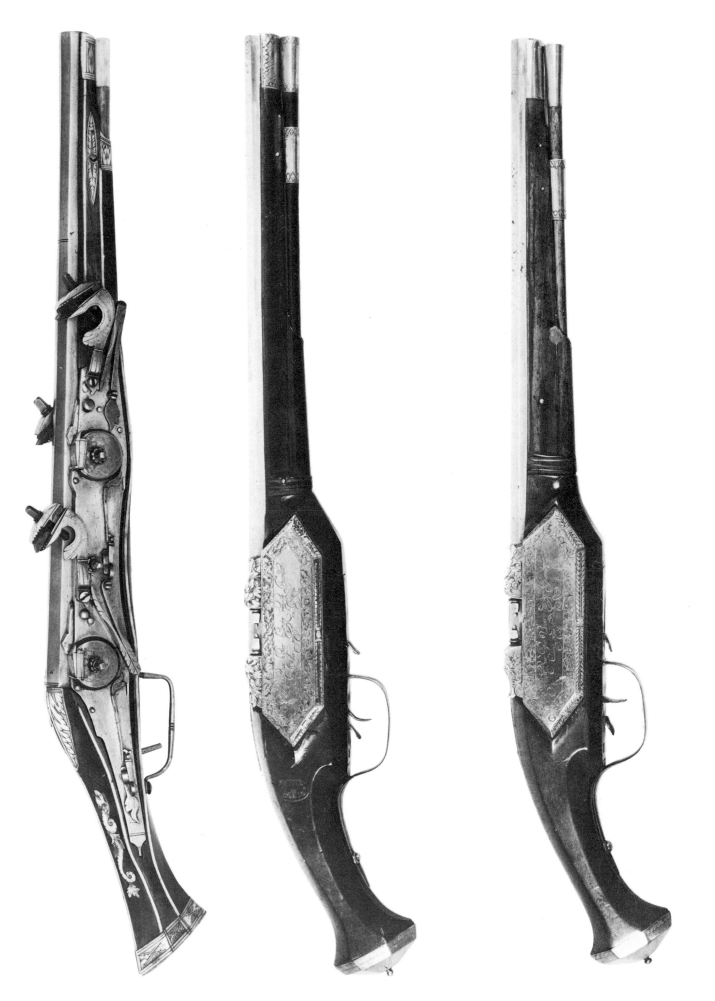

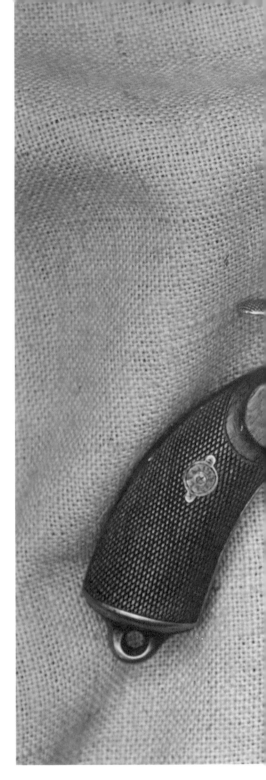

Above
Le Mat revolver – a Continental
percussion revolver designed with a
central barrel to discharge a single round
of buckshot. Barrel selection was made
by adjusting the nose of the hammer.

Left
Moveable lock fitted on a superimposed
load gun by H. W. Mortimer & Son,
c 1800. The touch-holes are protected by
pivoted covers; the lock is moved
backwards after each shot. Winchester
Gun Museum, New Haven, Connecticut.

time; the process could be repeated for all four shots.

Although, as will be shown, by the middle of the nineteenth century reliable revolvers were available, multishot weapons were still made. They were usually justified as being designed for some specific task rather than as a general-purpose weapon. Big-game hunting was a popular sport during the late nineteenth century, and it was standard practice that any wounded animal had to be tracked down and killed. In following such an animal it was often necessary to penetrate thick undergrowth where a rifle was inconvenient and a weapon of normal calibre might prove inefficient in coping with a large, dangerous animal. For situations such as this the gunsmith offered a large-calibre weapon usually known as a 'howdah' pistol'. It took its name from the basket-like container strapped to the back of an elephant in which the 'sahibs' sat when they went hunting tiger. It was recommended that one such pistol should be kept at hand in case the tiger sprang on to the back of the elephant. Howdah pistols were commonly double-barrelled and about .577 calibre (14.7 mm), and were produced in percussion, pin-fire and cartridge forms. They normally 'broke', that is, the barrels were lowered for reloading by means of a lever often positioned beneath the trigger guard, or by means of a catch on top of the breech. Their heavy bullet gave them considerable stopping power, and for this reason they were favoured by British Army officers serving in the Sudan campaigns in the late nineteenth century. Soldiers found that the normal-

Below
Lock of a four-shot, superimposed-load shotgun. An accidental touch on the wrong trigger, so firing the rear charges first, would have had disastrous results. Dominion Museum, New Zealand.

Bottom
Muzzle of a Roman Candle gun. The way in which the block is built up from four sections is shown by the faint joins visible. Tower of London Armouries.

Right
Pair of double-barrelled percussion pocket pistols of unusual design with twin barrels in a solid block, made in about 1830. The pistols have silver escutcheons, blued triggers and a platinum plug touch-hole.

calibre bullet was insufficient to stop a charging warrior rendered impervious to pain and fear by religious fanaticism, drugs and hatred of the enemy. Despite several hits by a standard revolver bullet, the fanatic could keep on coming with enough energy to inflict a serious wound. The .577 (14.7-mm) bullet was sufficient to stop a charging fanatic, or a wounded tiger, before either could get too near.

A popular, four-barrelled, howdah-type pistol was supplied by Charles Lancaster, a London gunmaker, in whose name it was patented in 1881. The Lancaster had four barrels drilled in a single metal block. A lever at the side opened a catch which permitted the barrels, hinged at the base, to be dropped so that the centre-fire cartridges could be loaded. The trigger caused an internal bolt and firing pin to rotate through 90° each time it was operated so that the four cartridges were struck in turn. Its shape was smooth and its calibre, .45 in (11.4 mm), was effective in dealing with most targets.

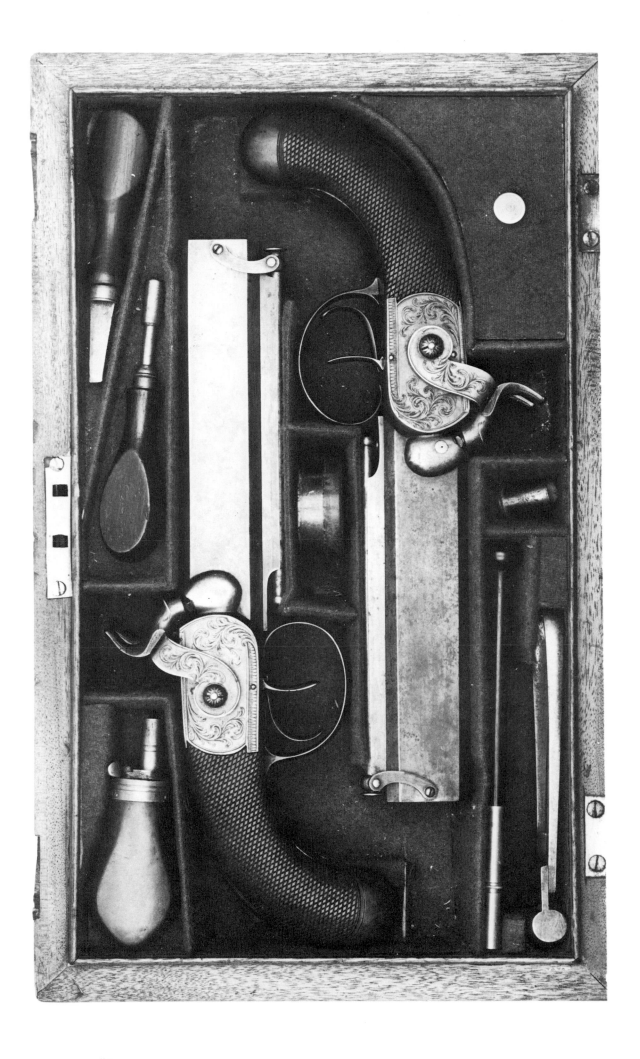

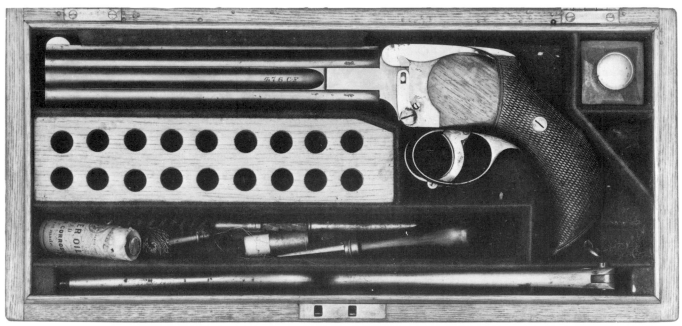

Above
Tipping & Lawden four-barrelled pistol made using the Sharp's patent in which the firing pin is rotated to discharge each barrel in turn. The trigger is sleeved, for safety reasons.

Above left
Flintlock pistol with belled barrel by Henry Nock, a noted London gunmaker. Nock was an innovator who experimented with a number of fresh ideas and produced a large range of weapons.

Left
Two four-barrelled Lancaster pistols.
Above Cased example of the model with the extended trigger, which is here folded back.
Below A .476 (12.1-mm) pistol with the normal trigger.

Besides the more conventional multishot weapons using several barrels were others that attempted to solve the problem in a different way. Many used a 'magazine' holding a series of charges which were positioned in turn in the breech of the weapon. The magazine came in a variety of forms and shapes. One system, patented in 1862 in France and the USA by Jarre, used a flat bar with 11 chambers to take pin-fire cartridges. The action of the trigger moved the bar through the breech so that the top hammer could strike each cartridge in turn. The bar sticking right through the pistol made it very awkward to carry, either about the person or in a holster. To overcome the problem some models were made

so that the barrel assembly could be folded for convenience, but this meant that the weapon was not ready for instant use. The bar with its spaced holes rather resembled a mouth organ in appearance, and the weapon became known as the 'harmonica pistol'.

A simpler, more compact, four-shot pistol was patented by a Swiss, Burkhard Behr, in Britain in 1898 and in the USA a year later. A small, oblong bar holding four cartridges fitted flush into the breech. The top cartridges were positioned behind the two over-and-under barrels, and the trigger operated pins to fire them in turn. The bar was then released by a catch and rotated through 180° to bring the lower cartridges into the

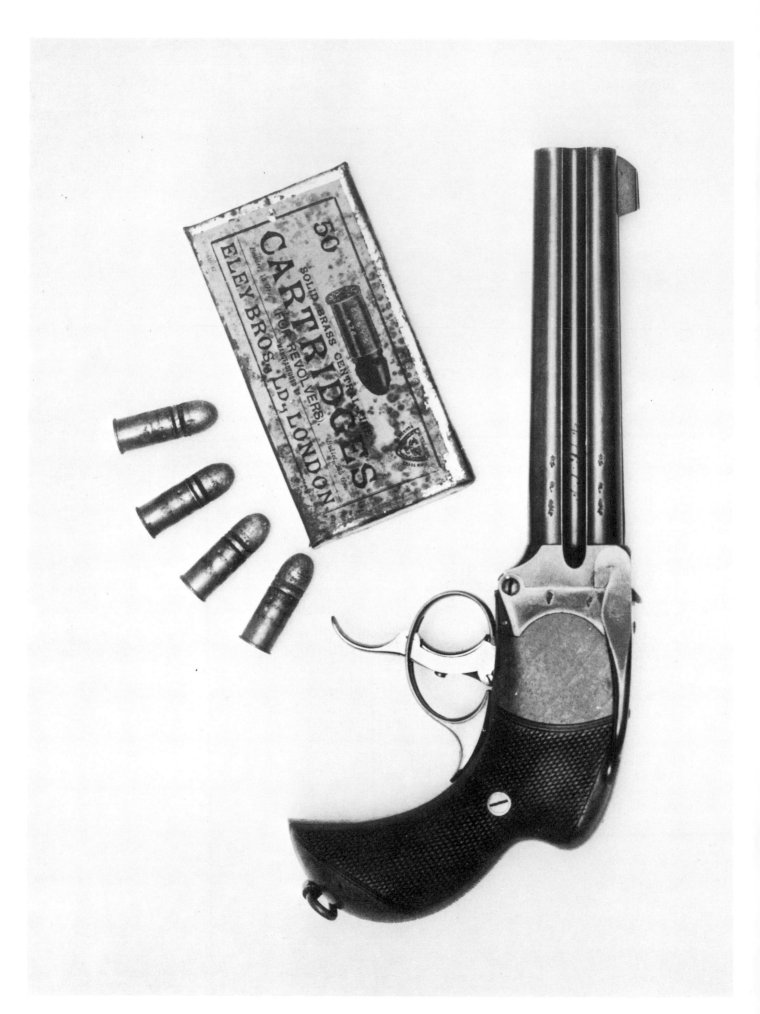

firing position. An ejector rod was screwed to the butt as each fired case had to be pushed out by hand.

Another variant on the 'flat' magazine was the turret pistol patented in April 1837 in New York by John Cochran. It had a flat disc with seven chambers drilled into it, each fitted with a nipple near the centre of the disc. The hammer was situated beneath the breech and struck upwards to hit the nipple. As each radiating chamber was lined up manually with the barrel, the trigger could be pulled to discharge a shot. A small spring catch clicked into position as each chamber was correctly positioned.

Possibly the most ambitious of all multishot systems was that made by an unknown, probably French, gunmaker. It consisted of a metal breast-plate to which were fitted 19 pivoted cartridge pistols. In the 'safe' position these pointed downwards, and when loaded and in the 'fire' position, they pointed forward. The pistols could be cocked by means of a hook fitted at the end of an attached chain, and they could be fired in groups of four or five by means of various studs and levers. The effect on the wearer, as the salvoes were fired, is not known! Even when the 19 pistols had all been fired, the owner was still not defenceless provided he could mount his horse, for with this extraordinary breast-plate came a pair of stirrups, each of which concealed two pistols. These were fired by pulling a strap; but from the shape of the stirrups it is not clear whether the pistols were designed to be fired to the front or the rear!

Far left
Lancaster four-barrelled howdah pistol with original tin of .476 (12.1-mm) centre-fire cartridges. These heavy-calibre weapons were popular with British Army officers serving in the Sudan in the 1880s and '90s, and also with big-game hunters.

Left and below
Two multishot pocket revolvers.
Left Small .32-in (8.1-mm) centre-fire cartridge, double-action pepperbox revolver with folding trigger. By Charles Nephew & Co, Calcutta.
Below .22-in (5.6-mm) rim-fire eight-shot pepperbox revolver marked 'Rupertus Pat. Pistol Mfg. Co. Philadelphia'; it has a sheath trigger.

Self Defence

The advantages that a pistol offers as a firearm are its size, weight and general convenience. It is much smaller than any musket or rifle and can be carried in a pocket or any convenient receptacle, and yet always be ready for use. It can be held in either hand when being fired, leaving one hand free.

However, its size imposes certain limitations on its performance. All other factors being equal and, within certain limits, the longer the barrel the more accurate a weapon will be. Since pistols seldom have a barrel more than 12 in (30 cm) long, their accuracy must be less than that of a carbine, a musket or a rifle. The smaller breech will also impose limits on the charge or cartridge which can be used without risking damage to the weapon. The size of the powder charge or cartridge affects the speed and power of the bullet. The lower power of the pistol means a shorter range and less 'punch' from the bullet.

Despite all these disadvantages there are certain circumstances in which a pistol is the ideal weapon. When conditions make it necessary to have a weapon readily available at all times, it is much more convenient to have a small pistol than any long arm. Equally, it is far easier to conceal a pistol than a long arm, and in

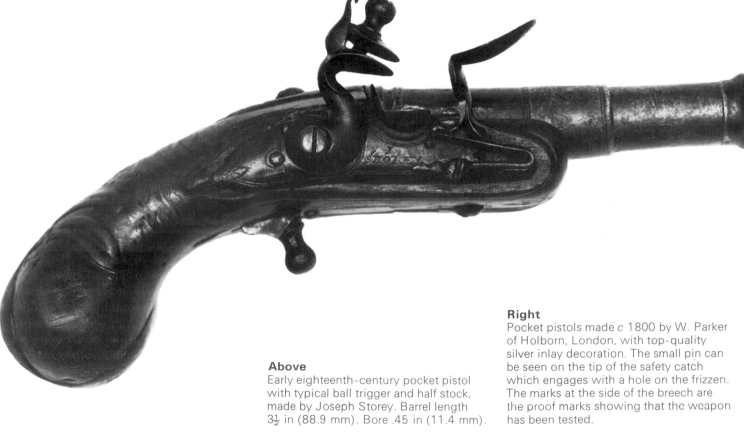

Above
Early eighteenth-century pocket pistol with typical ball trigger and half stock, made by Joseph Storey. Barrel length 3½ in (88.9 mm). Bore .45 in (11.4 mm).

Right
Pocket pistols made *c* 1800 by W. Parker of Holborn, London, with top-quality silver inlay decoration. The small pin can be seen on the tip of the safety catch which engages with a hole on the frizzen. The marks at the side of the breech are the proof marks showing that the weapon has been tested.

confined spaces the pistol has obvious advantages.

Pistols only became practical weapons from the sixteenth century when the wheellock system was adopted. It was simple to produce a matchlock small enough to go into a pocket, but there was no way that such a weapon could be carried ready for instant use. The glowing match meant that no matchlock could be put in a pocket or tucked under a coat. The wheellock was a very different matter, for the pistol could be loaded, spanned and tucked in a pocket, ready to fire. However, the earliest surviving wheellock pistols are hardly suitable for carrying in the pocket. Most were made at Augsburg or Nuremberg in southern Germany and one, dated 1534, measures about 19 in (48 cm) long. It is straight, with the butt in line with the barrel, a form which seems to have been common to most early pistols.

By the mid-sixteenth century the straight-line shape was still in general use but there was now a dip in the stock just behind the lock, whilst the tip of the grip was fitted with an egg-shaped pommel. There was, too, an increase in the use of decoration on the stock, with inlays of horn, ivory and metal. Most stocks were of wood but the German gunmakers also produced a number of all-metal weapons.

During the second half of the century there were two basic patterns of pistol being produced by the makers of Nuremberg and Augsburg. One style retained the relatively straight stock, but the grip was now sloped at a slight angle and terminated in an almost disc-like pommel, just large enough to prevent the hand from slipping off the end. The second form was more common and had a much sharper angle to the butt with an ovoid pommel. From the 1580s this pommel was large and elaborately decorated. Known as 'puffers', these pistols were designed to be carried in holsters fitted at the front of the horseman's saddle. The large pommel was not intended for use as a club but simply as a device to prevent the hand slipping off the butt.

The size of these earliest wheellocks would seem to indicate that these pistols were considered to be horsemen's weapons, and were clearly not designed for carrying about the person. However, the idea of a more personal weapon, immediately ready to hand, was beginning to develop and at the end of the sixteenth century a new feature appeared: the belt hook. This was a narrow, flat bar secured to the stock on the side opposite the lock. It stood about $\frac{1}{2}$ in (12 mm) away from the stock and ran parallel to the barrel, and could be slipped over a belt or even through clothing, so that the pistol hung conveniently ready to hand. The belt hook was fitted to a variety of pistols until well into the nineteenth century, and was a common feature on many Spanish pistols.

Although the wheellock mechanism made it possible to design firearms that were more personal, the problems involved in their design and the high cost of manufacture precluded their becoming common. It was the introduction of the snaphaunce and flintlock mechanisms which made the small, easily portable firearm more generally available, and pistols small enough to slip into a pocket or purse became popular. Their potential danger was also recognized, and in December 1594 a proclamation forbade people to carry 'small dags called pocket dags'. The term 'dag' was used in Scotland to describe all-metal pistols; it also occurs in English manuscripts but it is unclear whether the texts refer to all pistols or only to those of all-metal construction. In January 1612 a further proclamation forbade the 'manufacture, use or importation' of such weapons; it also ordered the surrender of any then held, although it seems unlikely that the proclamation had much effect.

From the mid-seventeenth century onwards, flintlock pocket pistols became relatively common. Most were simply smaller versions of the standard pistol. A number differed in the method of loading, and were fitted with a turn-off barrel, which could be easily unscrewed from the breech. To load one of these pistols the barrel was unscrewed and the powder placed directly into the small breech, the ball was placed on top and the barrel

Right
Plain pocket pistol typical of large numbers produced by many gunmakers in the late eighteenth and early nineteenth centuries. There is a small lug underneath the barrel to engage with the key used to unscrew it. The pistol was made by Barbar of London c 1780. G. Kellam, Broadstairs, Kent.

Below right
Simple, silver-wire inlay decorates the slab-sided butt of this pocket pistol by Johns, c 1790. The figure '1' at the breech indicates that it was one of a pair. S. Durrant, London.

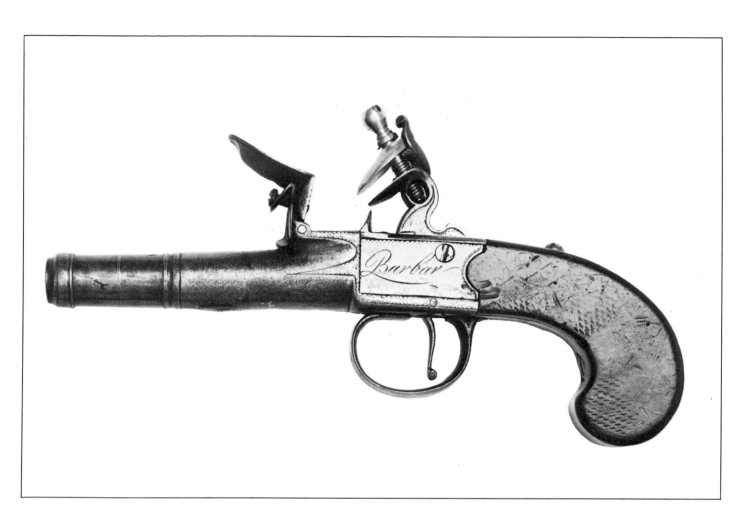

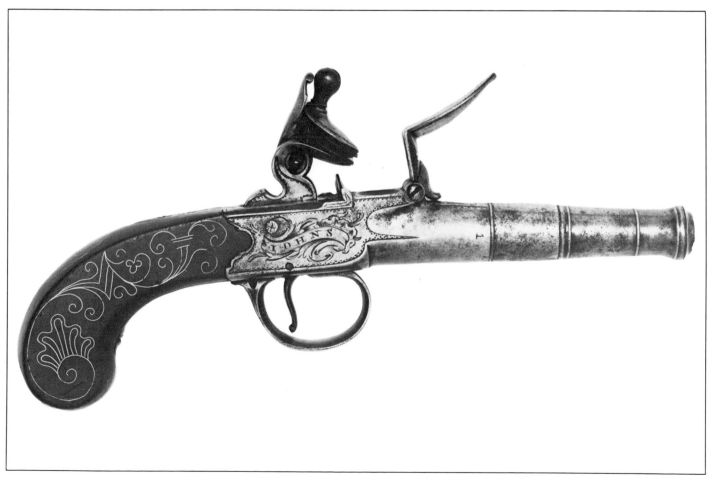

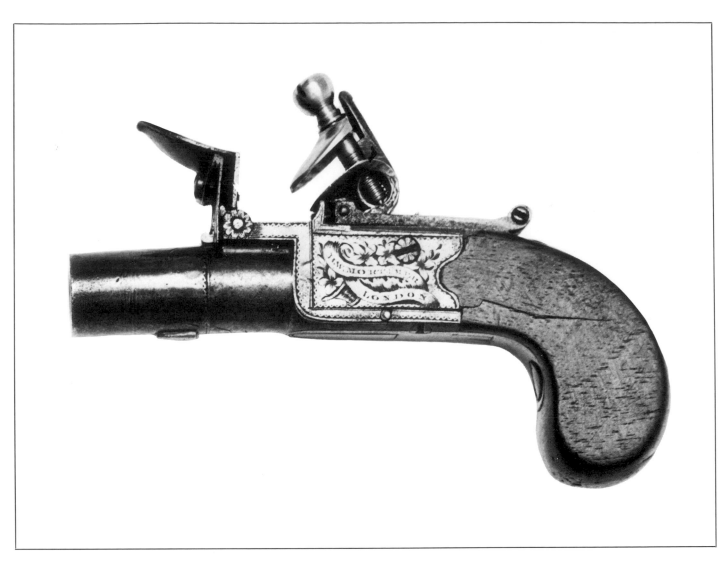

In order to improve the chances of stopping an attacker, some pocket pistols had quite a large bore. In this pistol by H. W. Mortimer of London it is .4 in (10.2 mm). S. Durrant, London.

screwed back. This method simplified loading and also ensured increased power since the ball could be made to fit much more tightly so that there was less gas leakage and more punch from the same charge of powder. Many larger pistols were also made to use this form of loading, and to prevent accidental loss of the barrel during loading an ingenious link was devised which allowed the barrel to be unscrewed but at the same time secured it to the breech.

Many seventeenth-century pocket pistols have no trigger guard, and the trigger is often in the form of a small knob rather than the flat bar form of most firearms. Most fire a bullet in the region of .3–.4 in (7.62–10.16 mm) in diameter. Since the charge was extremely small, the range would have been very limited. This was no great disadvantage because pocket pistols were never intended to be used at any great distance, but rather were designed for the situation when an

attacker was close and it would be hard to miss.

Although these small pocket pistols were quite useful as a personal defence weapon they were not without their problems. Their very shape, with the frizzen and pan sticking out, the trigger pointing downwards and the flint and cock mounted at the side, must have made them extremely awkward to slip in or out of a pocket. It must have been a not infrequent occurrence that just at the very moment when the weapon was most needed it would snag on the owner's clothing, possibly with fatal results. What was needed was a design which would eliminate as many of the odd projections as possible.

Around the middle of the eighteenth century, gunsmiths developed the box-lock. This differed from the standard lock only in design, the function being exactly the same. The cock and frizzen were removed from the side of the pistol and mounted

The perils of travel in the early nineteenth century are revealed in this Rowlandson illustration to *The Tour of Dr Syntax* by William Combe, as the hero is stopped by footpads.

centrally. The pan was dispensed with and a saucer-shaped depression encircled the touch-hole. The sides of the pistol were now smooth, but still the cock made an inconvenient projection. The trigger and its guard were less of a problem since they were smoother in outline.

Another improvement was the introduction of the concealed trigger.‘ When the pistol was loaded and the mechanism set in a half-cock position, no trigger was visible, and a smooth line was left beneath the butt. When the cock was pulled back to the full-cock position, ready for firing, this activated the internal mechanisms which allowed the trigger, a simple flat bar, to drop down. Not only did this remove one bulge, it also made for greater safety since it reduced the chances of the trigger catching and accidentally firing the weapon.

There was another serious problem: when the weapon was loaded, primed and slipped into the pocket, there was a danger that the frizzen could be knocked open, so letting the priming fall out of the pan. To overcome this a simple, double safety device was introduced. It consisted of a flat bar lying flush against the top of the butt and encircling the cock. If this bar was pushed forward, a projecting pin passed through a small, metal fence around the touch-hole and engaged with a corresponding hole in the closed frizzen. At the same time another section of the bar engaged with the rear of the cock and locked it in the half-cock position. The weapon was now reasonably safe to carry about half-cocked and with no danger of losing the priming. In a variant, a safety catch was operated by pushing forward the trigger guard, and this locked the mechanism in the half-cock position.

Since the vast majority of these pocket pistols were fitted with a turn-off barrel, they were supplied with a key for unscrewing it. There were two main types. The more common one had a short bar with a ring of appropriate diameter at the end. This ring was slipped over the barrel and a cut slot engaged with a lug beneath the breech end of the barrel which could then be easily unscrewed for loading. A few more elaborate models had a permanently attached, hinged arm fitted beneath the barrel which facilitated unscrewing but increased the risk of snagging in the pocket.

Other pocket pistols had four or five deep notches cut into the inside of the muzzle of the barrel. A tapered, square-cut bar with a 'T' handle was pushed into the barrel and the corners engaged with these notches. The key was then turned to unscrew the barrel.

These pocket pistols were usually sold in pairs and they were frequently numbered 1 and 2. They were available in various sizes and modern collectors usually refer to the smallest size as a 'muff pistol', although this was not a contemporary term, neither was the pistol especially intended to be carried in a hand-warming muff. A larger version is described as an 'overcoat pistol', but this is a modern, convenient term. It is, however, not inaccurate, since a traveller on the dangerous roads of the eighteenth and nineteenth centuries might well have carried a somewhat larger pistol. A holster pistol would have been just a little too inconvenient, and a small pocket pistol would not have been adequate for the possible dangers.

Judged by the number of surviving examples, these pocket pistols must have been very popular. They were produced in different qualities, many being very plain, lacking all decoration and having chunky, slab-sided butts. Others are far more decorative, their moulded butts inlaid with scrolls of silver wire and fitted with a cast silver butt mask.

When the percussion system was generally adopted in the 1820s and '30s, many of these weapons were adapted. This was simply done by removing the frizzen and screwing a nipple into the breech, and substituting a solid-nosed hammer in place of the cock. Many examples have survived with other, similarly crude conversions. Large numbers of

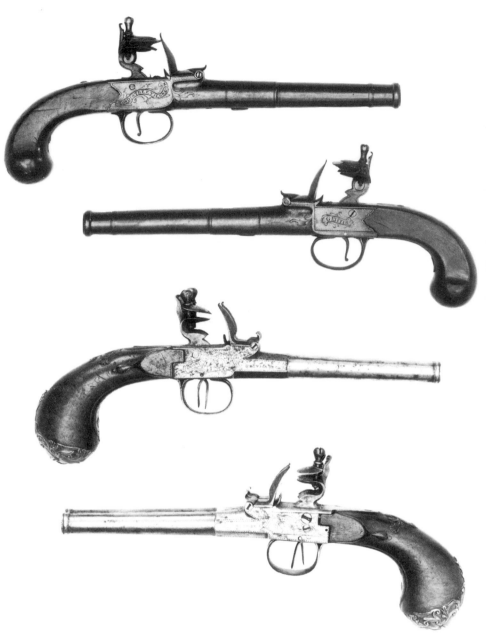

cheap pocket percussion pistols were produced for the popular market, both in Liège in Belgium and Birmingham in Britain. They were in continuous production until late in the nineteenth century and are to be seen on offer in gun catalogues dating from early this century despite the fact that they were rendered obsolete by the middle of the nineteenth century when the metal cartridge and the revolver arrived to offer a much more reliable self-defence weapon.

Whilst the majority of pocket percussion pistols can only be described as cheap and nasty, there was one particular weapon which caught the fancy of the market. This pistol was developed and produced by Henry Deringer, a gunmaker of Philadelphia, USA. The deringer

really had nothing particular to recommend it, but it was certainly in demand. It was a single-shot, percussion pocket pistol fitted with a back-action lock, *i.e.* one with the mainspring mounted behind the tumbler. The barrel ranging from 1 in (2.54 cm) to around 4 in (10.16 cm) long, was rifled, although the gain in accuracy with such a short barrel must have been very small. The deringer pistol was supplied in various bore sizes but most were around .4–.5 in (10–12.7 mm). Probably the pistol's most distinctive feature was the butt, which had a forward curve more pronounced than the British types. Like most pistols of the period deringers were supplied in pairs. The genuine article bore the name 'Deringer/Philadel.[a]'.

Left
Pair of plain, long-barrelled pocket pistols made by Griffin of Bond Street, London in the late eighteenth century. The longer barrel would have given slightly better accuracy and power but would have made the pistols less convenient to carry.

Below left
Pair of double-barrelled pocket pistols made in Liège. Each barrel has its own pan, frizzen and cock.

Right and below
Selection of late eighteenth and early nineteenth-century pocket pistols.
From top to bottom.
Pair of double-barrelled, over-and-under, tap-action pistols by Verncomb of Bristol.
Single pistol by Manton: the barrel has a pivoted lever attached to facilitate unscrewing.
Pair of percussion pocket pistols.
Pair of flintlock pocket pistols by Simmons.

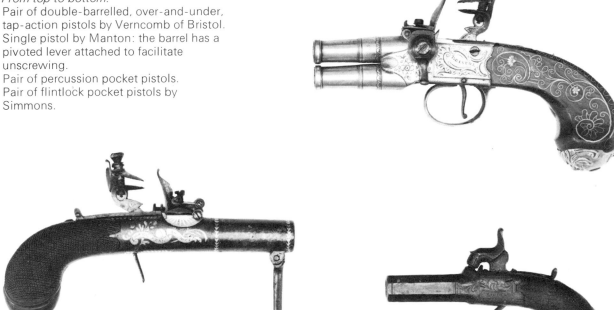

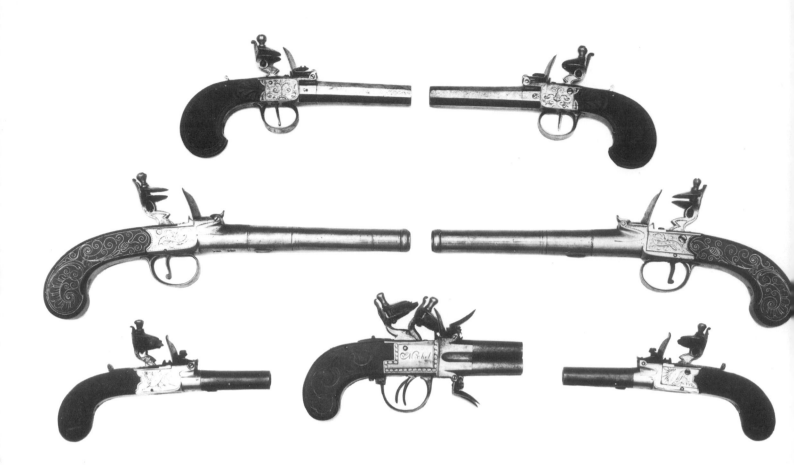

Deringer's pistol gained a certain notoriety as it was the weapon used by John Wilkes Booth to assassinate Abraham Lincoln in 1865. The American Civil War had ended on 9 April 1865, when General Lee surrendered at Appomattox Court House in Virginia. Booth was a supporter of the South who felt that he could, in some way, help its cause by killing Lincoln. He planned his assassination with care after learning that Lincoln was to attend the theatre. His successful attempt was part of a plot to dispose of several members of the government. Booth entered the box in which the President sat together with his wife and where his bodyguard, a policeman named John Parker, should also have been. In fact Parker was away having a drink and so, at 10.15 in the evening, during a roar of laughter occasioned by a scene in the play *Our American Cousin*, Booth was able to shoot Lincoln in the back of the head. In the struggle with one of the other occupants of the box, a Major Rathbone, the deringer fell to the floor. Booth's assassination weapon was a single-shot deringer of .41-in (11.22-mm) calibre with German

silver mounts; the latter was an alloy of copper, nickel and zinc used for many weapons' furniture since it was durable, decorative and cheap. Some 12 days later the assassin, John Wilkes Booth, was trapped and died of a shot which was almost certainly self-inflicted. The name deringer by then had become very well known, and the President's murder no doubt helped to popularize this weapon.

As the output from Henry Deringer's factory was limited, numerous competitors produced copies of his famous pistol. Henry Deringer fought several legal actions to prevent the exploitation of his particular design. Various legal devices were adopted to avoid his injunctions. One tactic adopted by his rivals was to label their copies 'Derringer', with a double 'r'. This form of the name has now come to describe any small personal pocket pistol.

Although the percussion derringer and other pocket pistols were very popular weapons, they were still somewhat bulky. It was only with the advent of the metallic cartridge in the mid-nineteenth century that really small, unobtrusive, pocket pistols

Above
Top Belgian-made flintlock pocket pistols with Liège proof marks, dating from the early nineteenth century.
Centre Pair of long-barrelled flintlock pocket pistols by Bunney of London.
Bottom Early nineteenth-century pair of pistols by Hull of London, flanking a four-barrelled Belgian pocket pistol made by Michael Berleur *c* 1780. The barrel block rotates to bring each pair of barrels into the firing position.

Right
Popular pistols of the late eighteenth century.
Top Brass-barrelled pocket pistol with spring-loaded bayonet.
Centre Silver-mounted pocket pistol by T. Ketland.
Bottom Small pocket or muff pistol by W. Parker of London.

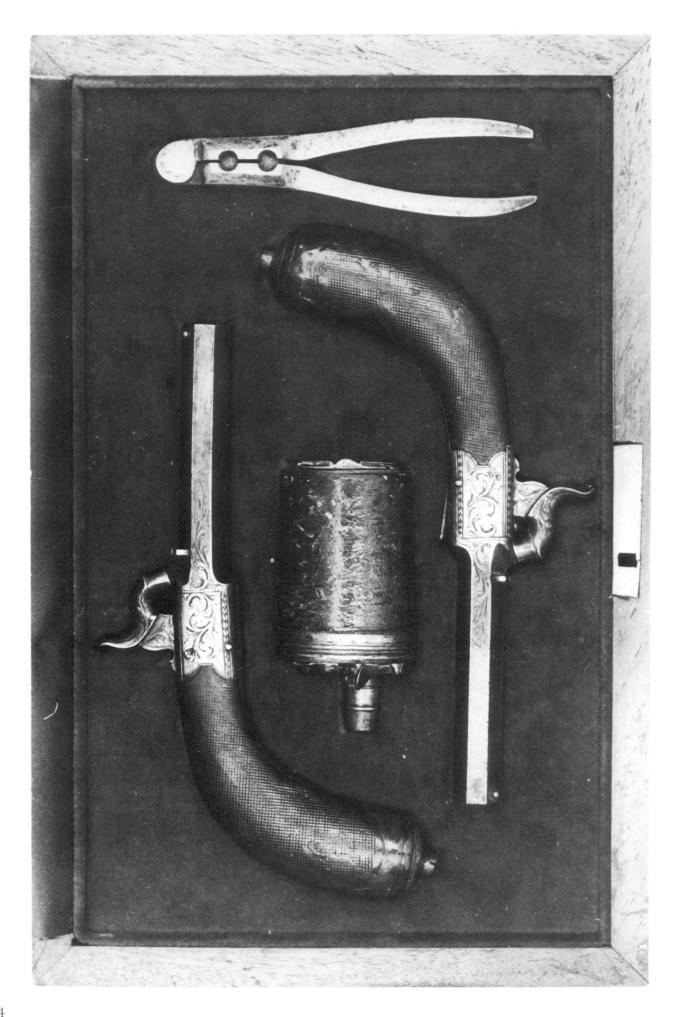

Above
Pocket pistol with inlaid silver-wire decoration and silver butt cap, bearing hallmarks for 1778, made by Perry of London. K. Giggal, Scotland.

Left
Cased pair of percussion pocket pistols by Joseph Egg & Sons of 1 Piccadilly, London, made c 1830. The pistols are unusual in that the sights are mounted not on the top flat of the barrel but at an angle.

could be produced. One unusual type of derringer was designed for use in any area where ammunition supplies might be scarce or unreliable. The Williamson derringer could fire an ordinary rimfire cartridge but should these not be available it could easily be converted. A small metal catch beneath the stock released the barrel, which could then be moved forward and a metal container inserted in the breech. The container held the black powder and had a nipple for the percussion cap; thus the weapon was converted into a percussion pistol. This convertibility meant that the owner could be more than usually sure of his ammunition.

In 1865 the famous American gunmaking firm of Remington produced a very small vest pocket pistol which was beautifully flat and, it was claimed, would fit into a lady's muff or into any waistcoat pocket without making a single wrinkle. It fired a very small cartridge, .22 in (5.6 mm) in diameter. Since the cartridge was completely enclosed there was hardly any loss of power, and, small though the bullet was, it was extremely effective at close range.

However effective these weapons might be there was always the chance that the owner might miss with his shot. Single-shot derringer or vest-pocket pistols gave him no second

chance. Remingtons quickly saw the need to market a multishot weapon and they produced the double derringer, which first became available in 1866. Two barrels were mounted one above the other, and the butt was somewhat like that of Henry Deringer's pistol, with a forward curve. The trigger was sleeved, that is, the frame of the weapon extended down either side of the trigger so that only when the finger was placed directly on the trigger could it be operated. This made it reasonably safe for the weapon to be carried in the pocket. The calibre was increased from the rather diminutive .22 in (5.6 mm) to .41 in (10.41 mm). The impact of two bullets of this fairly large calibre, even with only a small charge behind them, was, to say the least, considerable. The two cartridges were struck by the same firing pin which was so designed that, when cocked and fired the first time, the pin struck one cartridge. When cocked the second time, the firing pin position was changed to fire the second. To reload, a small catch was pressed and the barrels tipped up; the old cases could then be extracted and fresh cartridges inserted.

The popularity of this weapon may be measured by the fact that it went into production in 1866 and was made continuously and in quantity

Left
Pair of .22 Colt No 4 Model derringer pistols, made in 1859. The barrel pivots to open the breech.

Below
Palm pistol, 'The Protector', fired by squeezing the bar with the palm whilst the barrel projects between the fingers of the clenched fist. It takes seven .32-in (8.1-mm) cartridges. Tower of London Armouries.

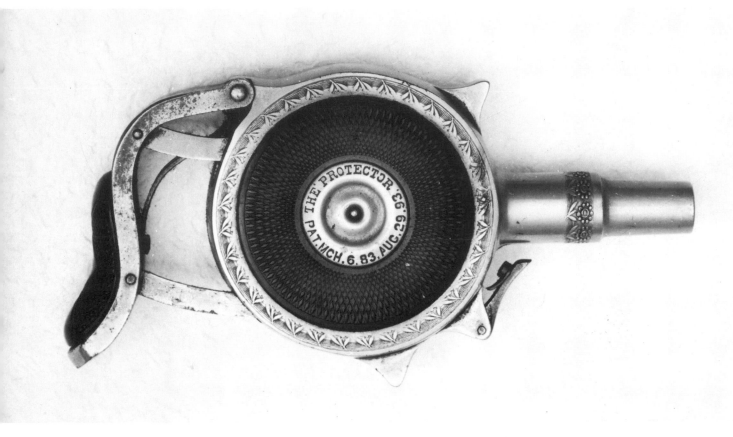

right up until 1935. The great virtue of the double derringer, as far as the shooter was concerned, was their very small, flat shape. They could be tucked away and hidden on almost any part of the anatomy and only a very thorough search would reveal them.

Seeing the considerable demand for the Remington derringer, many other firearms companies joined in their production. In 1870 the firm of Colt, one of the best-known names in the history of firearms, entered the field of small, personal derringers. Colt took over the National Arms Company and continued selling that company's derringers without adding the name 'Colt' to the pistols. In July 1870 Colt took out a patent for a new form of improved derringer with a spring-operated ejector. Colt's Model 1 derringer had a 2½-in (63.5-mm) barrel firing a .41-in (10.41-mm) cartridge with an all-metal butt which had a pronounced forward curve rather like an old-fashioned umbrella handle. To eject or load, the barrel was pivoted to swing down to the left. The pistol was available with a variety of different finishes, with barrels blued or plated.

A second Colt derringer was slightly more graceful and had wooden grips somewhat similar in shape to the original pistol of Henry Deringer. Both Models 1 and 2 were marketed by Colt from about 1870 to 1890.

Above
Brass-barrelled pocket pistol (*c* 1780) by Twigg of London, fitted with an under-barrel spring-operated bayonet.

Right
Pocket pistol by Grice of London with an unusually long barrel. The inlaid decoration is not silver but chiselled steel. The sliding safety càtch at the top of the butt can be seen, also the notch in the back of the cock with which it engages. A. Warren, Bracklesham, Sussex.

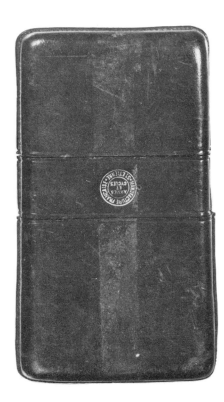

Similar to the palm pistol is this 8-mm six-shot Gaulois squeezer pistol made at St Etienne, France. It could be carried in the double-ended leather cigar case shown.

This Protector palm pistol holds 10 6-mm cartridges and is dated 1878. With it is the original leather purse container.

Their No. 3 Model was probably the most popular of all Colt's derringers. It was designed by F. Thuer, an employee of the company. Its shape was different and the barrel pivoted sideways to the right for ejection and loading. So popular was this model that production continued until well into this century, and in 1959 popular demand encouraged Colt to reintroduce a derringer into their range of weapons. The No. 4 Model is basically the same as the No. 3 except that it was made for a .22 cartridge. In 1963 the line was discontinued but there was, surprisingly, still a demand, and in 1970 a pair of these pistols, under the title Lord and Lady Model derringers, was made available in a presentation case. The Lady Model had simulated pearl grips!

One unusual tiny pistol was the Kolibri automatic pistol, made in Austria. Two versions fired either 2.7-mm or 3-mm bullets. Despite their very small calibre they were capable of inflicting a very nasty flesh wound at close range.

Although the majority of the later derringer pistols were really never intended for serious use, in World War II a single-shot personal pistol was reintroduced that was most certainly intended to see service. The United States Office of Strategic Services (OSS) co-operated with the Underground Resistance movements of Europe which were doing such an effective job of annoying and tying down large German forces. The planners of OSS decided that the Resistance forces had need of a weapon easily concealed, cheap to produce and suitable for close personal combat. The outcome of this was the so-called Liberator pistol, nicknamed by some the 'tin can pistol'. Despite this unkind title it was an efficient weapon designed for a specific purpose, and capable of achieving it. The Liberator had a 4-in (10-cm) barrel of steel tubing without any rifling, and the entire mechanism was made as basic as possible. It fired a .45-in (11.4-mm) cartridge, but in order to keep the whole thing as simple as possible there was not even an ejector. When the cartridge had been fired the empty case had to be pushed out by a small

Right
This brass and leather purse conceals a
five-shot, .22 pin-fire revolver. The
device is made to Frankenau's patent and
dates from about 1870.

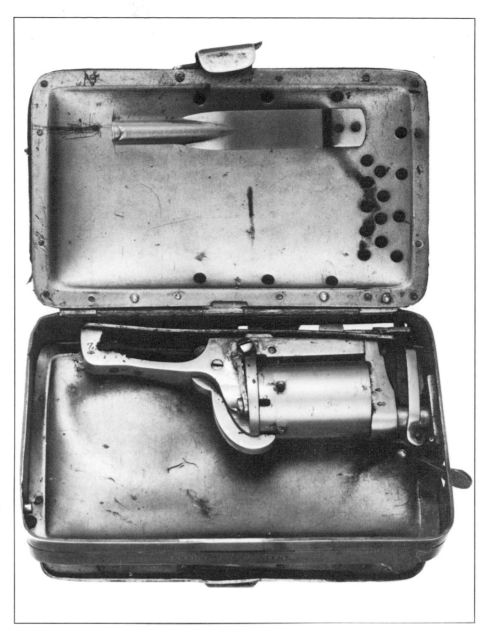

Below right
Another version of the squeezer pistol
showing the method of holding and firing
such weapons. This model is a
Rouchouse pistol.

wooden rod which was supplied with
the weapon.

The derringer and other pocket
pistols were small and could easily be
concealed in a pocket or bag. However, there was also a demand
towards the end of the nineteenth
century for a personal protection
weapon which could be concealed in
the pocket but might also be hidden in
the hand. To meet this demand, a
whole variety of curious weapons was
developed. The Protector was first
patented in 1883 in France, and was
also covered by patents in Belgium,
England and Italy, and an American
patent was granted in 1893. It was a
multishot weapon and could be
concealed in a clenched fist with only
the muzzle of the weapon projecting
between the fingers. The cartridges
were loaded into a thick, flat, metal
disc which was placed in a flat, circular
container with the barrel projecting
from one side. The weapon was laid in
the hand, and the firer's fingers were
looped around it above and below the
barrel, whilst the firing lever rested
against the ball of the thumb. When
the hand was squeezed, the lever

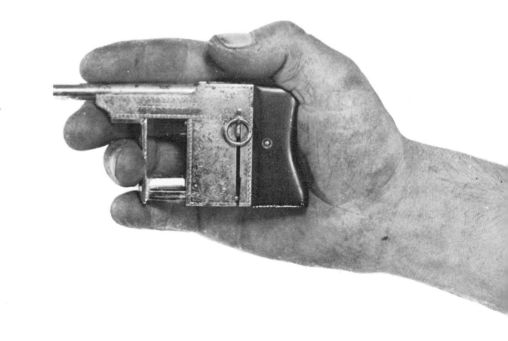

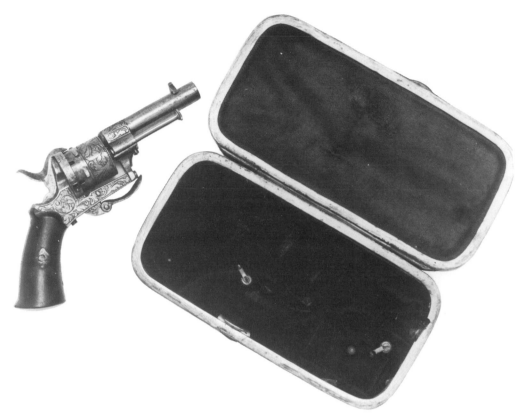

Left
Pin-fire revolver with etched decoration, folding trigger and a side ejector rod, with case. Quite a number of these purse weapons were produced during the latter part of the nineteenth century.

Right
Cased pair of highest-quality pocket pistols by Mortimer of London, *c* 1815. They have concealed triggers, silver inlay decoration on the butts and finely engraved barrels. The accessories include the key for unscrewing the barrels, seen in the compartment above the screwdriver. W. Keith Neal, Guernsey.

operated the firing mechanism. These weapons were produced in several calibres: the American one used a short .32-in (8.1-mm) cartridge and held seven shots, and the French version appears to have held 10 shots and used a slightly smaller-sized cartridge.

Whilst the Chicago Protector gun and the Gaulois, a somewhat similar design, might be very convenient to hide in the hand, it could be a disadvantage to have to keep the pistol in the hand ready for action. Another group of enterprising manufacturers argued that if the situation arose when a weapon was needed, it might be as well if the weapon could be concealed or disguised as some everyday object. The victim could produce an apparently innocuous, household domestic item and dispose of the attacker or thief with a single, well-aimed shot. One popular system was to conceal the weapon in a purse. One of the most popular was the Frankenau combination pocket book and revolver, patented in 1877 both in the United States and in Britain, where it was known as a 'revolver purse'. The weapon was a six-shot revolver which fired a small bullet of 5 mm. The gadget was in two sections, one of which was an ordinary purse whilst the other side held the pistol which had a concealed trigger.

The purse could be offered to the thief and the weapon fired without the necessity of opening the purse section.

Another popular hiding place was in a walking stick. These were especially popular with poachers since the gamekeeper would, hopefully, never suspect the unarmed walker striding along with his cane. These are commonly known as cane guns. There was a British patent as early as 1814 for one such gun which concealed a small, folding trigger, flintlock pistol. As can be appreciated, the flintlock in such a weapon caused certain problems of concealment, but with the introduction of the percussion lock cane guns became much easier to produce. In 1823 John Day, a Devonshire gunmaker, patented his cane gun in which the main body of the stick was made up by the barrel; the nipple was situated just beneath the handle, and the hammer was a flat metal bar. The muzzle was blocked by a wooden plug which formed the ferrule or cap at the end of the cane. In 1858 the Remington company patented a cane gun which offered a variety of handle styles. The weapon was cocked by pulling the handle back, and the barrel section of the cane was then charged and a cap placed on the nipple. The trigger was a small button just near the handle. In 1878 the firm offered a cartridge

version of the same gun. These and other cane guns could be used with bullets or shot. There were also one or two instances of umbrellas being adapted to carry a pistol. In 1978, in an apparent revival of the umbrella gun a Bulgarian defector, Georgei Markov, died in London after being jabbed by a stranger carrying an umbrella which, police believe, injected a minute poison-filled capsule into his thigh.

Small-calibre pistols have been concealed in other, no less obvious objects. There have been pipe pistols, while pens and pencils, by virtue of their shape, are easily adapted to single-shot pistols; several such weapons have been manufactured.

One very strange device was a belt pistol. A leather belt was fitted with a metal plate and in the centre, fixed at right-angles, was a very short barrel with the nipple at the rear, next to the plate. The hammer and firing mechanism were mounted flat against the plate, and the action was tripped by a length of cord. Presumably, the idea was that the victim of a hold-up could raise his arms and still, by means of the string, fire the shot.

A more lethal version was tested by the Nazis: this appeared to be no more than a thick metal buckle but the plate concealed four short, pivoted barrels. Pressure on two small

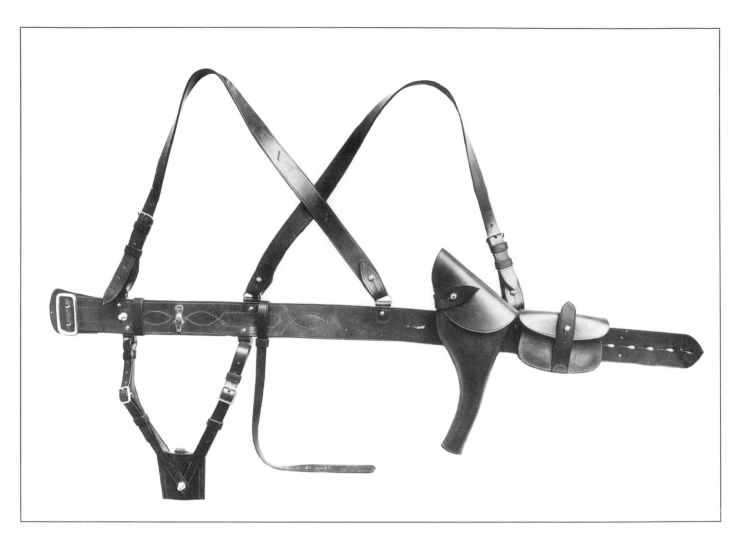

levers sprang the barrels forward, and this pushed up the front plate revealing the four barrels ready to fire, either individually or as a volley.

In 1929 a patent was granted for a sleeve pistol. This was secured to the wearer's forearm and fired by means of a short cord attached to a ring worn on the finger. The wearer would certainly need to be very careful when wearing this gadget: a sudden, unthinking move of the hand and the results could be disastrous.

One of the strangest fads in concealed weapons came with the growth of cycling as a hobby in the late nineteenth century. A few gunmakers in France and Belgium produced special small, six-shot pistols which fitted into the ends of the bicycle's handlebars. Obviously, cycling in those days had its added dangers!

Besides the weapon which could actually be concealed about the person, there were a number of weapons which were carried on the person by means of a holster. In its early days the pistol – a large,

cumbersome and rather heavy weapon, much used by cavalymen – was usually carried in holsters mounted at the front of the saddle. This meant that when the soldier dismounted he was either unarmed or he had to carry the pistol in his hand. It became clear that it would be more satisfactory if some means could be found to carry the weapon with him, especially if it could be done in such a way that his hands were left free. Mention has already been made of the belt hook, which appeared at a very early date and was to continue in use certainly until the mid-nineteenth century. Some adventurers such as pirates, who had need of firearms in quantity, wore a belt across the chest and on this carried as many as four or five pistols, held in place by belt hooks: an inconvenient, unwieldy and distinctly noisy method – or so one would have thought.

Some form of holster to hold the firearm was in use by the close of the eighteenth century. During the time of Napoleon I, French army

Full Sam Browne belt with cross braces, scabbard straps, holster and ammunition pouch. It was designed by a general who, having lost an arm, found it difficult to cope. This design was used and adapted by many forces throughout the world.

Small .25-in (6.35-mm) automatic designed by Browning and made in Belgium. Although small in size and correspondingly easy to conceal, the value of such pistols as practical weapons is today questioned by many experts.

standard-bearers carried two large, bucket-shaped holsters fitted to a baldric or cross-belt. It was not, however, until around the middle of the nineteenth century that personal holsters became commonplace. In general, the earlier ones were of leather, and many had a flap which closed over the top. Despite misconceptions created by Western films, where almost everybody wears open-topped holsters, the flap was very desirable. It protected the weapon from rain, dust and knocks, and made it extremely unlikely that it could fall from the holster. The fact that these flap-over holsters were carried by almost all armies suggests that either all armies were stupid and backward in their thinking, or that the flap indeed had some practical value.

The Sam Browne belt, first introduced by General Sir Samuel Browne, VC, was adopted in various forms by many armies. In the latter half of the nineteenth century the holster flap was secured by means of a brass stud which engaged with a

corresponding slit in the leather flap. Most modern armies still use the flap-over type of holster although leather has, in many cases, been supplanted by cheaper and more easily workable materials such as webbing or even moulded rubber. From the mid-nineteenth century there was a tendency for the flap to be discarded by non-military wearers. Those whose existence and safety might well depend on rapid possession of the firearm began to dispense with the flap and just a single, retaining strap across the top of the holster was substituted. Sometimes, as in the case of the open-topped, Western holster, a small loop of leather was secured at the top front, and this could be hooked over the hammer of the weapon, being sufficient to hold it in place but easily removed should necessity make it essential to perform a quick draw.

With the introduction of large-calibre revolvers and automatics, the size of the weapon made it far more difficult to hide, and there was some

Small Spanish Ripoll flintlock pistol with applied sheet brass decoration. The ring at the top of the cock and the square pan and frizzen are typical of this type of pistol.

experimentation in the field of concealed holsters. The most common type is the shoulder holster. Patterns vary considerably but usually they consist of a holster fitted to a loop through which one arm passes, and some arrangement of straps or laces which secure the holster to the body. These are quite effective in concealing the weapon but their position under the arm and across the body can make the quick draw rather difficult. In general the solution has been to remove as much of the support leather as possible, and in many cases some spring device holds the weapon firmly in place but not so tightly that it cannot be quickly drawn. Another system uses a holster which holds the weapon with the butt hanging vertically, so that the drawing movement is a straight-down one.

The increasing use of firearms by police and security men has encouraged the use of what are known as 'hideaway guns'. These are small-calibre revolvers or some kind of single-shot derringer-type pistol, so small that they can easily be concealed as a reserve weapon. It is now possible to obtain holsters which will fit in the bra of a police or security women, and holsters that will go under the trouser leg and strap around the ankle. At the other end of the scale, automatic weapons such as the Israeli UZI submachine gun are fitted inside brief cases!

Combination Weapons

Although multishot systems increased the effectiveness of the pistol, such weapons, once all the shots had been fired, were then an empty, almost useless piece of equipment. How much more effective would it be if they could be made to serve as weapons even when empty. It was with this purpose in mind that the gunmakers tried many and varied combinations of the pistol with other weapons.

The idea was not new and some of the earliest known firearms appear to have been adapted to form combination weapons. In the late sixteenth century the so-called 'holy water sprinkler' was not uncommon. This was a very vicious club with a long wooden grip and a thick cylindrical head with a series of projecting spikes; swung about the head it must have inflicted some very nasty wounds. However, presumably its shape, with a long grip and a small head, suggested to early gunmakers that it could serve a double function. Into the head of some of these holy water sprinklers were fitted two, three or four small barrels. Sometimes they were obvious, sometimes the muzzles were covered by a hinged lid. The four barrels were complete, each with

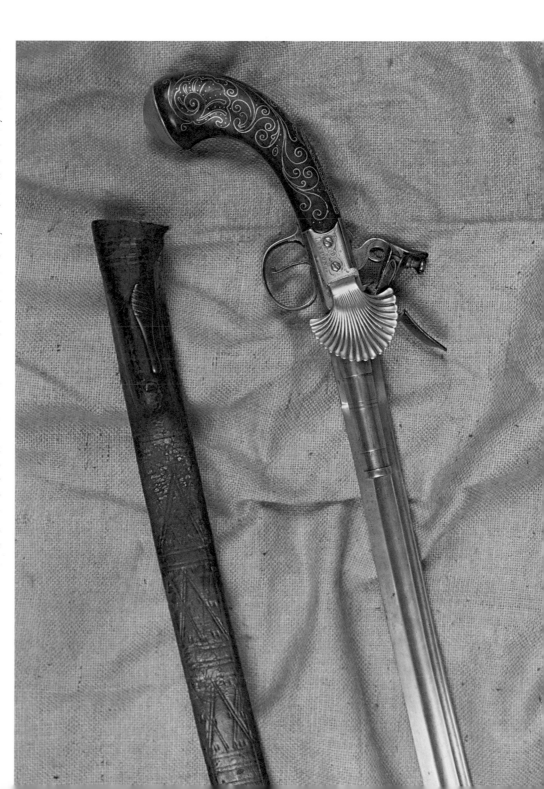

Pistol sword with silver shell guard and original tooled leather scabbard. The butt has silver-wire inlay decoration. This weapon was made by Hadley and the blade is by Harvey.

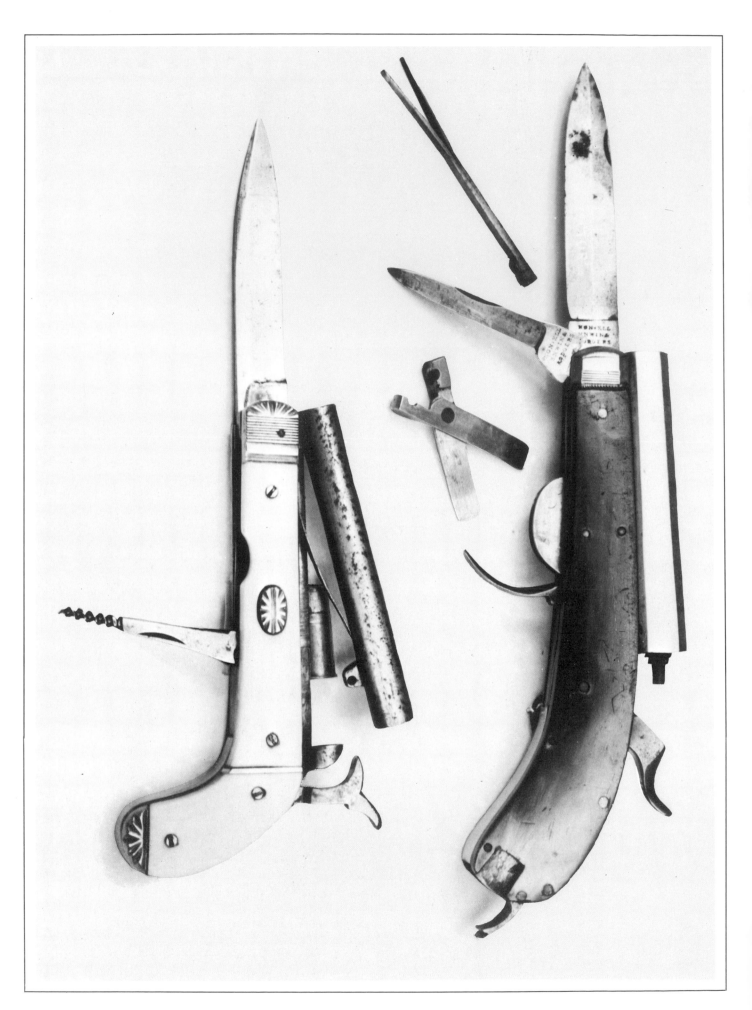

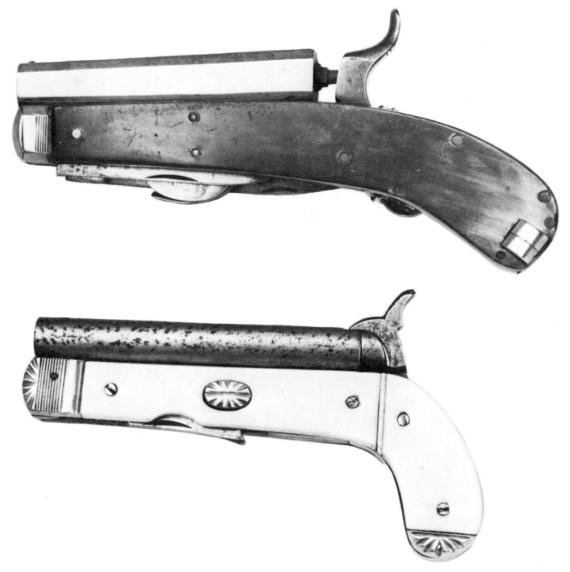

Left
Rim-fire cartridge knife pistol with its
barrel section raised for loading. The
cartridge is visible above the handle. To
its right is a percussion knife pistol with
the pistol action cocked; a pair of small
tweezers and a bullet mould have been
removed from the butt. The blade is
marked 'Unwin & Rodgers'.

Above
The two knife pistols in the closed
position. The handle of the lower, rim-fire
version is more butt-shaped than is usual
with this type of combination weapon.

its own pan and touch-hole, and by
tucking the haft of the weapon under
the arm the four barrels could be
discharged quite easily by a piece of
match held in the hand, whilst aiming
the head roughly in the direction of
the enemy. When the pistols had been
fired the holy water sprinkler was still
immediately available as a vicious
and unpleasant club.

This combination of club and pistol
was retained even when the wheellock mechanism was developed, and
there are a number of maces with
built-in wheellock pistols. The trigger
is usually situated just in front of the
grip and, of course, the hollow shaft
constitutes the barrel. Later the
flintlock mechanism was also incorporated into various forms of mace
pistol. Although the mace proved
very effective, for greater penetration
of armour it was important to concentrate the maximum energy over the
minimum surface area. For this
reason horseman's picks or war
hammers were preferred, for these

had a shaft which terminated in a
hammer head fitted with a long spike.
The haft lent itself naturally to
forming the barrel with the lock fitted
just above the grip. The majority of
wheellocks combined with maces or
horseman's picks date from the sixteenth century but in Eastern Europe
this combination continued for much
longer. Examples are recorded which
date from the early part of the
eighteenth century.

Another combination weapon
which lasted much longer than the
club or hammer was the pistol pole-
arm. At some point on the haft a firing
mechanism was fitted, and part of the
haft was modified to form the barrel.
Pistols were fitted to halberds, a type
of long pole-arm with an axe-like
head, and spontoons which were
primarily intended as emblems of
rank carried by army officers. Many
of these pole-arm pistols had only one
barrel but there are examples with
two or more. The system was used
with all types of ignition, with the

Above
Fork pistol with twin tines and the barrel
pointing towards the holder. The name
'F. Richter' is engraved at the base of the
grip.

Right
Top Hunting sword from the mid-
eighteenth century with shell guard,
modified to serve as a sword pistol. The
blade is engraved 'Ritson'.
Bottom Late eighteenth-century sword
pistol by George Jones of London. The
pistol butt has been straightened in order
to provide a better 'sword' hilt.
Private collection.

matchlock, wheellock and flintlock as
well as with pin-fire and centre-fire
cartridges.

Some of these pistol pole-arms were
primarily intended for the hunt and
were fitted with special firing devices
situated near the point of the weapon.
As the charging, or fleeing, beast was
impaled on the point, the impact
activated the trigger to fire a shot;
such weapons are often described as
'tiger spears'. The poor quarry was, at
one and the same time, stabbed and
shot.

One unusual variant of this idea
was a trident, the centre prong of
which was the missile. The rear
section of the pole was unscrewed to
permit the insertion of a .55 (14-mm)
percussion load, which could be fired
to discharge the steel dart.

It might well be argued that the
tiger spear had some real practical
purpose since the charging creature
could be killed quickly by the shot. It
is difficult, however, to see the
practical value of another weapon,
the shield pistol. The gunmaker may
have argued that when a shield was
held in front to protect its user, the
pistol could easily be aimed just by
turning the arm. Whatever the argument advanced, King Henry VIII
(reigned 1509–47) of England ordered a number of circular, metal
shields some time around 1544–7.
These were probably made by a
Signor Giovanbattista from Ravenna
in Italy. The centre of each shield was
fitted with a small matchlock pistol
which was loaded at the breech by the
insertion of a small metal chamber
holding powder and shot.

Most combination weapons em-
phasize the worst features of both
components and few have ever been
really successful. They are usually
rather clumsy and the effort to ensure
that one component is effective results
in loss of efficency in the other.
Possibly the most successful group of
all, certainly it was the most common,
was the sword or knife pistol. This
weapon has a long lineage going back
to the sixteenth century, and a good
proportion of them were primarily
intended for hunting rather than for
the battlefield. A broad-bladed hunting knife, known as a 'trousse',
sometimes had a wheellock pistol

fitted along the back edge. The
trousse was used to dismember the
quarry, and presumably the incorporated pistol could be used to kill off any
wounded beast, prior to its
butchering.

Hunting swords were fitted with
short blades, often slightly curved,
and these were frequently combined
with a small pistol. The pistol was
usually fitted at the side of the blade,
just below the guard, with the trigger
incorporated into the hilt. Specimens
with all types of ignition are not
uncommon and they probably served
some purpose in dealing with charging animals such as wild boar. Most
have only one barrel but some of the
later models were fitted with two, one
on either side of the blade. A few later,
more ambitious designs incorporated
a revolver, but they seem not to have
gained much popularity. The design
of these weapons called for a com-
promise: on some the hilt is deliber-
ately modified and has the appearance of a pistol butt, whilst on others
the sword hilt shape is retained.

The sword pistol was less common
in the East, although a few Indian
swords were fitted with a pistol. In
Burma there was some interest in an
elaborate 'dha-pistol sword' which, at
first glance, seems to be a matchlock
pistol with a very long stock. After the
pistol had been discharged, the
wooden section could be pulled clear
of the barrel to reveal a blade, with
the pistol serving as the hilt. The
Japanese produced one rather unusual false combination weapon
which was apparently a short dagger;
but when the weapon was drawn from
its sheath it revealed itself as a slim
percussion pistol. Presumably the
idea was to deceive an opponent into
believing that the owner carried only
a close-combat weapon before dis-
patching him at a reasonable and safe
distance.

Various types of dagger and knife
were fitted with wheellock, flintlock
and percussion pistols, but possibly
the oddest of all were small cutlery
sets of knife, fork and spoon made
early in the eighteenth century which
have small flintlock pistols mounted
in the handles. Because the barrel, in
the handle, points to the rear, that is,
in the direction of the holder, they

Left
Pin-fire knife pistol with a long bar hammer operated by the trigger situated under the handle.

Right
Knife pistol with unusual marks on the blade: the royal crown and 'VR', 'G.P.O.' and 'W. Cadman'. The small trapdoor at the base of the handle gives access to a small pair of tweezers. Private collection.

Far right
Elgin percussion cutlass pistol marked '109' and made by C. B. Allen of Springfield, Massachusetts.

have to be turned round to fire, so it is difficult to see their usefulness. It is likely that they were primarily novelties and most bear the name of F.H. Richter of Reichenberg, who perhaps made them one of his specialities. There are a few examples which are more in the nature of a very small pistol fitted with a knife blade or fork prongs, and on these the barrel points along the blade or prongs; one feels that these were perhaps a little more practical as weapons – they certainly were much safer for the user!

Whilst these cutlery pistol sets might be deemed to be novelties, there are one or two examples of combined knife pistols which were obviously intended for serious use. Some, made in India, combine the pistol with the katar, a dagger used in a punching motion. The grip was a crossbar held in the fist with the blade projecting forward as an extension of the forearm. A few of these katars were fitted with a pair of barrels, one on either side of the blade, so that a dagger thrust could be given or the trigger, fitted against the crossbar, could be used to fire a shot. One version in the Westgate Museum in Canterbury, England, has a guard of metal which goes over the forearm and back of the fist. A pair of forward-pointing flintlock pistols is mounted on this arm guard, and there is a spring-operated blade which can be kept locked back against the length of the guard. When released, the blade springs forward to lock into position, converting the armour into a combined katar pistol.

From the mid-nineteenth century onwards there was a vogue for penknife pistols mostly, but not exclusively, manufactured by two men, Philip Unwin and James Rodgers. The pistols come in a variety of shapes and sizes but generally they consist of a more or less conventional penknife with folding blades; mounted along the top of the handle of the knife is a short barrel usually about 2–3 in (50–76 cm) long. The earlier versions had percussion locks, but when cartridges became available Unwin and Rodgers simply adapted their models to take a small rim-fire cartridge, usually of .22 calibre. Often the knives themselves are quite elaborate with various folding attachments such as corkscrews, screwdrivers and even forks. Many of the Unwin and Rodgers weapons are quite conventional-looking, straight-handled penknives, perhaps with a slightly bulbous curve towards the end. In others the handle of the knife is much more butt-shaped.

Basically the penknife pistol was a practical penknife with the firearm as an extra to be used in an emergency. There is, however, one group of knife pistols in which it is difficult to tell which was intended to be the dominant component, the knife or the pistol. Perhaps as a result of the great publicity aroused by the exploits of Jim Bowie with his long-bladed knife, in July 1837 George Elgin of Georgia, USA, applied for and was granted a patent in the United States for a cutlass pistol. The weapon was basically a conventional, single-shot percussion pistol whose butt had a pronounced hook form; beneath the barrel was fixed a long blade with a clipped edge, rather like the famous bowie knife. The majority of these pistols were produced by two firms, C.B. Allen of Springfield, and Morrill, Mosman and Blair. The original patent model had a 13-in (33-cm) blade, but the only known official order for cutlass pistols from the US Government refers to them as being 11 in (28 cm) long. Although there is no mention in the patent, some models have a knuckle guard which springs from the trigger guard across to the tip of the pistol butt. Elgin cutlass pistols do not seem to have been in great demand, although quite a number were made. The nearest thing approaching recognition of these weapons was made by the United States South Seas Exploring Expedition, authorized by an Act of Congress in May 1836. Six naval vessels undertook an expedition to the Pacific which lasted for nearly four years, during which time they surveyed coastlines and explored over 300 islands. Elgin offered cutlass pistols with 5-in (12.7-cm) barrels and 11-in (28-cm) blades in a scabbard of black leather tipped with a German silver button. In the official order mentioned above, 150 were ordered for the expedition, and the

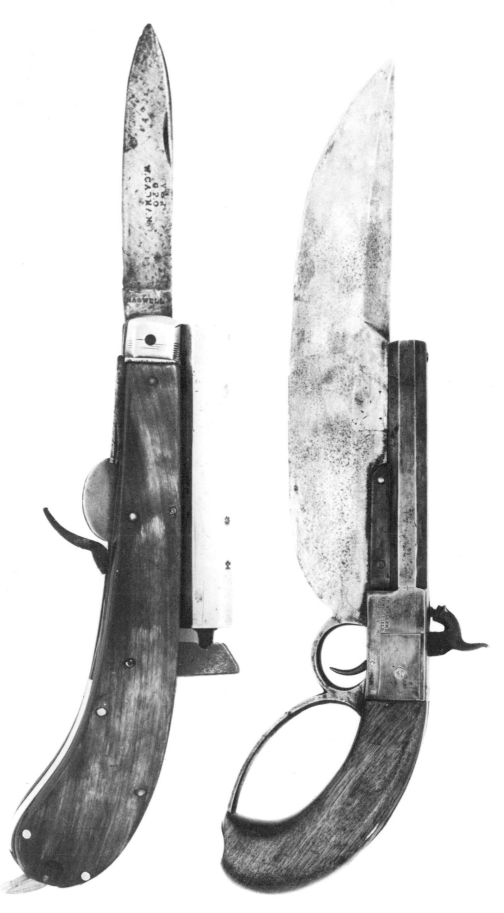

Left
Pistol sword by Gandon of London, made
c 1760. The butt has been modified to
serve as the grip, and the shell and
applied decoration are silver. A. Warren,
Bracklesham, Sussex.

Below
Brass-barrelled flintlock blunderbuss
pistol with spring-operated bayonet. The
blade is locked back by means of the
trigger guard.

Left
This sword pistol has two pistols, one mounted on each side of the blade. The hilt is ivory and the grip strap is signed 'Giuseppe Averan . The scabbard has steel mounts with a scallop-shaped guard at the neck.

Right
Pair of percussion pistols by William and John Rigby. The barrel is marked 'Dublin 78 99/7900' They are a little unusual in having side-mounted bayonets.

weapon apparently saw service. In the memoirs written by a lieutenant who served with the expedition, he mentions a fight with some natives in which a Mr Henry shot one of them with his pistol knife and cut down another with the same weapon.

Although the Elgin cutlass pistol never achieved great popularity the design was copied by numerous manufacturers, and when pin-fire cartridges became common various types of revolver were fitted with a similar cutlass blade, most of them being made by a Belgian manufacturer, Dumonthier.

One of the more ambitious forms of combination pistol and knife became popular during the latter part of the nineteenth century. It was invented by a Monsieur L. Dolne and received the somewhat fanciful nickname of 'Apache knuckleduster pistol'. The name had no real connection with the Apache Indians of the American Southwest, but was taken from the name given to a number of thugs who were terrorizing Paris late in the nineteenth century. Their cruel nature and behaviour was supposed to be such as to rival the Red Indians! The central feature was a small, pin-fire revolver which was essentially a cylinder without a barrel.

The butt consisted of a knuckleduster which could be folded away when not required. (A knuckleduster was a shaped metal bar with holes cut so that it could be slipped over the fingers; any blow struck with a fist so armed would be extremely powerful and dangerous.) Pivoted at the front

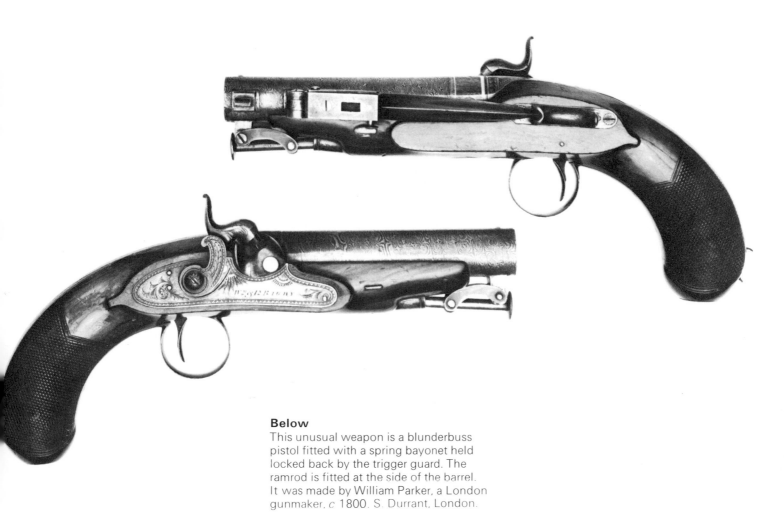

Below
This unusual weapon is a blunderbuss
pistol fitted with a spring bayonet held
locked back by the trigger guard. The
ramrod is fitted at the side of the barrel.
It was made by William Parker, a London
gunmaker, *c* 1800. S. Durrant, London.

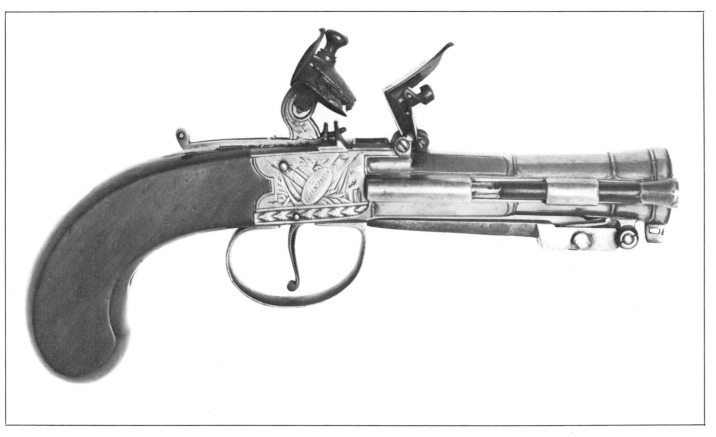

end of the frame was a short dagger, usually about 1½ in (38 mm) in length. The whole weapon could be folded to make a compact bundle which could be dropped in the pocket and, should the need arise, the owner had the choice of three weapons. If attacked he could take out the weapon, fold down the butt and lower the folding trigger to fire five or six shots. If the assailant survived this fusilade the owner could fold out the knife and impale him, or reverse the weapon, slip his fingers through the knuckleduster and beat him into insensibility! Early versions were for pin-fire cartridges but later ones used a small .32 (8.1-mm) centre-fire or a .22 (5.6-mm) rim-fire cartridge.

A similar weapon was made by a J. Delhaxe of France. This model had a very similar cylinder but with a fixed trigger, and the butt consisted of a rigid bar. The trigger guard formed part of the knuckleduster section which did not pivot. The lower end of the knuckleduster united with the base of the butt to give it a 'square frame' – its modern designation. A 2½-in (6.35-cm) blade was pivoted at the base of the butt and a short rod, used to push out the empty cases, also screwed into the base of the frame.

Towards the end of the nineteenth century combination weapons became even more elaborate, and numbers of patents were taken out for military swords with a whole range of pistols and revolvers mounted in the hilt with barrels pointing down the blade. One, patented in Britain by W. Davis in December 1877, had a six-chambered revolver fitted with a blade below the guard; but his novel contribution to combination technology was to make the sword scabbard fold up so that it could be attached to the hilt to convert the weapon into a carbine. This, like so many other combination weapons, was really more spectacular than effective. Possibly the only form of combined weapon which proved really effective was the bayonet.

The bayonet owes its origin to the limitation of the matchlock musket. Since the musket was single-shot and took time to load, the musketeer was left defenceless for those periods. One solution was to intersperse bodies of pikemen with the musketeers, the long pikes holding off any attack whilst the muskets were being loaded. If no pikemen were available, then the musketeer had to evolve his own defence. In a tight corner he pushed the hilt of his knife into the muzzle of his empty musket, so converting it into a crude, short pike. At first any knife was used but gradually, in the second half of the seventeenth century, a basic standard pattern, known as a 'plug bayonet', was evolved.

This had a tapering wooden grip with short crossguards, usually of brass, and a tapering, double-edged blade. Its name was probably derived from the town of Bayonne in France, long famed for its well-made hunting knives. The big problem with the plug bayonet was that the grip was simply pushed into the muzzle, which meant that the weapon could not be fired with the bayonet in place. It was obvious from the beginning that this system was very limited and means were sought to fit the bayonet to the musket in such a way that the weapon could still be fired. Eventually the socket bayonet was developed, which could slip over the barrel without obstructing the muzzle.

Very few early pistols were fitted with bayonets but, in June 1781, John Waters of Birmingham patented a device which was to become very popular. His idea was simple and consisted of a short, triangular blade mounted on the top, bottom or side of the barrel and pivoted at the muzzle. A small but strong spring exerted pressure against the bayonet when it was folded back along the barrel and the point engaged with a simple, sliding catch. When this catch was pulled back it disengaged the blade and the spring, which had been compressed, swung the blade forward; a simple spring clip then engaged in a small lug at the muzzle and the bayonet was locked into position. On some of the better-quality pistols the trigger guard was made to serve as the catch engaging with the tip of the bayonet when it was folded back under the barrel.

Spring bayonets were fitted on many pocket pistols as well as to a few larger, holster pistols. Blunderbusses, both the pistol and the large size, were commonly fitted with them.

Double-barrelled flintlock pistol by Burgon, fitted along the top with a spring-operated bayonet, locked back by a sliding catch on top of the breech. The escutcheon is silver. Barrel 9 in (22.8 cm). Blade 7½ in (19 cm).

Samuel Colt, in his US patent of 1836, included details of a bayonet to be attached to his revolvers. Franklin Wesson obtained a US patent in July 1869 for a 'dirk-knife' which, slotted into a double-barrelled derringer-type pistol, was ejected by a quick jerk and locked into place between the barrels. In January 1910 Henry Hull of Ohio, USA patented a spring-operated bayonet to be secured beneath the barrel of a cartridge revolver 'to enable the operator to have an auxiliary weapon of defence for use in close quarters or when the supply of cartridges is exhausted'. As recently as 1957 a US patent (No. 2,805,507) was granted for a pistol with a knife blade.

Numbers of cartridge revolvers were equipped with specially made bayonets. Harrington and Richardson, the American gunmaking firm, claimed in a 1902 advertisement that

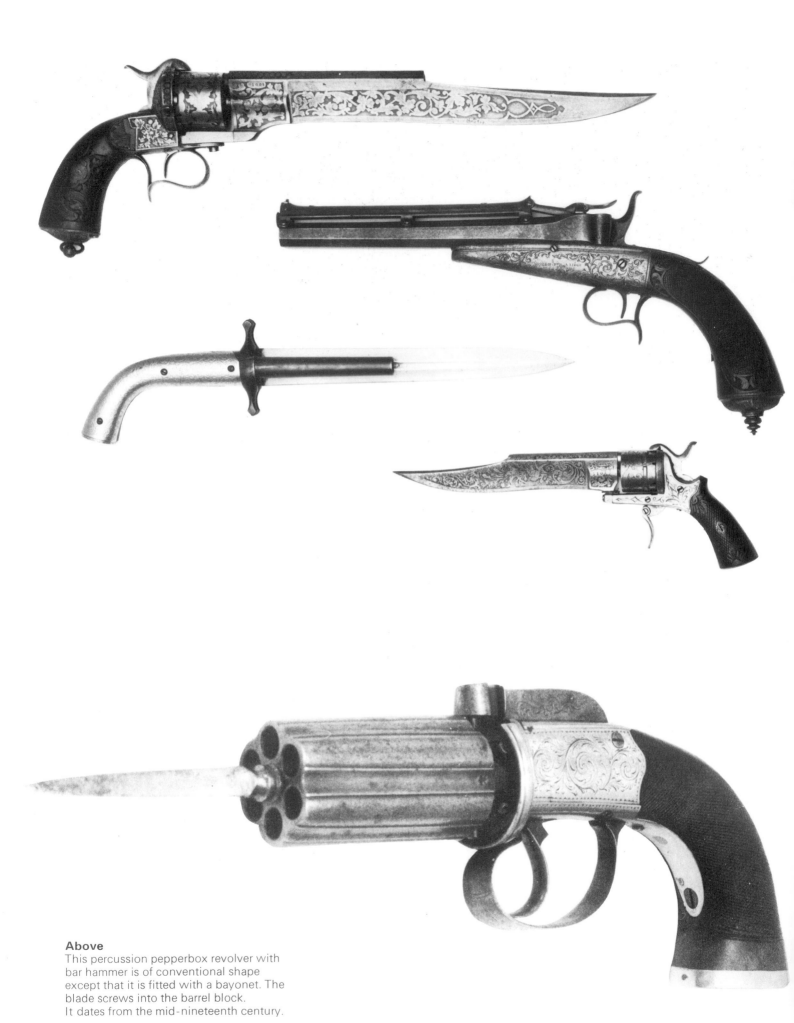

Above
This percussion pepperbox revolver with
bar hammer is of conventional shape
except that it is fitted with a bayonet. The
blade screws into the barrel block.
It dates from the mid-nineteenth century.

Left

From top to bottom.

Six-shot pinfire revolver fitted with long blade, the whole surface of which is etched with floral motifs. The revolver is marked 'Du Monthier'.

Unusual pattern of revolver with the magazine mounted above the barrel; the cartridges are fed in by gravity.

Plain, double-barrelled percussion sword pistol with one pistol on each side of the blade. The latter is marked 'Du Monthier Brevet/Dun'; the pistol was made *c* 1880.

Smaller pin-fire revolver knife pistol with folding trigger, also by Du Monthier and marked 'Du Monthier B.S.G. D.G.510'. Its date is *c* 1860.

Right

Percussion pistol sword of the mid-nineteenth century with brass-mounted scabbard. The pistol is marked 'Dumonthier & Charton'. The blade is 20⅞ in (53 cm) long and the weapon dates from the mid-nineteenth century.

they had received numerous requests for a bayonet revolver and this was why they offered 'The New Harrington & Richardson Automatic Bayonet Revolver'. The 2½-in (6.35-cm) blade was fitted beneath the barrel and could be folded back when not required. A detachable bayonet was designed for the British Webley revolver, and tradition has it that they were made for British Army motor cyclists serving in India.

Apart from the bayonet, none of the combination weapons ever really became popular and their value is doubtful, but this never deterred the inventor and some remarkable ideas were produced. Patents were granted for such devices as fish hooks which shot the fish; pistols which photographed the target as it was fired at, and a plough with a built-in gun! However, one of the most novel must surely be US Patent No. 1,183,492, of 1916, which was for a German-type, spiked helmet which concealed a pistol pointing forward: this was fired by blowing down a tube to inflate a bulb which operated the trigger. For good measure the top section of the helmet could be detached and used as a cooking utensil!

Revolvers

Despite all their efforts to overcome the single-shot limitation of early firearms, the gunsmiths were not really successful until the nineteenth century. Nearly every combination or multishot weapon that was developed had some snag. The solution only came between the 1830s and '50s, when the first really practical revolvers were introduced. They came about as an extension of the old idea of a rotating barrel block. Mention has already been made of the over-and-under barrel system – the so-called 'wender' – and it was from this basic idea that the solution was to be developed. The principle was to bring freshly loaded barrels into the firing position one after the other. One problem was that the long barrels, the breech block and, with flintlocks, the pans and frizzens combined to make the weapon very barrel-heavy. It was the difficulty of overcoming this handicap and other practical manufacturing problems that so long delayed the production of a really effective revolver.

Most of the early revolvers were hand-operated with some form of locking device which had to be disengaged and the barrels rotated to bring an unfired one into position. The mechanism was then locked, the shot was fired and the sequence repeated until all barrels had been discharged. The system worked but it was clumsy and limited. The problem caused by the projecting frizzens was overcome towards the end of the eighteenth century when a new type of flintlock revolver came into use. Examples usually had seven fairly short barrels which were fixed onto a cylindrical breech block. The revolver had a centrally mounted boxlock and the single frizzen served all seven barrels. Each of the barrels had its own pan which was so positioned that it came into place directly beneath the single frizzen. The priming powder was kept in place by a close-fitting collar which encircled the breech end of the barrels. To fire a shot it was only necessary to close the frizzen, cock the action and press the trigger, then the sparks fell through the encircling guard into the pan of the first barrel and fired it. The barrel assembly was then rotated by hand to bring the next barrel and pan into line under the frizzen; this was re-closed and the sequence repeated until all seven shots were fired. Although there were normally seven barrels only six operations were required to empty the weapon. The central barrel, around which the other six were located, shared a common touch-hole with one of the outer group of barrels; consequently there were five single shots and a double one.

With the adoption of the percussion system the whole mechanism was simplified. In place of the pans and retaining collar of the old flintlock weapon, the percussion version of the revolver had each barrel fitted with a nipple. This was normally set at right angles to the bore and distributed around the circumference of the barrel block. The end view of the

English percussion revolvers of the mid-nineteenth century.
From top to bottom.
Adams's self-cocking revolver; the spring behind the cylinder is a safety device.
Deane-Adams double-action revolver with bolt safety at the rear of the cylinder.
Daws revolver with double-action mechanism and Colt-like under-barrel loading lever.
Kerr revolver of 1858–9 with side hammer.
Pattern Room, Royal Small Arms Factory, Enfield.

barrel assembly with the holes resembles a very large pepper pot, and these weapons are commonly known as 'pepperboxes'.

The percussion pepperboxes enjoyed quite a spell of popularity around the 1840s and '50s. There was a variety of models, and one of the more advanced and certainly rarer examples was that produced by Edward Budding from Thrupp Mill, near Stroud in Gloucestershire, England. This ' was a hand-rotated pepperbox, as were most of the earlier examples, but its interesting feature was that instead of being at right-angles to the bore, the nipple was

mounted horizontally and screwed into the rear end of the breech. The hammer was an internal one mounted inside a central barrel block. When the trigger was operated the hammer, instead of moving through a vertical plane, moved forward horizontally. The system made for a very neat outline but it introduced the problem that, in order to reload, the whole barrel block had to be removed from the frame.

The Budding, being hand-rotated, required both hands to operate it, but early in the 1830s the self-cocking pepperbox appeared. The earliest patent for this action was granted to a

well-known gunmaker, Ethan Allen, in Massachusetts, USA, in 1837, and the patent also covered the bar-hammer. This was a flat bar terminating in a solid disc which projected over the breech to reach just above the nipples. As the trigger was pulled the bar was raised until, at a certain point, the trigger was disengaged from the bar so allowing the mainspring to drive it down to strike the cap on the nipple. At the same time as the bar was rising a small, slightly curved lever known as the 'hand' engaged with a series of ramped teeth cut into the back of the breech. As the trigger was pressed the hand rose

111

FORGE

MILLING ROOM

FACTORY

RIFLING ROOM

FITTING ROOM

Left
The total number of pistols and revolvers produced in the United States since the time of Colt is enormous. This picture in *The Scientific American* of January 1880 dealt with the production of the New Model No 3, introduced in 1878 at Smith & Wesson's factory at Springfield, Massachusetts.

Above
Snaphaunce revolver with six chambers, possibly made in London by John Dafte *c* 1680. The mechanical operation is very similar to that patented by Samuel Colt in the nineteenth century. Tower of London Armouries.

vertically to lock behind one of the projecting teeth. As it lifted under the trigger pressure it turned the entire barrel assembly. At the top of its rise the blocks were so positioned that an unfired barrel was in position under the hammer. When the trigger was released the hand slipped back over the teeth to engage with the next one. The two actions, hand and hammer, were so united that the bar fell at just the right moment when the nipple was in the correct position.

This style of pepperbox was produced in quantity, with minor variations, until the 1860s both in Europe and America. The Continental versions were frequently fitted with a ring trigger and the index finger was pushed through the ring at the end of the bar. These weapons also differ in that the nipples are often set, like the earlier Budding pepperbox, in line with the bore. Unlike the British version these Continental pistols normally fire the bottom barrel first.

Undoubtedly the pepperbox offered certain advantages. It was a weapon which could be loaded with six shots in one go and then fire a shot whenever required. However, it was in many ways an inconvenient wea-

pon for the very solid barrel assembly, even though drilled out with six bores, was heavy and uncomfortable to carry for any length of time. As each of the bores was smooth-bored, the accuracy was not of a very high order.

Attempts were made to overcome these difficulties by producing what is often described by collectors as a 'transition revolver'. These had a truncated pepperbox assembly with a rifled barrel fitted in front and in line with the top bore. It was a very simple form of revolver but at best it was makeshift, at worse it was feeble, and it does not seem to have been very popular. The pepperbox system lingered on until the mid-years of the nineteenth century and, in a specialized form, persisted right up to the beginning of this century. Many combined weapons such as the Apache pistol were little more than a cartridge or pin-fire pepperbox. At the same time as the pepperbox was being developed, however, very important events were taking place in the United States.

The modern revolver is usually traced back and described as the brainchild of a Yankee Hartford businessman, Samuel Colt. He took

Above
Flintlock revolver with seven barrels made by John Tocknell of Brighton. The single frizzen and cock serve all seven barrels and the priming powder is retained in the pans by the collar around the breech. Art Gallery and Museum, Kelvingrove, Glasgow.

Right
American percussion revolvers.
Top Savage & North Second Model Navy Revolver 1861–2. The ring trigger acts like the British Tranter double trigger, rotating the cylinder and cocking the action, while the normal trigger fires the shot.
Centre Starr double-action revolver, a six-shot weapon with the unusual feature that on reloading it 'breaks' barrel-down for removal of the cylinder.
Bottom Remington percussion revolver with plated trigger guard. New Model Army revolver of .44-in (11.2-mm) calibre.

out a British patent for a revolver in October 1835, and in 1836 he took out similar patents in France and America. Among the claims that he made for his revolver was that it was simple and effective, and indeed it was. The action of all Colt's single-action revolvers was basically the same. Linked to the hammer was a small, upright hand which, as in the pepperbox, engaged with a toothed section at the rear of a solid cylinder. As the hammer was pulled back so the leverage lifted the hand which, in turn, rotated the cylinder. When the cylinder had turned the correct amount, a small locking device engaged with a recess in the circumference of the cylinder and held it securely in position. When the trigger was pressed the hammer which, as it had been pulled back, had compressed the main spring, swung forward to detonate the cap and fire the charge lined up with the barrel. Although Colt patented this action in 1835 the idea was not new, for a flintlock revolver working on a very similar principle can be dated to around 1680. It was probably made by a famous London gunmaker, John Dafte. Whether Colt had knowledge

of this system or had seen an example of Dafte's revolver is not known, but in many ways the systems are very similar.

Nor was Colt the first to put into production a rotating cylinder weapon. Some very efficient flintlock revolving arms were manufactured early in the nineteenth century. They are usually marked 'Collier' and were the work of Elisha Haydon Collier of Boston, Massachusetts, who lived in London. Collier's system was patented in London in 1818, but a Captain Artemas Wheeler of Massachusetts had been granted a very similar patent in the same year, and in France another American, Cornelius Coolidge, had also patented an almost identical device. Who was the originator of the idea is not at all certain! Most of the surviving examples bear the name of Collier and it is to him that the credit is given. Collier's rotating revolver underwent certain major modifications. His first patent had the cylinder powered by a coiled spring. When the weapon was loaded, the cylinder was rotated against the coiled spring so that it was under tension. As the action was cocked, a mechanism allowed the

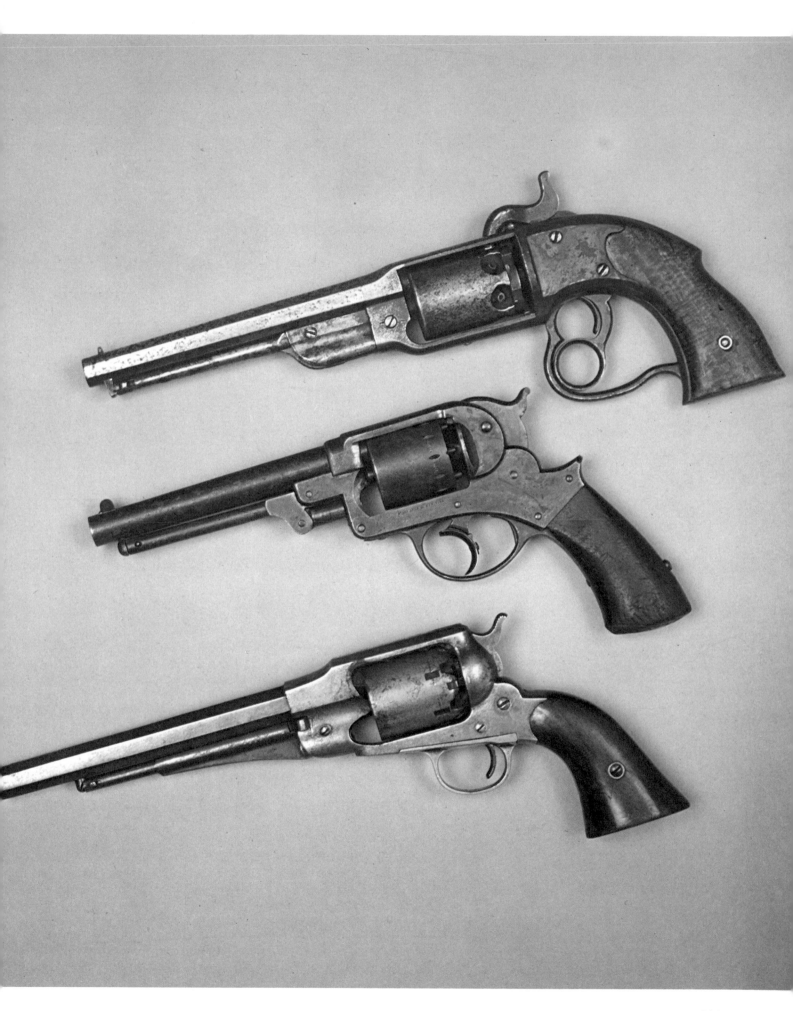

Flintlock revolvers by E. H. Collier.
Top Revolver with external cock, a fluted cylinder and an octagonal barrel; it is probably slightly later than the model below.
Bottom The first five-shot pistol, this model has a smooth cylinder which was rotated by hand; the priming is automatic. It was made *c* 1819.
Victoria and Albert Museum, London.

cylinder, driven by the spring, to rotate to bring the next chamber in line with the barrel. Presumably Collier decided that this system was perhaps a little too complex, and all surviving examples of his revolver have a cylinder which is hand-rotated.

One of the problems which was to bedevil all revolvers, indeed it continues to do so, is the effect known as obturation, a rather obscure name for a simple and obvious fact. If the barrel is not attached directly to the cylinder which contains the charge, whether it be in a cartridge or loose powder, obviously there will be a gap between the face of the cylinder and the rear of the barrel. This means that at the moment of explosion a certain amount of gas must necessarily escape through this gap. Even with the most modern of revolvers this effect is still present. The amount of gas leakage affects the velocity of the bullet. Obviously, if a large amount escapes through this gap there is less gas to drive the bullet forward. It is a very serious and important problem. Collier dealt with it by countersinking the end of the chamber and pressing the

cylinder forward over the end of the barrel to produce a very tight fit. When the cylinder had to be rotated, it was pulled back slightly to disengage it from the barrel in order that it could be turned to bring the next full cylinder into line. In this way the escape of gas was kept to an absolute minimum although, clearly, the forward and backward movement of the cylinder introduced certain mechanical complications. Whether Colt was familiar with the Collier action or the Dafte-type flintlock revolver is not really important, however, because nothing can take from Colt the credit for introducing nineteenth-century technology into the arms trade.

Samuel Colt was a man apparently full of energy and enthusiasm, sometimes misplaced; he was perhaps a little vain for he delighted in the use of the title of Colonel although it was little more than a courtesy rank in the Connecticut Militia and he should really have been addressed as Lieutenant-Colonel. He was, though, outstanding in promoting his products. He had faith in his ideas and managed to acquire the capital necessary to set himself up in business,

Top
Colt's Paterson Belt Model, available in .31-in (7.9-mm) and .34-in (8.63-mm) calibres with concealed trigger and no attached loading lever. The barrels varied from 4-in (10.16-cm) to 6-in (15.24-cm), and a few were 12 in (30 cm) long. Winchester Gun Museum, New Haven, Connecticut.

Above
Colt single-action Army revolver, with 7½-in (17.8-cm) barrel. One of the best-known revolvers in the world, it was made in various calibres and with several barrel lengths. Winchester Gun Museum, New Haven, Connecticut.

and put the Patent Arms Manufacturing Company of Paterson, New Jersey, into production. He made the famous Paterson Colt revolver with its folding trigger, as well as revolving carbines, shotguns and rifles. Despite the many virtues of Colt's system he did not achieve anything like the sales he expected, and in 1843, after only seven years, the company became insolvent.

For four years Colt sought to promote and encourage an interest in his percussion weapons and, fortunately for him, in 1847 the United States Army ordered from Colt 1,000 heavy .44 (11.2-mm) holster pistols. His experience with the Paterson Colt had stood him in good stead. He realized, or perhaps it had been pointed out to him, that his early weapons

had structural weaknesses; his new .44 pistol, by contrast, was extremely sturdy. It had an attached loading lever to ram home the balls into the chambers, the cylinder was strong and there was a substantial trigger in place of the rather suspect folding trigger on the Paterson. A firm trigger guard gave protection against accidental discharge and altogether the components combined to form a very substantial revolver weighing over 4 lb (1.8 kg). The weapon itself comprised three main sections: the frame which included the butt and the trigger and spring mechanisms; the cylinder, and the barrel. The cylinder slipped over a central spigot to which the barrel was secured by a flat bar which pushed through the barrel assembly and the spigot.

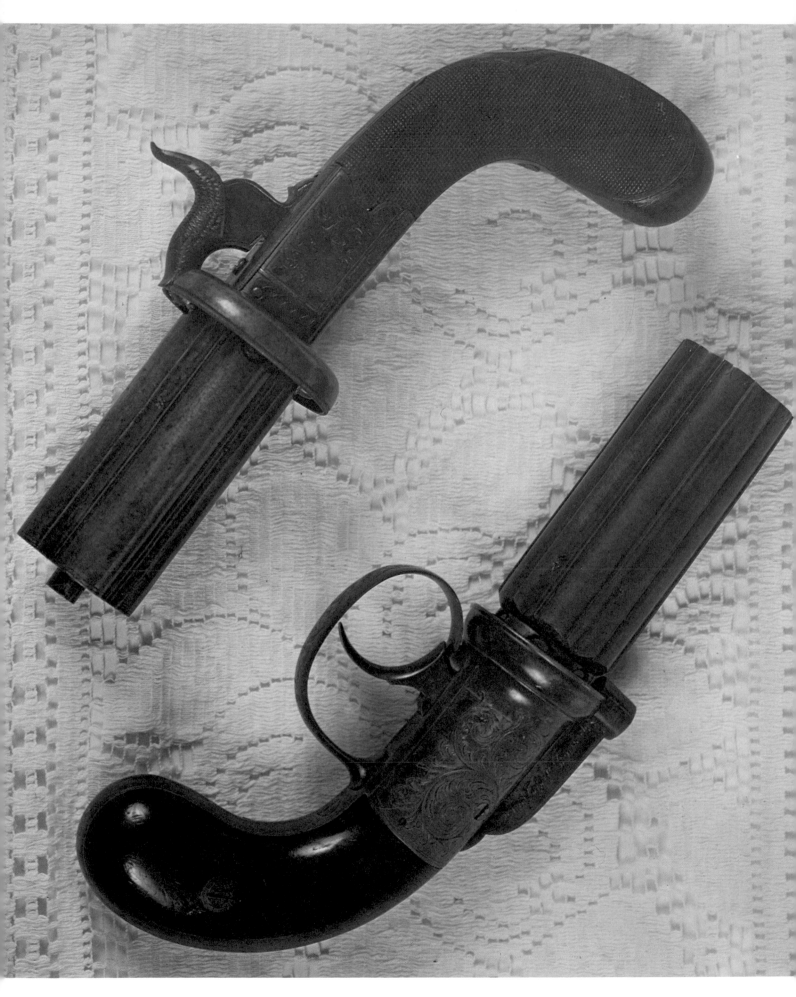

Left
Pepperbox revolvers made in about 1850.
Top A conventional bar-hammer type.
Bottom An earlier form with the
conventional percussion hammer and
large nipple shield.

Above
Example of the so-called transition
revolver, which was really a combination
of a short-barrelled pepperbox fitted with
a rifled barrel.

After his unfortunate beginnings Colt lacked the means to manufacture these revolvers, and called upon another well-known gunmaker, Eli Whitney. Then, with the growth of interest in his products, Colt was soon able to set up his own factory in Hartford, Connecticut; from 1848 onwards, until his early death in 1862, his enthusiasm, skill and technical 'know-how' made a lasting impression on the firearms industry. In 1848 he began production of his big, six-shot, Dragoon or Old Model Army .44 in (11.2 mm) calibre. This was a rather heavy weapon, and to accommodate less ambitious shooters he

produced a five-shot Model 1848 Pocket Revolver in a variety of barrel lengths from 3–6 in (76–152 mm) and firing a much smaller ball, only .31 in (7.9 mm). Most of the early models had no attached loading lever and in 1849 he produced another pocket revolver, a six-shot one this time, most of which were fitted with an attached ramrod lever.

In 1851 he compromised between the small pocket pistol of .31-in (7.9-mm) calibre and the army .44, and produced the so-called Navy Colt or Belt Revolver in .36-in (9.14-mm) calibre. The standard model had a 7½-in (19-cm) barrel which gave it

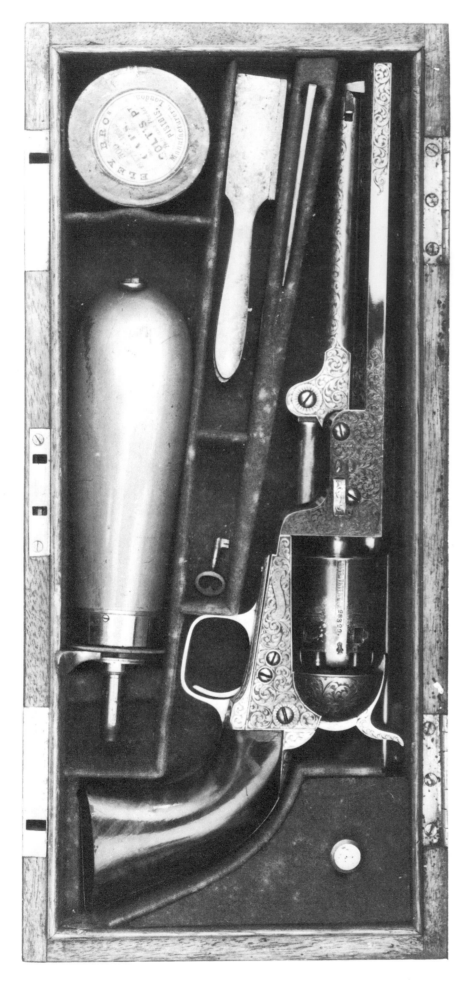

considerable accuracy, and it was an extremely popular weapon. The name 'Navy' was derived from the naval battle scene, between Texan and Mexican ships, engraved on the cylinder. The battle took place in May 1843 and some of Colt's early Paterson revolvers were used in the fight. In 1855 Colt put into production one revolver which was very different from all his other models. The Model 1855 Sidehammer Pocket Revolver was a five-shot weapon in .28-in (7.1-mm) and .31-in (7.9-mm) calibres. Although this weapon had many features in common with other Colt revolvers, it differed in having a hammer which was mounted externally, on the side of the frame. The barrel and frame were made in one piece and the trigger was sleeved and not fitted with a trigger guard.

In 1860 Colt decided that it was time for a replacement for the Dragoon, and in that year he produced another army revolver in .44-in (11.2-mm) calibre with a 7½ or 8-in (19 or 20.3-cm) barrel. In the next few years Colt introduced several new models of revolver as well as a variety of long arms.

Quite apart from his ability in designing revolvers, Colt was perhaps even more deserving of credit for introducing modern technology into the production of firearms. During the early nineteenth century emphasis on the individual, craftsman-made pistol was diminishing, but Colt saw the necessity for what would today be called mass-production techniques. One great virtue which Colt always claimed for his products was that all parts were interchangeable. From stock, any Colt Navy 1851 cylinder could be fitted on to any other Colt 1851, and the same was true for all the fittings. He designed or modified many of the machines which were used in the production of his revolvers, and was never afraid to experiment.

In 1851 in London there was staged the Exhibition of The Works and Industry of All Nations, better known as the Great Exhibition. Colt heard of this grand event and decided that he should be represented in the American Gallery. His stand was decorated with patterns of his weapons, and he

Left

1851 Colt Navy Percussion Revolver, cased and with its original fittings. The weapon is engraved and has an escutcheon with a crest, a rampant stag, and the name 'Edward Micklam R.E.' (Royal Engineers).

Below

Although the Colt Company closed their factory in London they maintained an agency and continued to advertise widely in Britain. This small ad is from the *Illustrated London News* of December 1900. The New 'Service' revolver was introduced in 1898.

Bottom

When Smith and Wesson held the master patent on the breech-loading cylinder, manufacturers devised many systems to avoid the limitation. This was the Thuer Conversion used by Colt, patented in 1868, which allowed the weapon to be loaded from the front. Illustration from *The Mechanics' Magazine*, July 1869.

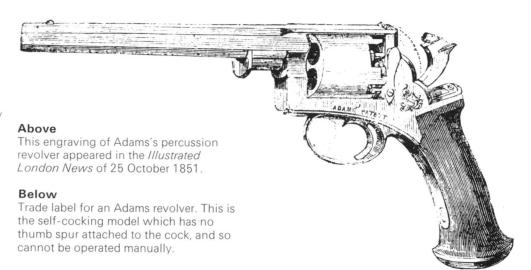

Above

This engraving of Adams's percussion revolver appeared in the *Illustrated London News* of 25 October 1851.

Below

Trade label for an Adams revolver. This is the self-cocking model which has no thumb spur attached to the cock, and so cannot be operated manually.

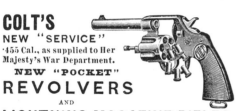

COLT'S
NEW "SERVICE"
·455 Cal., as supplied to Her Majesty's War Department.
NEW "POCKET"
REVOLVERS
AND
LIGHTNING MAGAZINE RIFLES.
Price Lists Free.
COLT'S PATENT FIREARMS M'F'G CO.,
26, Glasshouse Street, Piccadilly Circus, London, W.

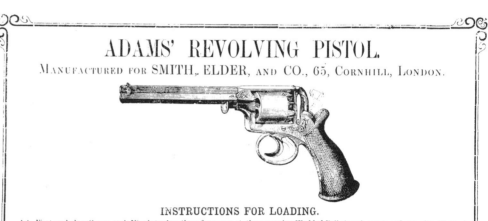

ADAMS' REVOLVING PISTOL.

MANUFACTURED FOR SMITH, ELDER, AND CO., 65, CORNHILL, LONDON.

INSTRUCTIONS FOR LOADING.

1st. First explode a Cap on each Nipple to clear them from any accumulation of oil or other deposit, to ensure certainty of fire.
2nd. Pull the Trigger into the position of the dotted Trigger; this will draw the Hammer back; then press in the Stop Spring with the thumb, and hold it there, while allowing the Hammer to return to its position at rest. The Chambers will now revolve freely. Put the Powder into each of the Chambers with a flask,

then press in a Wadded Ball *close down upon the powder*—the wad next the powder, put on the Caps, and the loading is complete.
To Fire, pull the Trigger five times in succession.
To take out the Chambers press in the Stop Spring and draw the Spindle towards the Muzzle, when the Chambers may be readily
To disengage the Stop Spring, pull the Trigger. [removed.
Keep the Spindle clean, and oiled occasionally.

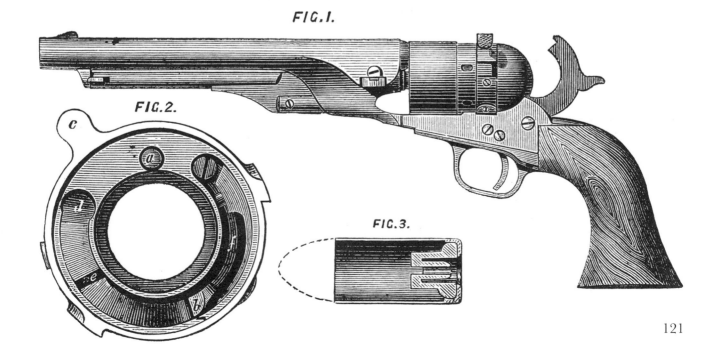

FIG.1.

FIG.2.

FIG.3.

Cased pair of Adams percussion revolvers, *c* 1851. They are self-cocking with no spur to the hammer, and are fitted with Adams rammers situated beneath the cylinder on the side of the frame.

This is the large Colt Dragoon six-shot revolver produced, with minor variations, between 1848–62. This particular weapon, the 3rd Model, has a pewter heart set in the butt – the badge associated with XXIV Corps of the Federal Army.

missed no opportunity to boost the sales of his products by presenting specially engraved or ordinary model weapons to virtually anybody who might, directly or indirectly, influence his potential sales.

He found to his great astonishment, that there was no equivalent British product and that his percussion revolver unquestionably led the world. Not unreasonably, he felt that if he could set up a factory to make his weapons in London the market potential was very considerable. He consequently instructed his agents to rent a suitable property that he had seen in Pimlico, a district of London, and the factory was leased in 1852.

It took time to equip the factory and train operators for the various machines, and it seems that London production did not begin until January 1853. About 200 workers were

employed in addition to some 30 American technicians. The various presses were powered by belts which ran off a central spindle turned by a 30 horse-power steam engine. Much of the shaping of the various parts was done by American drop-hammers, and many of the specialized machines were designed by Colt's own staff. Charles Dickens, the famous British writer, visited the factory and described the scene in detail. Despite his excellent modern approach to the business, Colt did not immediately receive large government orders; in fact it was not until 1854 that 4,000 of his Model 1851 Navy Revolvers were ordered for the Royal Navy.

The impact of this breezy, hard-headed, commercially minded American on the British gun trade was more than considerable. The British gunmakers resented his meth-

123

Below
Engraving from a book on revolvers that shows Robert Adams loading an example of his percussion revolver.

ods, they resented his intrusion and, above all, they feared the competition, and if an opportunity arose to denigrate Mr Colt or his products, few of them were sufficiently strong-minded to resist. Some of the evidence given to a committee set up by the British Government 'to consider the cheapest and best way of providing small arms for the Government forces' by some well-known members of the British gun trade, would appear, on the face of it, to be somewhat biased. Colt made much of his claim of interchangeability, and it is not surprising that some prejudiced evidence sought to play down this feature. Despite the criticisms of the trade, however, some of the users of Colt's weapons gave them very high praise.

The outcome of his industrial venture was not quite what Colt had

expected. Although he maintained an English business interest with an agent to sell his weapons, he decided that the factory was not really a success, and late in 1865 Colt virtually ceased manufacture in London.

The only serious British rival of Colt's percussion revolver was one designed by Robert Adams which differed from the Colt in several important respects. The Colt had a separate barrel, whereas on Adams's revolver the barrel and frame were fashioned as a single piece. The rotating actions were not dissimilar and the cylinder on both was basically the same, with centrally placed nipples parallel to the axis of the bore and separated by a metal shield. This was to prevent what was known as chain-fires, where the explosion of one cap set off all the others in turn.

One of the biggest differences

Far left
Five-shot Beaumont Adams percussion revolver, cased with its accessories. The double-action mechanism was patented in 1855. This model was marketed by Dickson & Son of Princes Street, Edinburgh.

Top left
Double-action percussion revolver made by the London Armoury Company Ltd. The special features of this weapon were patented in 1858–9 by James Kerr and were designed to make the weapon very easy to service with easy access to all parts.

Above left
Beaumont Adams percussion revolver with five shots. The loading lever or rammer is housed along the side of the barrel. This model is more profusely engraved than usual.

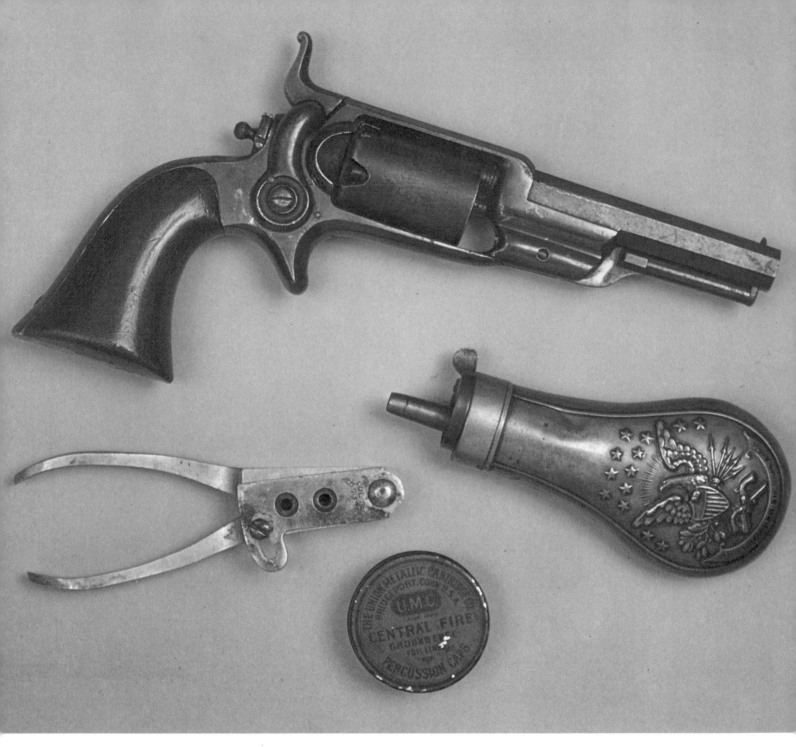

between the two weapons lay in the method of firing. The Adams was of the type known as self-cocking: as with the pepperbox, the trigger raised the hammer to a certain point and then allowed it to fall and fire the revolver. The Colt revolver had to be cocked manually for each shot. There was, and still is, much discussion as to the virtue of each system; both have something to offer. Manual cocking certainly makes for slower and probably more carefully aimed fire, the trigger pull is light and an aim can easily be taken and held. Self-cocking makes for more rapid fire but this in itself is not necessarily an advantage

and the strength of pull needed is considerable. Despite some rather exaggerated claims made for both weapons, there was little to choose between them as far as efficiency and effectiveness were concerned.

In February 1855 a Lieutenant Beaumont of the Royal Engineers patented a mechanism which permitted the use of both cocking systems on a single revolver. This design of trigger mechanism was incorporated into the Adams revolvers, and the Beaumont Adams revolver came into production shortly afterwards. It could be cocked with the thumb, so offering the advantage of the Colt, but

A Colt side-hammer revolver, unusual in having a solid frame as well as the unconventional, externally attached hammer. This type of Colt revolver was first made in 1855 and continued in production until 1870. It was available in .28-in (7.1-mm) and .31-in (7.9-mm) calibres.

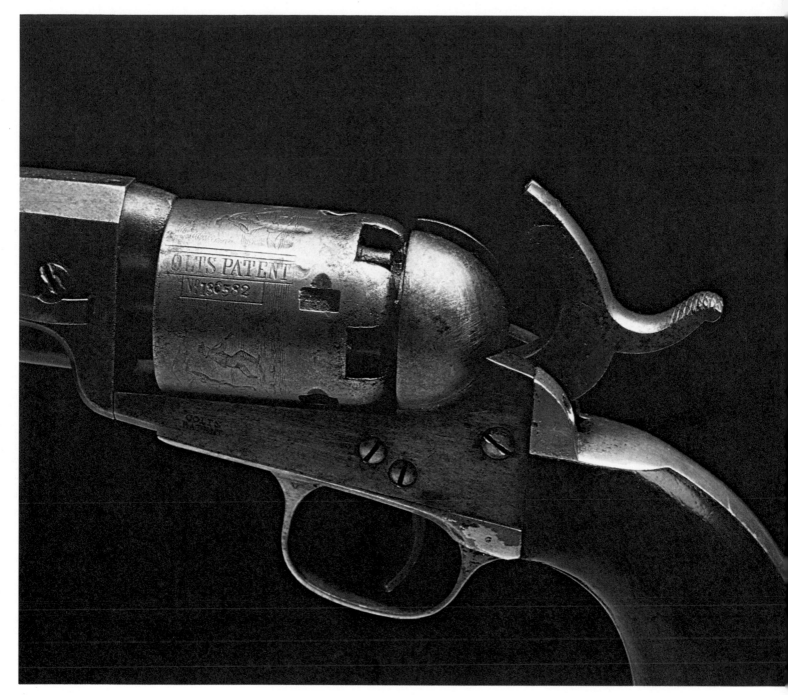

Colt's patent cylinder — the recipe for the first mass-produced revolver. This cylinder marking and number are from a Model 1849 Pocket Revolver.

it could also be fired by means of the trigger alone. The Beaumont Adams revolver also had an attached ramrod, a feature lacking on the original self-cocking Adams. There were two main types, the Kerr rammer which was pivoted at the front of the frame and secured to the side of the barrel, and the one patented by Robert Adams which was secured below the cylinder by the side of the butt.

The 1850s and '60s saw a great increase in the production of percussion revolvers, and there was little to choose between the English and the American. On the whole the English tend to have a slightly better finish

and are probably of better-quality workmanship. One feature which a large number of the British revolvers adopted was a small, rear-projecting spur near the top of the butt, rather reminiscent of the saw handle on some of the early nineteenth-century duelling pistols. George Daw, a London gunmaker, produced some percussion revolvers which were very similar to the Colt, with an under-barrel loading lever and a separate barrel. Daw was not the only manufacturer: two brothers, James and Philip Webley of Birmingham, were producing percussion gunlock systems as early as 1835. Their Webley revolvers were made

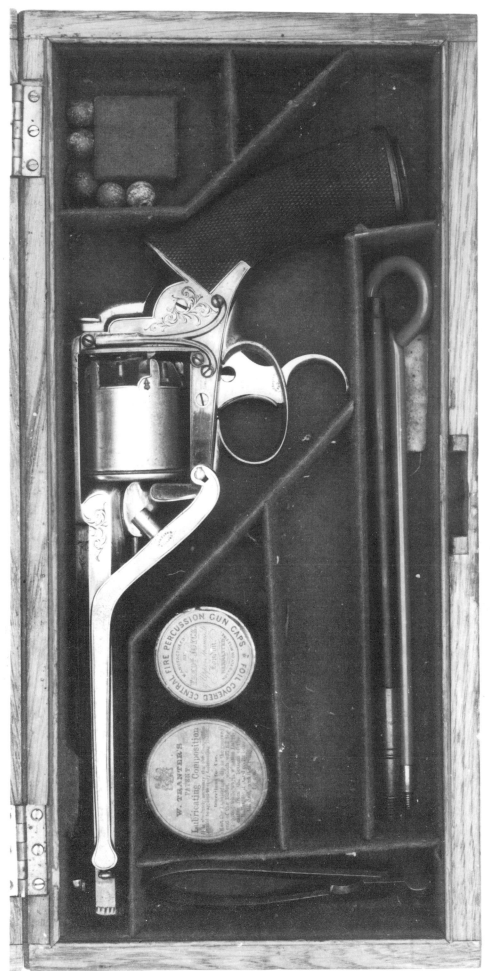

Left
Double-trigger percussion revolver by
William Tranter retailed by B. Cogswell of
224 Strand, London. The loading lever is
detachable and the spring by the cylinder
is, like that on the Adams revolver, a
safety device.

Above right
A Belgian-made revolver from Liège, this
slightly unusual pattern is a six-shot pin-
fire weapon of 9-mm calibre, made
c 1870. The ivory butt is pivoted, as is the
side plate, to allow easy access to the
springs and mechanism. It is marked
'Bayft RE 5 Brevette'.

Right
Pinfire revolver elaborately ornamented
with applied silver decoration. It has a
folding trigger and side ejecting rod.

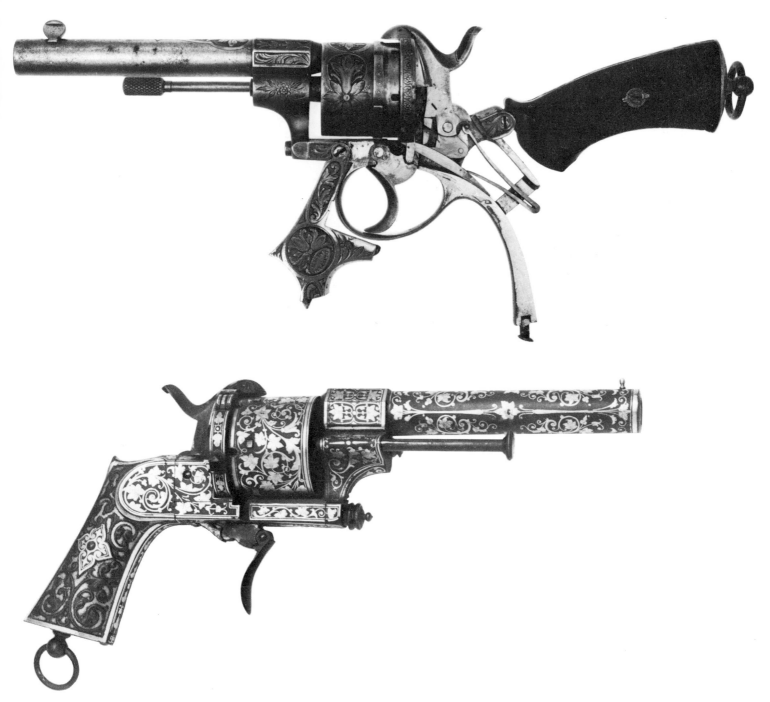

with both single- and double-action systems, and the earlier models were characterized by a long, gently swept-back butt. Webleys also adopted both the under-barrel loading lever and the Adams type of ramrod mounted along the side.

One interesting model in the British field was William Tranter's revolver, produced under a patent of 1853, which was an attempt to benefit from both systems of cocking. Tranter revolvers were fitted with a long, double-recurved trigger, the end section of which protruded through a slit in, and extended below, the trigger guard. When the lower section of the trigger below the guard was pressed, the cylinder rotated and the action was cocked. In order to discharge a shot the top section of the double trigger, within the trigger guard, was pressed; this released the hammer to fire the shot. The lower trigger could be pressed to bring a fresh chamber into position, and then the aim could be conveniently held until the right moment came to fire.

The 1860s saw a further expansion of revolver production, and a whole range of new models, many claiming to have some distinctive feature or other, appeared on the market. In America pistols were produced by the Massachusetts Arms Company, Remington, Witney, and many others. In Britain they were made by Kerr, Deane Harding, Webley, Daws, Adams, and some less well-known companies. The majority of the pistols were loaded by means of paper cartridges and the bullet rammed home into the chamber by means of the attached lever. Armed with a pair of such revolvers, the military man or the hunter had 10 or 12 shots immediately available. For some, 12 shots were insufficient and

there were revolvers firing more than the standard six. One, patented by John Walch in 1859, was in effect a superimposed-load revolver with two charges in each of the six chambers. Another oddity was the double-purpose revolver patented by Dr Le Mat from New Orleans. It was basically a percussion revolver with nine shots but it had a second barrel mounted below the normal, rifled barrel. This discharged a round of buckshot, and was detonated by adjusting the nose of the hammer to

strike a special nipple. A number of the Le Mat revolvers saw service during the American Civil War.

One of the more bizarre patents to increase the firepower potential of the percussion revolver was that granted to Enouy Joseph in 1855. The basic weapon was a conventional percussion revolver, but an elaborate spindle extended from the tip of the butt and onto this spindle was fitted a wheel of cylinders, seven in all. The first one was placed in position, and the six shots discharged; then the

Above
This was the first Colt weapon produced for metal cartridges. Of .41-in (10.16-mm) calibre, it was introduced in 1871 and remained in production until 1876. Most were only four-shot, but some five-shot versions were also made.

Right
John Adams Mark II Service Revolver with an ejector rod of 1872 patent. Although a service pattern, this example has been decorated with engraving and gilding and carved ivory grips, probably for the Asiatic market. Its calibre is .455 in (11.6 mm).

From an 1887 edition of *Harpers New Monthly Magazine* comes this print of 'New York's Finest' carrying out a river arrest. Firearms have long been part of the United States police forces' equipment, and here two officers use their revolvers to arrest a group of suspects.

wheel rotated to bring a fresh cylinder into place which, in turn, could deliver six shots, so that the whole pistol offered a potential firepower of 42 shots. The weapon was big, clumsy and, to say the least, rather impractical.

Most revolvers of the 1850s and '60s were the normal percussion type and were reasonably efficient and reliable. Even the best malfunctioned at times, as for example the famous Australian bushranger, Ned Kelly, has recorded. This particularly audacious outlaw once wrote a justification of his actions, and in his letter he described an encounter with an Australian policeman, Constable Hall, in 1870. Kelly wrote: 'Hall got up and snapped three or four caps at me and would have shot me but the colts patent (*sic*) refused.' If the Colt had functioned the career of Kelly might well have ended there and then, and he would never have gone on to fight the police wearing his

celebrated home-made armour.

In 1854 a pin-fire revolver was patented by Casimir Lefaucheux. It was, in some respects, basically the same as the modern revolver with the cylinder bored through so that the cartridges were loaded singly from the rear. An ejector, fitted beneath the barrel, was used for pushing out the empty cases. Their ease and convenience of use made these revolvers very popular, and they saw considerable service in the European and American campaigns of the late 1850s and '60s. One drawback lay not in the design of the pistol itself but in the cartridges, for the protruding pin from the base of the cartridge was always a potential source of danger.

In 1855 Rollin White of Connecticut took out a US patent for a breechloading revolver in which the cylinder was bored through in much the same style as the French pin-fire revolver. Slightly earlier, in 1850, a French patent was granted to a Monsieur

Right
This leaflet was issued in 1867 warning of copies of the Smith and Wesson revolvers.

Below right
Harrington and Richardson of Worcester, Massachusetts produced a wide range of revolvers that enjoyed some popularity. The model advertised is a hammerless type; the date is 1899.

No. 1.—POCKET PISTOL.

Seven Shot, weight 11 ozs., Plated Body, Rosewood Stock, length of Barrel 3 inches.

No. 1½.— POCKET PISTOL.

Five Shot, weight 16 ozs., Plain Body, Rosewood Stock, length of Barrel 3½ and 4 inches.

No. 2.—BELT PISTOL.

Six Shot, weight 24 ozs., Plain Body, Rosewood Stock, length of Barrel 5 and 6 inches.

MESSRS. SMITH & WESSON beg to caution dealers against the various imitations of their Revolvers sold in Europe, which are far inferior to the genuine ones, and in most instances higher in price than their own.

None are genuine that do not bear their full name and address, to obtain which they beg to refer to their Agent,

Mr. J. H. CRANE,

Gun Maker.

3, ROYAL EXCHANGE, LONDON, E.C.

Houllier for a whole range of cartridges, one of which incorporated a ring of detonating compound deposited internally around the flange at the base of the case. This form of rim-fire cartridge was taken up by two American designers, Daniel B. Wesson and Horace Smith. By 1857 they had developed an efficient copper case, .22-calibre (5.6-mm), rim-fire cartridge which was loaded into the cylinder of their revolver from the rear. The design of the cartridge was slightly modified into the rim-fire type as used today with a small circumference of detonating powder, as opposed to the complete coverage of the base which had been used on the earlier model. The Smith and Wesson revolver was fitted with a hinged barrel which, when the catch was operated, tipped up and the cylinder was removed from a spigot. The cartridges were loaded into the cylinder which was replaced and the barrel was then locked back into the

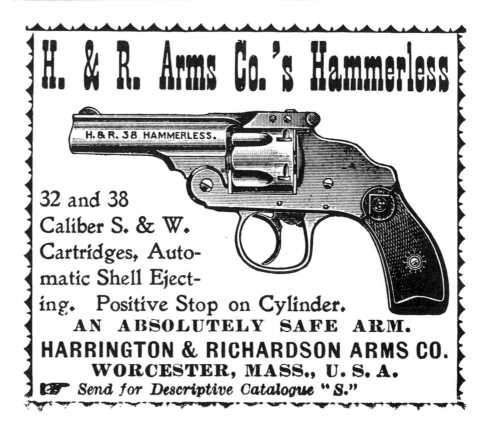

H. & R. Arms Co.'s Hammerless

H. & R. 38 HAMMERLESS.

32 and 38 Caliber S. & W. Cartridges, Automatic Shell Ejecting. Positive Stop on Cylinder.
AN ABSOLUTELY SAFE ARM.
HARRINGTON & RICHARDSON ARMS CO.
WORCESTER, MASS., U.S.A.
Send for Descriptive Catalogue "S."

Left
British military revolvers.
From top to bottom.
John Adams .45-in (11.4-mm) cartridge
revolver. This is the Mk II pattern of
1867.
Enfield Revolver Mk I 1880, of .476-in
(12.1-mm) calibre.
Enfield Revolver Mk I 1880, of .476-in
(12.1-mm) calibre with rifled chambers
in the cylinder.
Enfield Revolver Mk II 1882, also of
.476-in (12.1-mm) calibre.
Pattern Room, Royal Small Arms Factory,
Enfield.

Above
The glamour of the Wild West and its
characters aroused interest all over the
world This picture, from a December
1890 edition of *Le Petit Journal* of Paris,
shows Buffalo Bill (William Cody) in
action against the Indians.

normal position. The procedure had to be repeated for unloading, and here the central spigot served as a fixed ejector to push the empty cases out of the cylinder. The Smith and Wesson revolver was a great success, and since they held the master patent for the drilled-through cylinder no other US competitor was able to copy their design.

One weakness of the weapon was that a .22 bullet was not really effective for certain purposes; in 1860 they increased the calibre to .32 in (8.12 mm), but even this size is rather limited. The problem was that in order to expel the larger calibre bullet with effective force, a fair-sized charge of propellant was needed and this meant that the cartridge case had to be strong enough to withstand the explosion. This, in turn, meant that it was difficult to make the base thin enough to allow the hammer to detonate the internal rim deposit of priming.

The Rollin White patent was effective until 1869, and until that date Smith and Wesson effectively had a monopoly of breech-loading cartridge revolvers. However, the expiry of the patent opened the flood gates and a wide range of cartridge revolvers came on to the market.

Smith and Wesson made one more very important contribution to the technology of firearms when, in 1869, they produced a .44-in (11.2-mm) calibre revolver with the novel feature that the barrel was hinged so that it could be swung down, and the cylinder was made an integral part of the barrel assembly, which made loading easier. They also overcame yet another small problem, that of ejecting the empty cartridge case, by a simple but ingenious arrangement of cam and spring. As the barrel was tilted down, a cam operated a spring-loaded arm with a star-shaped projection at the end, which pushed out the empty cases and then snapped back to fit flush with the face of the cylinder.

One great limitation in revolver design which still had to be overcome concerned the strength of the cartridge case. The problems in making a satisfactory rim-fire case thin enough to permit detonation and strong enough to resist the force of the propellant, were considerable. In 1859 a French gunmaker, Perrin, had patented a revolver which was designed to use centre-fire cartridges with the primer mounted at the centre of the base. A centre-fire cartridge of good design had been patented in 1858 and this was adopted in 1861 in Britain by Daw but, at first, it seems to have been used only for rifles. In 1866 a British Colonel, E. M. Boxer, patented a rifle cartridge which was later adapted for a .45-in (11.4-mm) revolver. The case was of solid, drawn brass and the primer was mounted at the centre of the base. This design meant that the case could be quite thick for there was no need to crush the rim in order to produce detonation. The primer was set in the centre of the base where a

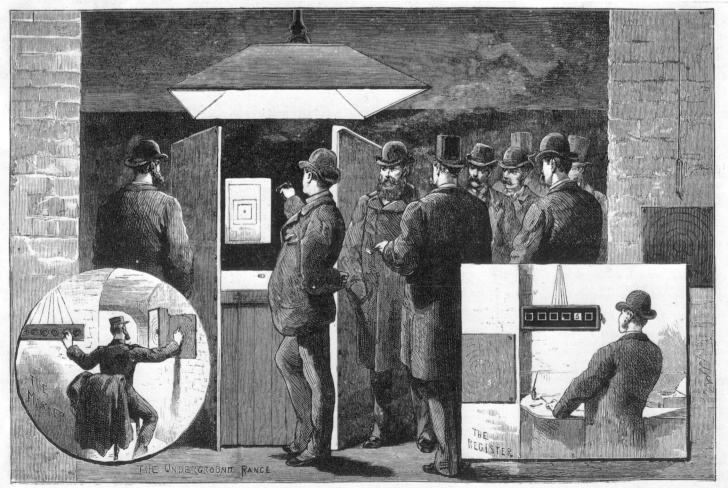

THE UNDERGROUND RANGE

THE UNITED SERVICE REVOLVER CLUB, CURSITOR STREET, CHANCERY LANE.

Below left
This engraving of a Victorian revolver range suggests a rather casual approach when compared with today's. The shooters wear no ear protectors and the safety precautions seem minimal. The firing stance does not, however, differ greatly from the modern one.

Right
Frederic Remington saw the Wild West as it really was. This famous engraving of 1888 shows a gunfight shorn of all the frills added in film and TV versions. Note the holster worn high on the right and not tied down low, the fashion so favoured by film heroes.

Below
Chief Petty Officer Norton of the Royal Navy takes aim with his Webley revolver at Bisley, the main shooting centre in Britain, in 1922.

small hole permitted the flash to pass through and ignite the propellant. In 1867 John Adams developed a special, double-action revolver to take this cartridge; so effective was it, in 1868 it was adopted as the official British Army revolver. Thus by the 1870s the modern revolver had emerged virtually in its present form. In 1873 the famous Single Action Army Revolver was introduced by Colt, and this excellent weapon has remained in almost continuous production.

There remained only one major new development and that was the 'swing-out cylinder'. The cylinder was mounted on a housing which was pivoted on the frame. When unlatched, this mounting swung out to bring the cylinder well clear of the frame. An ejector could then be

operated to push clear the empty cases. This was in use as early as 1865 when William Mason of Massachusetts, a Remington employee, patented a device featuring the swing-out cylinder. When Mason later went to work for Colt, he patented in 1888 a double-action revolver with a swing-out cylinder and an automatic ejector.

With the basic design now well established, the gunmakers were able to concentrate on improving details such as sights, grips, cartridge sizes and a host of other features. Today the emphasis is on the use of new materials as well as improved cartridges for, so far, rocket pistols and super-power guns have not proved to be of any great potential.

Above
Webley Fosbery 'Automatic Revolver', in an unusual .38-in (9.6-mm) calibre, showing the channels which engage with the lug to operate the cylinder and cocking mechanisms. The two projections in front of the cylinder are common on many military weapons, and are designed to ensure that the cylinder does not snag on the holster.

Right
From top to bottom.
M.1880 German revolver of 11-mm calibre.
M.1880 German 11-mm revolver; this is the short version.
Model 1874 French 11-mm revolver produced at the St Etienne Arsenal.
German revolver designed by an Austrian, Gustav Bittner; it uses a clip of 7.7-mm cartridges, and was made *c* 1893.
Pattern Room, Royal Small Arms Factory, Enfield.

Automatics

By the last quarter of the nineteenth century a wide range of revolvers was available to the shooter. They were in calibres going from .22 in (5.6 mm) up to the large .577 in (14.56 mm) size, and had a great variety of barrel lengths. Some revolvers 'broke' open for reloading and others had swing-out cylinders. There were revolvers which had to be cocked manually, but the majority were self-cocking. There were large holster pistols and small, easily concealed weapons with folding triggers and diminutive barrels. Some had the butt so designed that a detachable stock could be clipped on permitting the weapon to be used as a carbine. There was a profusion of cartridges each of which, according to the manufacturers, had some particular virtue.

Despite the number of different designs, shapes and sizes all the revolvers suffered, in varying degrees, from one great drawback. No matter which model was used, all these weapons were slow to reload. In a weapon such as the Colt Single Action Army Revolver each empty case had to be pushed out by the ejector rod fitted beneath the barrel. The new cartridges then had to be dropped, one by one, into the chambers as the cylinder was rotated – a slow job. Break-open weapons were much simpler: a catch was disengaged and the barrel assembly was pressed down. This movement activated the spring arm which ejected

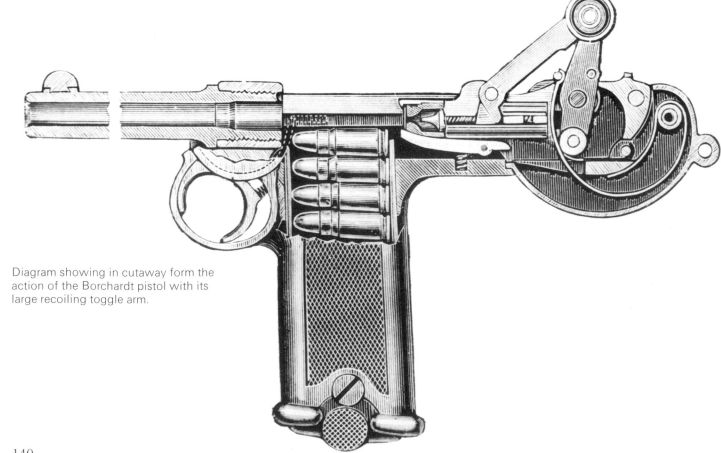

Diagram showing in cutaway form the action of the Borchardt pistol with its large recoiling toggle arm.

140

Right
A Luger with the butt safety catch which
ensured that the weapon could not be
fired unless the butt was gripped and the
catch depressed. This feature was
dropped from the 1908 pattern.

Below right
Small 6.35-mm automatic pocket pistol
made by Lignose of Berlin, the firm which
succeeded Bergman. It is a variation on
the Model 2 and has a larger magazine
capacity of nine rounds.

the cases, and then the new rounds
could be inserted into the chambers.
Swing-out cylinders were probably
just a little slower for the cases usually
had to be ejected by hand before new
cartridges were loaded.

To reduce loading time, various
ingenious devices were developed.
One type, patented in 1914, was
known as Prideaux's Patent Instant-
aneous Revolver Magazine. Basically
it consisted of a circular frame which
held six cartridges so positioned as to
permit the shooter to deposit them
simultaneously into the chambers
with one movement. Modern speed-
loaders work on the same principle,
the cartridges being released by
pressure on a button or spring. These
devices are pre-loaded and carried in
belt pouches ready for instant action.
Another system uses flat pouches,
each holding six cartridges, and is so
designed that the cartridges drop into
the hand ready for loading.

Although these devices reduce the
loading time they can only produce a
limited improvement, for their use
still requires both hands as well as
time taken in reaching across to draw
them from the pocket or pouch.

Yet another limitation was imposed by the design of the revolver,
for it was difficult to fit more than six
charges into the cylinder. The only
way to increase that number was to
increase the diameter of the cylinder,
and then the weapon became heavy
and unwieldy. Some pin-fire revolvers had enormous cylinders taking
over 20 rounds, but for the conven-

Bergman automatic of .26 (6·5-mm)
calibre, an early automatic which relied
on the gas blowback to extract and eject
the fired case from the breech; later
models incorporated an extractor. The
plate below the barrel was swung down
to permit reloading.

141

tional, practical revolver six rounds was about the maximum. Some models, such as the Walch superimposed-load revolver, offered 12 rounds; and the Le Mat offered perhaps about eight rounds as well as a charge of buckshot, but this was pushing the capacity of the revolver pretty well to its maximum.

Another limitation of the revolver was its rate of fire. In the hands of an expert quite incredible rates of fire can be achieved, but for the average shooter speed is usually achieved only by the sacrifice of accuracy. Manual cocking is obviously slow, so rapid revolver fire is achieved by the use of a self-cocking action, and this requires considerable trigger pressure. The trigger has to be pulled back quite some distance and the pressure required is fairly heavy. With rapid fire this quick, heavy pressure naturally increases the tendency for the muzzle to wave about. Rapid, accurate fire with a revolver is a difficult proposition.

Gunmakers and designers were well aware of the problems and sought ways whereby the time and effort required to insert a fresh cartridge into the breech could be reduced. If the action of cocking and loading could be speeded up, then there were obvious advantages. If rounds could be held in some kind of handy container, and when one charge of shots was expended the empty container could be removed and a full one inserted, that would help matters. Such containers, or magazines, could simplify loading and so speed up the rate of fire. The idea of a magazine in a pistol was not new. In the seventeenth century a German gunsmith, Peter Calthoff, who at one time had worked in the Netherlands and later in Denmark, designed a flintlock magazine pistol. By moving the trigger guard, a charge of powder and a ball were fed into the breech from the appropriate magazines. Another magazine primed the pan, cocked the lock and closed the pan cover. It was quite a complicated system and the problems due to fouling (the deposit left by burning black powder) must have been quite considerable. Later another maker, Michele Lorenzoni, who worked in the latter part of the seventeenth century and the early eighteenth century, made magazine repeating pistols. John Cookson, an English gunmaker working in Boston, Massachusetts, early in the eighteenth century, and other makers from Genoa and Augsburg, also worked on very similar systems. All these systems used a breech block which had a chamber and a recess for one ball. This chamber was rotated, usually by a lever fitted at the side of the body. The pistol was tilted, muzzle-down, and the lever turned through 180° so that the hole was then lined up with a magazine in the butt which held powder, and some then filled the chamber. At the same time a ball fell into the breech from a second magazine, and the lever was then turned back, so moving the now-loaded cavity back in line with the barrel. On some of the pistols using this system the lever also cocked the mechanism and on some it also primed the lock. Development was limited because of the problem of coping with loose black powder and further improvements had to wait for the appearance of the metallic cartridge.

The first step along the path to the modern, self-loading pistol was taken

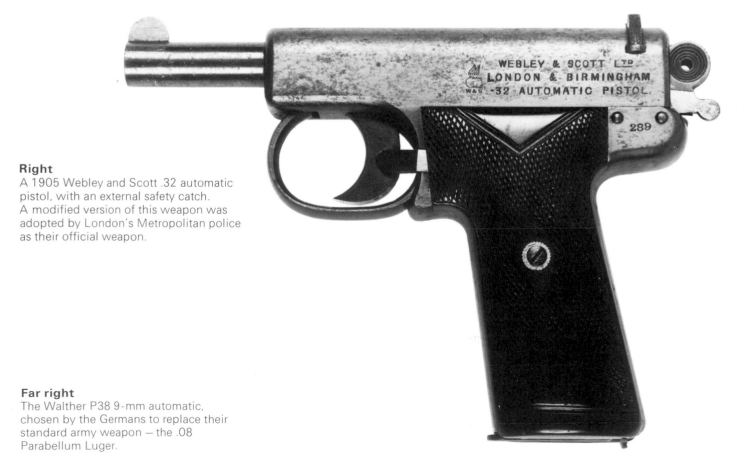

Right
A 1905 Webley and Scott .32 automatic pistol, with an external safety catch. A modified version of this weapon was adopted by London's Metropolitan police as their official weapon.

Far right
The Walther P38 9-mm automatic, chosen by the Germans to replace their standard army weapon – the .08 Parabellum Luger.

by a New Yorker, Walter Hunt. In 1847 he designed a rocket ball which was a bullet containing the propellant in its base. This bullet-cartridge proved so successful that it was used in a magazine rifle known as the Volitional Repeater, patented by Hunt in 1849. The Volitional Repeating Rifle led to the development in 1854 by Smith and Wesson of a pistol which operated on virtually the same principle and was later known as the Volcanic. In 1854 Smith and Wesson patented their pistol and began to manufacture the weapon at a factory in Norwich, Connecticut, and a company, The Volcanic Repeating Arms Company, was formed in July 1855. The pistols were produced with two lengths of barrel, 4 in (10 cm) and 8 in (20 cm). The cartridges were loaded into a tube set beneath the barrel and the operation of a ring-ended lever fed a cartridge from the tube into the barrel. The system worked, and was later to lead to the emergence of the Winchester rifle.

Although the Volcanic became the best known of all these magazine-type pistols, it was but one of many which appeared during the last two decades of the nineteenth century. Despite all the systems developed, however, none offered much advantage over a revolver. To operate them some lever such as a trigger guard, a ring bar or other motivating device had to be moved to feed the next cartridge into the breech. The systems would only offer a real advantage if they could be made to operate mechanically so that no physical effort was required by the shooter to feed a fresh cartridge into the breech. What was wanted was a system that would do it automatically! From this concept came the popular name for such pistols – automatics. Strictly speaking this is an incorrect name, for the weapon is not automatic and a more accurate description would be that of self-loader, or, possibly, semi-automatic! True automatic weapons continue firing for as long as the trigger is pressed or they run out of ammunition.

To achieve self-loading, there had to be some mechanical movement to transport the cartridge from a magazine or container into the breech. The power to carry out this movement had to be obtained from the pistol itself. One solution that the gunmakers worked towards was to use the recoil energy, for as the propellant exploded and forced out the bullet in one direction there was, as in all physical actions, an equal and opposite push in the other direction. If this reaction energy could, in some way, be utilized to operate a mechanical system it might be possible, with careful design, to move a cartridge from the magazine and transport it to the breech. There was, however, another problem for although the energy could be obtained from the cartridge, the cartridge case would still be in the breech. The same action which was to load the fresh cartridge also had first to remove the empty case from the breech. In addition to withdrawing the empty case and inserting a new one into the breech, this energy also had to re-cock the action.

There was another method, and this was to channel off some of the gas from the explosion to carry out these mechanical movements. Whichever system was used, there had to be some means of reversing the direction of the moving parts since the reaction would be in only one direction. Almost all the systems devised incorporated a spring which was compressed by the original movement and expanded to reverse the motion.

Attempts to produce such automatic or self-loading pistols were also held up by shortcomings concerning the propellant. Black powder, with the fouling or deposit it left could jam a mechanical system after a few shots. What was needed was a propellant which burnt away and left virtually no deposit. The discovery of smokeless powder took place in the 1880s, and from then on developments in many fields of firearm design pushed rapidly ahead.

One path was explored by Sir Hiram Maxim (1840–1916). Originally an electrical engineer, he had no connection whatever with the firearms trade, but his attention and interest were directed towards the problems of rapid-firing weapons. He tackled the job with a mixture of genius and inspiration. In 1883 he was granted a patent for a device

Right
Webley and Scott automatic taking the 9-mm Browning long cartridge. It was basically of the same design as the .32 Webley and Scott but was not popular.

Below right
Walther PP automatic pistol introduced in 1929 and available in .22-in, 7.65-mm and 9-mm calibres. A fine, self-cocking weapon, deriving its name from Police Pistol.

Bottom right
The Glisenti 9-mm automatic, used by Italian forces in both world wars. It was originally patented in 1906 but is known as the Model 1910. It holds seven cartridges, and was rejected by the US Government during tests held in 1907.

Above
Popular with many soldiers, including Sir Winston Churchill, was the 1896 Mauser 'Broomhandle' automatic. This one is shown with its wooden holster and leather harness dated 1915.

Above right
Mannlicher pistol of 1901. This example was made for the Argentinian Army and marketed as Md 1905. It was loaded from above the butt from a clip holding eight rounds.

which converted the lever-operated Winchester rifle from a single-shot to a semi-automatic weapon. He used the recoil from the shots to operate a device which, in turn, activated the loading lever. In 1884 he produced the Maxim machine gun which was based on the use of the expanding gas from the explosion to operate the mechanism. His gun was a great success and clearly demonstrated the possibilities of automatic systems.

Another contributory feature to the development of automatics was the improvement in bullet design. The old lead bullet was liable to distortion by accidental knocks and the sudden impact of the exploding charge. This distortion, more often than not, had little effect but on occasions it could jam a mechanism. A Swiss army officer, Major Rubin, around 1886–8 developed the modern type of bullet which has a lead core covered by a very thin cupro-nickel coating, just sufficient to strengthen the outside of the bullet and prevent this casual distortion.

By the 1890s most of the basic problems had been solved or at least considerably eased. The principle of recoil-operated mechanisms was reasonably well understood; the new propellants gave the power required, and the new bullets were capable of withstanding the pressures and ten-

sions of any automatic action.

In 1892 an Austrian, Anton Schonberger, produced the first commercially available automatic or self-loading pistol. His pistol had a fixed barrel and the breech was, during firing, locked firmly to it. The primer in the cartridge case was seated well inside the centre of the base. When a shot was fired the case was held firm but the primer was blown back and pushed against the bolt. This rearward movement, though only a fraction of an inch, was sufficient to unlock the breech from the barrel. Although the distance travelled by the primer was so short, it was time enough for the bullet to leave the

barrel. (Failure to hold breech and barrel locked during this time means a loss of power, since part of the propellant's force is lost by leakage.) Schonberger's pistol had an under-barrel magazine which held the cartridges, each of which was turned through 90° before being loaded into the breech.

In 1893 the forerunner of one of the most popular of all automatic pistols, the Luger, was patented. Hugo Borchardt of Connecticut, USA was the man who evolved the basic mechanism, which was later modified by Georg Luger. The Borchardt pistol was the first to use a metal magazine which loaded into the butt

of the weapon. The power to operate the mechanism was obtained by using the recoil of the cartridge to move the slide. In the forward position the bolt was held firmly in place by a jointed bar. As the bolt was pushed back by the recoil, the joint was 'broken' by lugs and this allowed the bolt to continue backwards to eject the case, cock the action and feed in a new round. As this toggle arm went back it provided the motive force to return the bolt to the forward position. The system worked but the shape of the pistol was not very convenient because of the coiled spring which was housed in a large section at the very rear of the breech. The general design

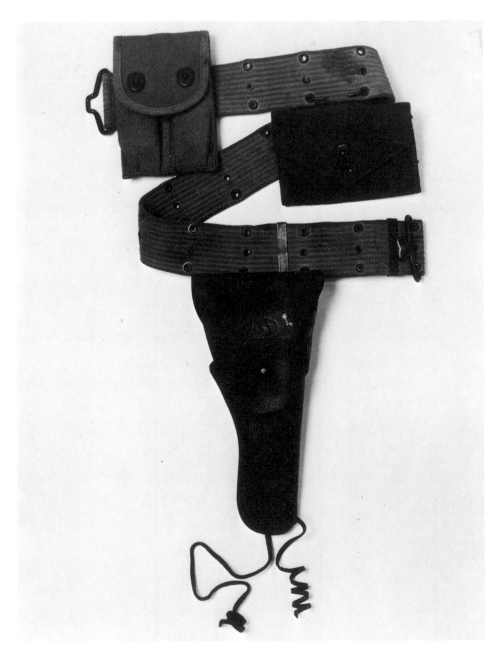

of the pistol made it awkward to handle and the action was really better suited to a carbine than a hand-held firearm. The designers may well have recognized this problem for the Borchardt carried a thick, shaped, wooden board which could be secured to the rear of the butt to convert it into a carbine-type weapon.

Borchardt was unable to obtain much support in America and the pistol was finally taken up by the firm of DWM in Karlsruhe. The problems involved in its use and operation were largely overcome by the efforts of Georg Luger, who was a salesman at the firm making the Borchardt pistol. The Luger parabellum was first produced in 1900 and was later modified. Luger removed the large coiled spring of the Borchardt, mounted the butt at the rear of the barrel assembly, and sloped it to make aiming much easier; the result was a good, sound automatic pistol. The basic design, using a toggle arm, was left much the same but there were many changes in detail.

Some pistols were fitted with a butt safety catch which ensured that the weapon could only be fired when the butt was gripped and the catch pressed home. The early models were all in the calibre of 7.65 mm, but the later 9-mm versions were more popular. The barrel length was originally $4\frac{3}{4}$ in (12 cm), but a carbine version was much longer at $11\frac{3}{4}$ in (30 cm); a Naval model was given a 6-in (15-cm) barrel, and that of the Artillery model was $7\frac{1}{2}$-in (19 cm). The magazine for all these models was a metal box which normally held eight rounds. In 1911, a large cylindrical magazine, or snail drum, was devised; this held 32 rounds but had to be loaded by means of a special tool, which was no easy matter. So successful, however, was the basic Luger pistol that it remained in production until 1943.

In 1895 the first patent for another very famous automatic was taken out in Germany. Peter Paul Mauser had made rifles and revolvers for some years, and he became interested in automatics in 1894 when some of his employees were experimenting with designs for such a weapon. By 1897 one of the world's best known automatics was in production – the so-

Left
At first glance this appears to be a Colt
.45 automatic but it is, in fact, a Star — a
Spanish-made copy. It lacks the grip
safety fitted at the rear of the butt on a
true Colt.

Below left
Full 'rig' for the US Government's .45
(11.4-mm) automatic, comprising belt,
magazine pouches, brown leather holster
and first-aid wallet.

called 'Broomhandle' Mauser Model
96. It was a little unusual in that the
rounds were housed in a magazine
situated in front of the trigger and
were fed in by means of clips rather
like those used for magazine rifles.
The 1896 model was to undergo
minor changes but it remained in
production until 1939, when the
company discarded it.

One innovation, introduced in
1932, was the Schnellfeurer Pistole
which was a version designed to fire
either single shots or to function on
fully automatic. Whilst it was a
novelty its practical use was limited,
for the effort required to control a
handgun loosing off shots at a rate of
more than 800 rounds a minute was
beyond most people's ability. The
magazine held a maximum of 20
rounds and these were discharged in
approximately $1\frac{1}{2}$ seconds.

The 1896 model was normally
supplied complete with its holster,
which was of wood and so made that
it could be clipped onto the butt to
convert the weapon into a carbine; as
such it was very effective. The holster
had to be carried in a leather harness
which could be attached to a belt or
cross strap.

The Military 1896 model was by no
means the only automatic pistol made
by Mauser. From 1910 onwards the
firm produced a whole range of Vest
Pocket pistols designed for self protection which were only about 4 in
(10 cm) long. Later slightly longer
versions were produced, and in 1937
the firm introduced the HSc which
was commonly used by the German
Navy and Air Force during World
War II. The main feature of this
pistol was that it was self-cocking:
whereas most automatics had to be
cocked by pulling back the slide to
feed in the first round, the HSc could
be cocked by simply pressing the
trigger in the same way as a revolver.

In 1894 an Austrian, Ferdinand
Ritter von Mannlicher, patented a
slightly unusual variation in which
the barrel moved forward against a
spring. It ejected the case and then
moved back to pick up the next
cartridge. It was not, however, a very
practical system for the mechanism
had to be cocked by hand prior to
each shot so that the purpose of the
automatic was rather nullified. In
1903 Mannlicher patented another
automatic not unlike the Mauser, but
it was not so popular.

Above
A Colt .455 automatic of the 1911
variety. It differs from the 1911-A1 which
had a number of modifications to improve
its handling. This example is unusual in
that it is stamped 'R.A.F.' (Royal Air
Force). This pistol was originally issued
to the British Royal Marines and Navy
but in the 1920s it was withdrawn from
these forces and issued to RAF officers
and NCOs.

Theodore Bergman, of Gaggenau Baden, in 1894 designed a blow-back pocket pistol which found an appreciative market. This weapon was rather unusual in that the empty case was ejected not, as in most weapons, by a mechanical system but was blown out by the gas generated in the case. The magazine was in front of the trigger and, like the Mauser, was loaded from clips. After World War I the Bergman factory was taken over by Lignose of Berlin, who made a number of pocket pistols. One was the Einhand, which used the trigger guard to cock the pistol by pushing back the slide.

Another pioneer of early automatic design was Andreas Schwarzlose. He began designing them as early as 1893, and his first production model was made in 1896. It was the usual pattern with the barrel and bolt recoiling together, but after a short traverse the bolt was turned, by means of lugs, through 45° to unlock, so allowing the barrel to move back under pressure of a spring. In 1908 Schwarzlose produced another unusual pistol in which the breech was fixed and the barrel moved forwards.

These pioneers showed the way for later inventors such as John Moses Browning who was the outstanding firearms designer in America. His interest in repeating weapons had steadily grown, and in 1897 he took out a patent in the United States for various actions. In 1899 he produced a .32-in (8.1-mm) pistol. The weapon was manufactured in Liège, Belgium, by the Fabrique Nationale des Armes de Guerre and soon gained great popularity. The weapon found its way into many different countries and many different hands including that of a young Serbian student. It was a Browning .32 that shot and killed the Archduke Franz Ferdinand at Sarajevo in June 1914, and so sparked off the trail which led to World War I.

In 1910 Browning redesigned his .32 pistol and produced a weapon with a smoother outline. The internal mechanism differed also, with the barrel locking onto the frame by means of engaging lugs and the recoil spring encircling the barrel. A version of this weapon with a 4½-in (11.4-cm) barrel was produced in 1922, and the magazine capacity was increased from seven to nine rounds.

At the turn of the century there appeared a curious hybrid weapon which was neither revolver nor automatic but something between the two. It was an automatic, self-cocking revolver made by Webley and Scott

A Savage pistol competed with the Colt .45 automatic when the US Army were considering adopting a self-loader. This is a .32 (8.1-mm) model of 1907 with a magazine holding 10 rounds.

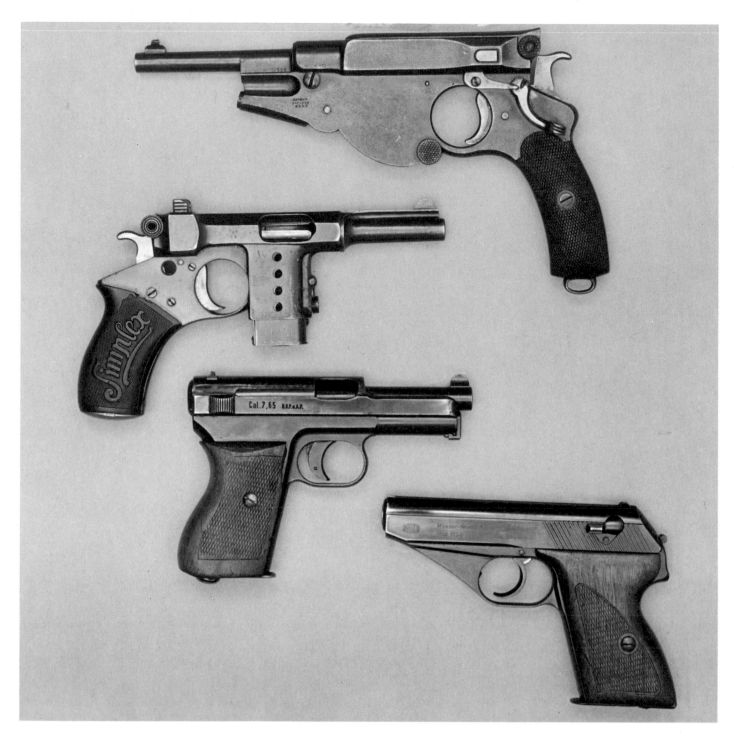

German and Austrian self-loaders.
From top to bottom.
One of the early self-loading pistols – the
6.5-mm Bergman. The magazine below
the barrel held five rounds.
This pistol, the Bergman Simplex, fired an
8-mm cartridge housed in a magazine
below the barrel.
Used by the Austrian Navy, this 1934
Pocket Mauser automatic fired a
7.65-mm cartridge.
The Mauser HSc, an early, self-cocking
automatic. It had a magazine capacity of
eight rounds.
Pattern Room, Royal Small Arms Factory,
Enfield.

and based on the patents of G.
Fosbery, which were taken out in the
late 1890s. The weapon, of .38-in
(9.6-mm) or .455-in (11.6-mm)
calibre was made up of a frame,
comprising the butt and trigger
action, and a top section which
consisted of the barrel and cylinder. A
zigzag groove was cut into the
cylinder's surface and this engaged
with a lug. When a shot was fired, the
recoil forced back the top section and
the lug caused the cylinder to rotate,
so bringing an unfired cartridge into
the firing position. The rearward

movement also cocked the action so
that only a slight touch on the trigger
was needed to fire the next shot. It is a
strange weapon to fire with the large
mass of metal, cylinder and barrel
moving backwards and forwards.
There was little real advantage in the
design, although the heavy pull
needed on most revolver triggers to
fire them was obviated, and only a
slight touch was required to fire the
Webley Fosbery.

The British firm of Webley and
Scott in Birmingham had a long
history of designing and making guns,

Top
Browning was a master of design and responsible for many innovations. This is one of his pistols made at Herstal, the .32 ACP or 7.65-mm automatic.

Centre
The Colt .25 (6.35-mm) automatic pistol was first introduced in 1908 and continued in production until 1941. Although well made, for practical purposes it is of small calibre and low-powered.

Bottom
French Pistolet MAS 35, first planned in 1935; it used a 7.65-mm cartridge which fitted no other pistol. The title comes from the initials of Manufacture d'Armes St Etienne.

Smith and Wesson .35 (8.9-mm) automatic, first issued in 1913 and fitted with two safety devices; one is at the rear of the butt and one below the trigger guard.

and in 1903 they experimented with a .455-in (11.6-mm), self-loading pistol, but with little success. In 1904 the firm did produce a more practical weapon with the square, upright appearance common to all early Webley and Scott pistols. It worked well, although it was far too heavy for comfortable shooting, and was remarkable for its minimal recoil.

The first decade of this century saw a great increase in the number of self-loading pistols appearing on the arms market. Another well-known manufacturer, Carl Walther, designed a pocket pistol in 1906 which fired a 6.35-mm bullet. Walther produced nine models of this pistol, all slight variations on the original pattern, then in 1929 a new pistol was introduced. This was the Police Pistol, known as the PP, which fired a 9-mm cartridge. It was a double-action pistol, and could be cocked by pulling back the slide or by pressing on the trigger. A smaller version was designed to take the 9-mm short cartridge, and since the German word for short is *Kurz*, the pistol was known

as the PPK. Its size made it convenient for bodyguards and security men, and although it is a normally reliable weapon it received some adverse publicity in 1974. Princess Anne of England was attacked whilst in her car near Buckingham Palace. Her police bodyguard was armed with a PPK which jammed at the crucial moment.

The Walther company produced a very fine .22-in (5.6-mm) target pistol for use in the Olympic Games of 1932 with either a 9-in (22.8-cm) or 5-in (12.7-cm) barrel, and in 1936 offered an even better version – the Walther Olympic Pistole.

Although German designers rather dominated the field, other countries were working on their own weapons. In Italy the old established firm of Beretta supplied a range of pistols including a .32-in (8.1-mm) model which was adopted by the Italian Navy. The Italian Army preferred a model using a 9-mm cartridge, made in 1910 by Glisenti.

Undoubtedly one of the finest automatics ever produced was the

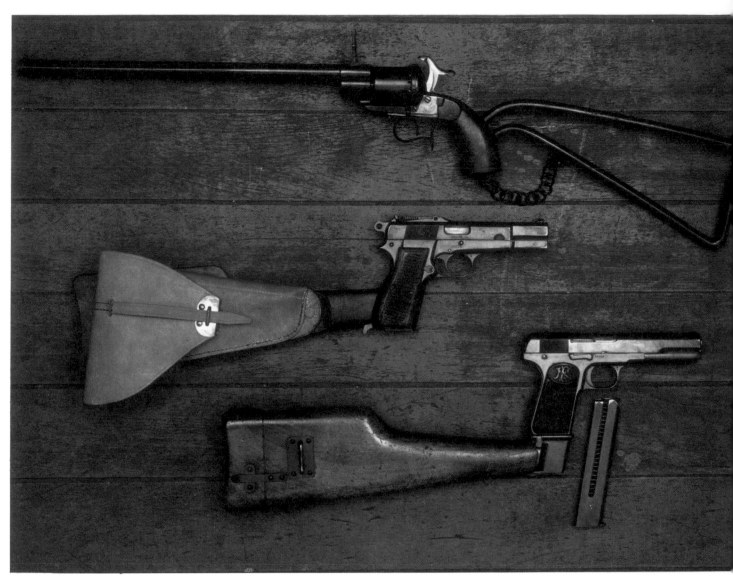

Many pistols were made so that a shoulder stock could be attached to permit their use as a carbine.
Top French pin-fire revolver by Lefaucheux with skeleton stock.
Centre Browning Hipower with combined holster and stock.
Bottom 1903 Browning with longer-than-usual magazine.
Pattern Room, Royal Small Arms Factory, Enfield.

Colt .45 (11.4 mm). This famous handgun was a descendant of the .38-in (9.6-mm) model designed by John Browning. The United States Army was displaying interest in acquiring an automatic weapon, and in 1906 decided to hold tests: the testing committee specified that the weapon should take a .45-in (11.4-mm) cartridge. A Colt automatic had been designed to take this cartridge and was submitted along with eight other weapons, including a .45 Luger. After a stiff programme of tests the board rejected all except the Colt, Savage and Luger automatics and two revolvers. There was, and still is, considerable debate as to the relative virtues of revolvers and automatics. Generally the automatic is considered to have advantages in the number of rounds that it can hold, its ease in reloading and its reduced recoil which can help to improve accuracy. The disadvantages are basically to do with the mechanical systems, for these can jam and so render the weapon totally useless. Broadly, revolvers have a better reliability record. However, the US Board preferred the automatics, and decided to field-test the Colt and Savage pistols. Troops tried the weapons and found that both were lacking in some respects, but the Colt was thought to be the better weapon.

Browning slightly redesigned the pistol, and so was born the Model 1911 Colt .45. Its heavy bullet had great stopping power and its rugged construction made it a popular weapon with fighting men. In 1923 certain minor changes were introduced, and the present Model 1911-A1 began its long life. The new model differed only a little, but it was more comfortable to handle and proved popular with many police and armed

From top to bottom.
Walther P38 9-mm pistol. This weapon
was accepted as the standard German
Army weapon in place of the Luger.
Beretta M.51 9-mm pistol.
Beretta M.33 7.65-mm pistol.
Heckler & Koch P9s 9-mm pistol.
Pattern Room, Royal Small Arms Factory,
Enfield.

Webley and Scott 9-mm automatic model
of 1909. It has a grip safety, a 5-in
(12.7-cm) barrel and an eight-round
magazine.

Top
Fully automatic Schnellfeuer Mauser 1930. This example bears Chinese markings, and many of these pistols were exported to the Far East. Selection was by turning the selector to 'N' for normal single-shot working or 'R' for fully automatic (or Repetition).

Above
French-made 7.65-mm MAC Model 1935S, made at Chatelleraut; similar weapons made at St Etienne are labelled 'MAS'. This was the official service weapon of the French forces and used a 7.65-mm long cartridge.

forces. To reduce the heavy cost of practice – .45 cartridges are expensive – a conversion kit was produced. The barrel, extractor and various other pieces of the operating mechanism were changed, and, while the pistol then functioned exactly as before, it now fired .22 cartridges. The weapon could just as simply be converted back to fire .45 ammunition. Some quality target versions were also produced, and today the weapon is preferred by many practical pistol shooters. Colt also manufactured a number of .22 target pistols including the Woodsman, a particularly fine weapon.

From the 1920s onwards the arms industries of most countries produced automatic pistols of various calibres and patterns. One of the most popular was the Browning Hipower, first marketed in 1935 and selected by many armies. Russia developed the Tokarev; Poland had the Radom, Finland the Lahti and Japan adopted the Nambu pistols.

Much research went into the ammunition for automatics and most of them have always used the rimless case. In the great majority of weapons the cartridges were fed out of the magazine directly into the breech and

Top
Steyr 9-mm automatic – an Austrian-made weapon with a built-in magazine which is loaded from a clip inserted into the top of the pistol. The eight cartridges are then pushed down into the magazine and the clip removed.

Above
A 9-mm Beretta M.1951 automatic. The official weapon of the Italian services, it was also at one time used by both Israel and Egypt.

157

Left

From top to bottom.
SIG 9-mm automatic, Model P210-6 with custom grips.
Smith and Wesson .22 (5.6-mm) Model 41 with muzzle brake.
Metropolitan Police pistol, a Webley and Scott .32 (8.1-mm) model.
Pre-war Commercial Browning Hipower 9-mm automatic, adopted by many armed forces.

Right

Two-handed shooting with a .45 automatic. This is the style of grip favoured by those who seek to achieve the best results quickly and with the greatest ease. Note the ejected case in the air above the muzzle.

it was important that this cartridge movement was smooth and unimpeded. The lip or rim found on most revolver cartridges could hamper this sliding action, so a case was designed which had no lip. However, most mechanisms for ejecting the empty case needed some means of gripping it, and without the lip this was difficult. The solution was to cut a groove into the wall of the case near the base; this gave the ejector claw something with which it could engage. This shallow groove did not impair the easy movement of cartridges. The head of the case, which gripped the bullet, rested against the end of the barrel and prevented the cartridge slipping in too far. Though the majority of automatics use these rimless cartridges, .22 target pistols use rim-fire cartridges with the conventional lip.

Over the last decades there have been many experiments and attempts to improve the automatic, and some notable weapons have emerged. The Czech arms industry, always very alert and imaginative, came up with the 7.65-mm VZ 61, usually known as the Scorpion. It is more than a simple automatic and is capable of fully automatic fire, so that it is in the nature of a machine pistol. It has a pivoted skeleton shoulder stock and is available with a silencer and an infrared sight. Poland has developed the 9-mm Machine Pistol Wz-63, also capable of automatic fire.

One of the finest of all modern automatics is the 9-mm SIG P210, made in Switzerland. It is accurate

and is beautifully made. Like the Colt automatic it can easily be converted to take the .22 cartridge for practice.

New materials have been pressed into service, and stainless steel is gaining in popularity although there have been some problems with rusting. Much research has gone into the sights, and on the top-grade target pistols electronic devices have been employed to achieve positive firing with minimum trigger pressure. Generally the standard of reliability is now about as good as that of revolvers, and several United States police forces, previously equipped only with revolvers, are going over to automatics. Safety devices have been improved, and in comparison there is now little to choose between revolvers and automatics.

Top
Small pocket automatic by the German firm of Dreyse. It held six rounds of 6.35-mm cartridges and was patented in 1909. The weapon is stripped by first lifting the rear sight.

Centre
Small Webley and Scott 6.35-mm automatic with external hammer — a weapon small enough to go into a waistcoat or vest pocket.

Bottom
Two miniature automatics.
Right A Kolibri 3-mm pistol; though tiny, it has sufficient power to cause a very nasty flesh wound.
Left Menz Lilliput 4.25-mm automatic.

Military Pistols

When cannons first made their appearance in the wars of Western Europe in the fourteenth century, the only people with sufficient resources to obtain the components to make gunpowder and have the heavy barrels cast were kings or the more powerful nobles of the realm. As pistols and muskets developed, so costs fell and more people could afford to own them, and gunpowder mills went into production. It now became possible to arm large numbers of troops with the new weapons.

The matchlock musket, which began to develop in the sixteenth century, was the prime weapon of the infantry. Pistols in the sixteenth century were essentially wheellock weapons·and their complexity and expense, as already pointed out, precluded their issue to large units on the grounds of cost alone. Normally the only troops who carried the pistol were the cavalry and certain selected bodyguards. However, as the demand for pistols and other firearms grew in the private sector, so the number of gunmakers increased to meet this demand.

During the latter part of the sixteenth century colonies of gunmakers grew up at certain centres of production. In England the centre was London, in France, Paris, and in Germany, Nuremberg and Augsburg. The growing use of firearms caused certain problems for the

British cavalry armed with revolvers charge the Egyptian guns during the campaign of 1882.

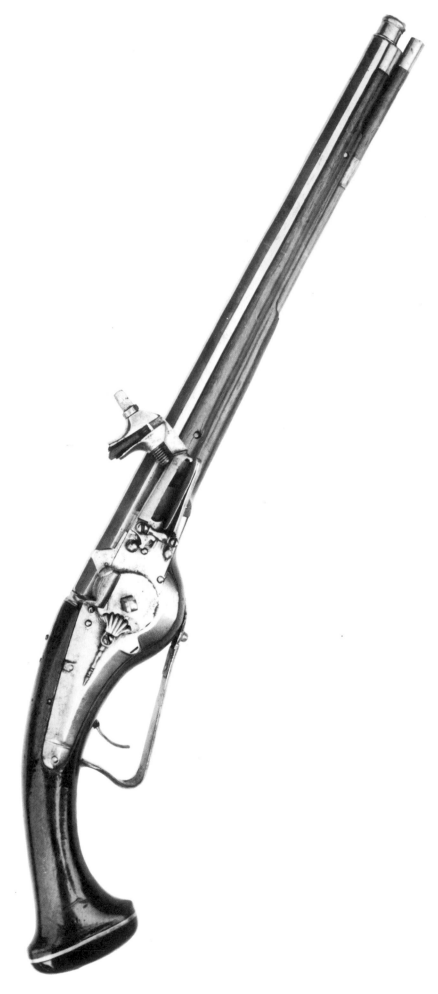

Left
Military wheellock pistol of about 1630
with typical shaped butt and general
lack of decoration. W. Keith Neal,
Guernsey.

Right
Most Scottish pistols were very
functional and plain, quite unlike this pair
made c 1760 by Murdoch of Douane in
Scotland. The barrels are blued and inlaid
with gold, and the butts have enamel
plaques. This elaborate pair of pistols was
presented to Sir Henry Clinton by
George III.

military authorities. The business of
supplying an army was always difficult in the sixteenth and seventeenth
centuries, but the introduction of
firearms and gunpowder complicated
matters even further. It meant that
supplies of match, gunpowder and
bullets – heavy and bulky items – had
to be made and transported with the
army. If a number of different-calibre
weapons was in use the supplies of
bullets or moulds had to be large
enough for all the different pieces. It
was therefore to the advantage of
central governments if their troops
could be armed with a smaller
number of more or less standard
weapons. There gradually grew up,
during the seventeenth century and
particularly during the eighteenth
century, the concept of standard
military weapons. Although the
pattern might be decided by the
central authority, the production was
in the hands of a large number of
contractors and in consequence the
'standard weapon' was never quite
standard. There were slight differences between the pieces supplied by
the different gunmakers both in
design and general quality.

During the religious and political
wars of the early seventeenth century
there was an increasing use of wheellock pistols. These were not the
beautifully ornate and decorated
pieces of the nobility but simple,
totally functional weapons. The
wheellocks were quite plain and,
apart from some fairly simple engraving on the metal, were devoid of all
forms of decoration. The mechanism
was covered with a very plain plate
and the wood had a pronounced
swelling to accommodate the lock.
The whole stock was fairly straight
with just a slight downward curve for
the butt which was normally cut

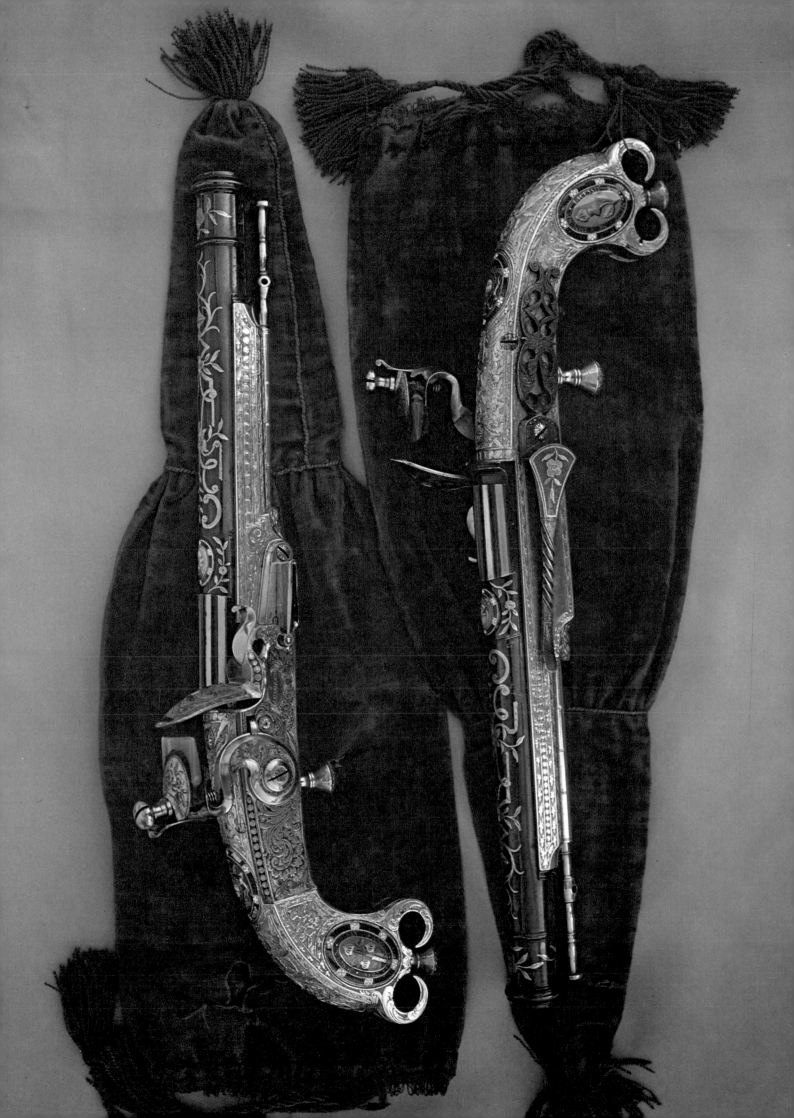

1. *To Horse.* 2. *Uncap your Pistol.* 5. *Span your Pistol.* 6. *Prime your Pistol.*

3. *Draw your Pistol.* 4. *Order your Pistol.* 7. *Shut your Pan.* 8. *Cast about your Pistol.*

Plate 1 of the 'Ancient English Horse Exercise'. Although these engravings were made later, they accurately represent the seventeenth-century pistol drill for cavalry.

square with a reinforcing ring round the tip. Sweden was still using such a military wheellock as late as the 1680s, although other ignition systems were being introduced.

The snaphaunce and flintlock mechanisms offered considerable advantages to the military as their production was fairly simple and consequently their cost was low. It was now possible to equip all the cavalry with a pair of these pistols. However this, in turn, created another problem, that of getting the weapons supplied. At this date, the early seventeenth century, very few countries had any centralized production systems. In Britain, for instance, the manufacture of firearms was largely in the hand of the Gunmakers Company. Prior to the formation of the Gunmakers Company the manufacturers of firearms had been members of other Companies, a situation which made for problems. To simplify matters the gunmakers had petitioned for and received Letters Patent in 1605. After some difficulties the gunmakers were eventually granted a charter to become a City Company in 1638. New entrants to the body were required to serve a long apprenticeship before they qualified to set up in their own right.

In Britain and most other countries the government contracted for the numbers of weapons required. Thus the pattern might be agreed and barrel length and calibre were normally specified, but the details as to quality of wood, type of finish, fittings and furniture might well vary from one manufacturer to another. All weapons supplied by the gunmakers had to be tested by the Officers of the Board of Ordnance. Proof was very important and consisted of loading the barrel with a larger than normal charge and firing it. If the barrel burst, bulged or showed any defect it failed proof. The Gunmakers Company adopted a view mark of a crowned 'V' (signifying that a weapon had been inspected) and a proof mark of a crowned 'G.P.' Barrels for government weapons in the eighteenth century were struck with the royal cypher and crossed sceptres for proof, and the royal cypher and a

broad arrow. On the lock was en-graved the maker's name.

The seat of government was in London as was the principal muni-tions centre, the Tower of London. It was not surprising therefore that in the area around the Tower, known as the Minories, large numbers of gun-makers were to be found. This system of contracting-out was to remain in use until well into the nineteenth century and the same story is true of most other countries.

Military pistols were simple with little decoration, but in order to indicate that they were government property and to prevent misuse or loss, the weapons were normally marked in some way, usually on the lock plate. This carried the crown and the royal cypher, which in Britain was 'J.R.' for James II, 'C.R.' for Charles II, 'G.R.' for the Georges I to IV, 'W.R.' for William IV, and finally 'V.R.' for Victoria.

Although the actual weapons were made by contractors, somebody had to design and approve any particular pattern. This normally fell within the province of the Master General of the

Ordnance, whose headquarters was the Tower of London. When a pattern had been approved several specimens were made: these were the official patterns and indicated the design and quality to which the local contractors were bound to aspire. The finished weapons were then sub-mitted to the Tower for official approval, they were inspected and, if satisfactory, were marked and accepted by the Board of Ordnance which was responsible for the overall supply of all forms of ammunition and weapons to the forces of Britain. The weapons were then stored at the Tower and shipped out to equip the various regiments and military organizations.

Although naturally there were variations, most military pistols were similar in that they were plain and substantial. As far as Britain was concerned, basically the pistols were long- or short-barrelled, either 12 in (30 cm) or 9 in (23 cm) in length. The stocks were of walnut, the fittings of brass and the barrel circular in section. The lock was plain but effective and was normally engraved

These cuirassiers are shown using wheellock pistols; each carries a second pistol in a holster attached to the saddle. They wear three-quarter armour, although as the century progressed armour was worn less and less. Engraving from *Art Militaire à Cheval* by Jacques de Wallhausen, published at Frankfurt in 1616.

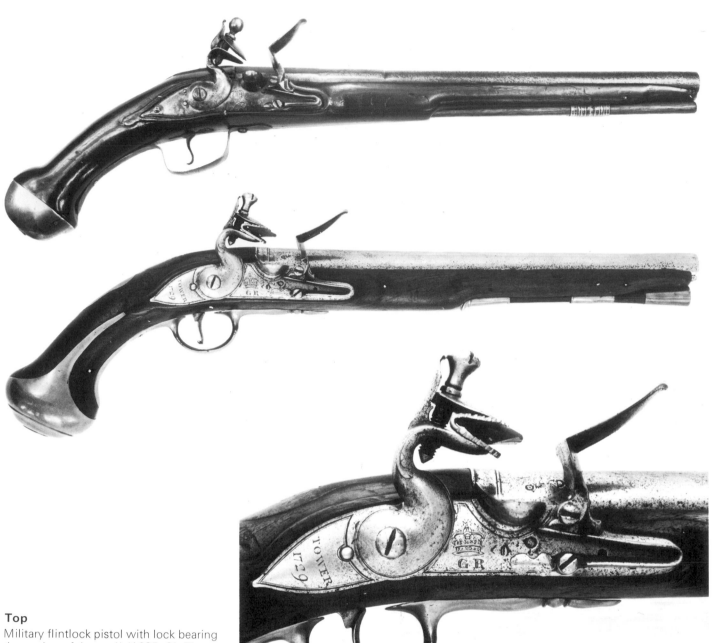

Top
Military flintlock pistol with lock bearing the cypher of James II (1685–8). The butt cap lacks side arms and the trigger has the backward curl typical of pistols of this period.

Centre
Heavy dragoon cavalry pistol with lock dated 1729 and bearing the royal cypher 'GR'. G. Kellam, Broadstairs, Kent.

Bottom
Detail of the lock on the 1729 dragoon pistol. The lock carries its date and the word 'Tower', which indicates that it was accepted by the Board of Ordnance. The crowned 'GR' also indicates government ownership. G. Kellam, Broadstairs, Kent.

Right
The artillery were often equipped with different weapons from the infantry. This French Horse Artilleryman of 1814 is armed with a sabre and a flintlock pistol. His busby is not dissimilar to that worn by the Hussars.

with the name of the supplier and the date of production. This form of dating was, however, discontinued from 1764 when it was felt, probably with good cause, that units were loath to accept pieces with an early date on them, feeling that they were, in some way, inferior to those with a more recent date.

The flintlock itself was a fairly standard pattern with a rather graceful S-shaped cock which was later replaced by the ring-neck pattern. The early examples of these weapons had a rather large lock with a flat face, and indeed many cocks themselves are also flat in section. Later locks and cocks have a convex section. Their military purpose is often indi-

cated by some marking, usually on the barrel, where the regimental number and title were abbreviated: thus '2RHG' might well stand for the Second Royal Horse Guards. Pistols were normally supplied only to the cavalry, and regimental markings are usually confined to the various British cavalry regiments. Pistols were also supplied to the Royal Navy, where they were primarily intended for the use of boarding parties.

Holsters were not normally supplied and the weapon was carried about the person by means of a belt hook. This was a narrow, flat bar fixed to the side of the stock opposite to the lock and standing clear of it by about $\frac{1}{4}$ in (6 mm). This could be

J. lith. de Delpech.

Artillerie Légère.

Canonnier en grande tenue.

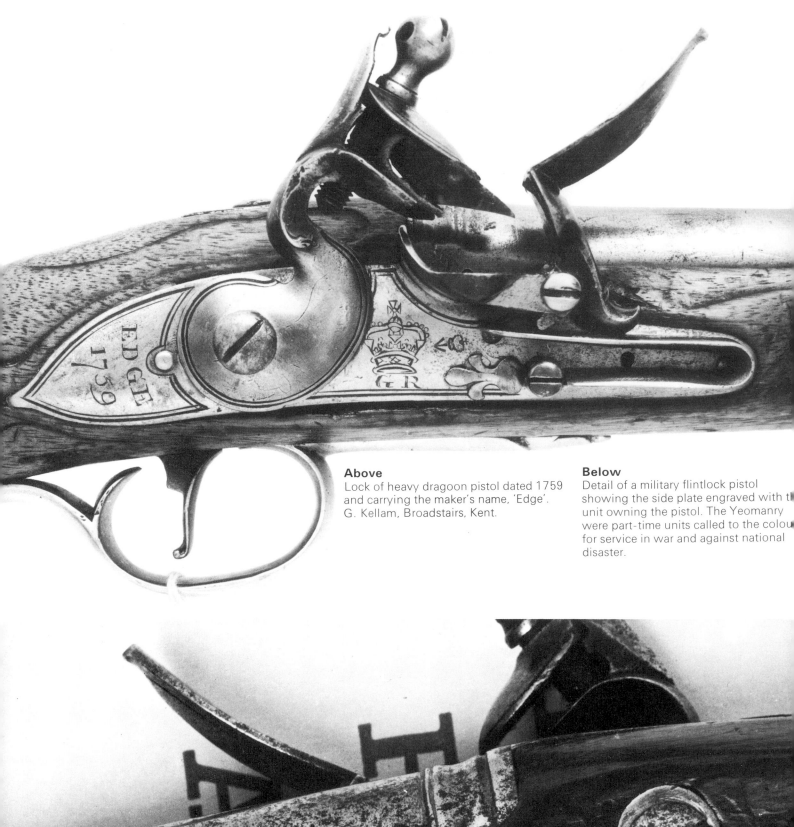

Above
Lock of heavy dragoon pistol dated 1759 and carrying the maker's name, 'Edge'. G. Kellam, Broadstairs, Kent.

Below
Detail of a military flintlock pistol showing the side plate engraved with the unit owning the pistol. The Yeomanry were part-time units called to the colours for service in war and against national disaster.

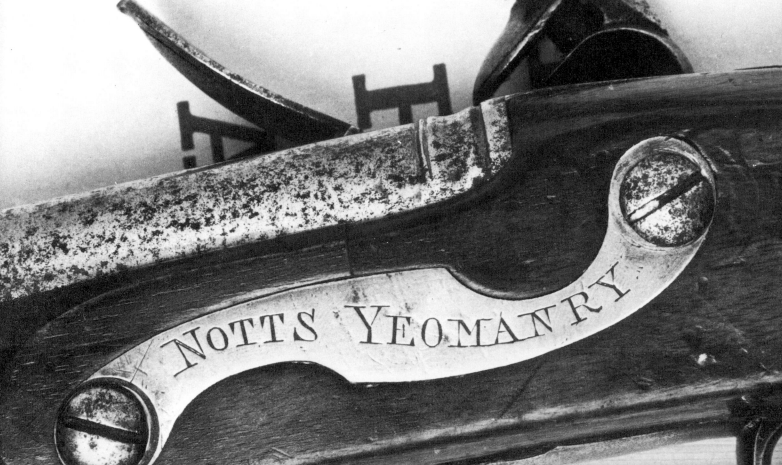

pushed into the waist-band of the trousers, into the pocket of a coat, or hooked over a belt, where the weapon could hang ready for instant use. Most of these military pistols are fitted with a fairly substantial brass butt cap. On the early models it is usually little more than a brass hemisphere, but later two arms were extended along the side of the butt to give a little extra strength. At first the arms reached well up the side of the butt, then as the eighteenth century progressed they became shorter and shorter until they were little more than a slight rise in the edge of the butt cap.

Production of military weapons was often a matter of urgency for governments, who were seldom prepared for war when it started. Some countries explored the possibilities of setting up official centres of firearms manufacture. The sites were usually selected becaused of their geographical position: perhaps they were on a convenient trade route or close to supplies of coal or mineral ore. St Etienne, near Lyons, was one such place and there, as early as 1515, King Francis I had created a royal arms manufactory. An inspectorate of supply was formed in France at a very early date, and in 1717 selected officers were given the job of supervising the manufacture of the royal weapons at Maubeuge, Charleville and St Etienne.

At Charleville, situated by the River Meuse, the authorities were instructed in 1667 to reserve for the central government all the weapons produced in the principality (as it then was). Just as the Tower of London was the central depot of all British arms, so the Bastille in Paris, or, to give it its full title, The Royal Magazine of the Bastille, played the same role in France. Various royal manufacturers such as those at Charleville and St Etienne sent their products there for dispatch to the various units.

The French described their weapons by the term 'Model' and the year of its introduction. The Pistol Model 1763, for example, was a cavalry pistol with a barrel 233 mm long and a calibre of 17.17 mm. The lock was marked with the name of the factory and the town in which it was made – thus 'MRE de Maubeuge', etc.

The stock of this weapon differed from the British pattern in having a less pronounced curve to the butt, but in other respects it was very similar. A big difference between Continental and British pistols was in the method of securing the barrel to the stock. French weapons had a screw passing through the tang (the extension of the barrel) into the stock, and a long nose cap of iron or brass which encircled the muzzle and the stock. The British used a system of pins passing through the stock and a lug beneath the barrel.

The French at this early date adopted the ring-necked cock, a feature which did not appear on British weapons until much later. Big changes were made to French pistols in the Model 1777. Although the cock was similar to the earlier patterns, this was about the only feature in common with that of 1763: the whole pistol was smoother in outline and the lock and trigger guard were all affixed to one metal section, and virtually the only piece of stock was the butt which had a brass cap. The ramrod was situated by the side of the barrel rather than underneath it as on most other models and it fitted into the lower section of the lock. The lock-plate had, in script, the name of the arsenal where it was made. Stamped into the butt were various identifying marks relating to the unit holding the pistol. Later models, such as that of Year IX, that is 1800/1801 in the old-style pre-Revolution calendar, reverted to the more conventional form with a full stock and a brass nose band.

The French government adopted the percussion system in 1840, and most of the old flintlock pistols were adapted to the new system in the normal way by removing pan and frizzen and substituting a solid nose hammer and a nipple and block at the touch-hole. When the pistol was made as a percussion weapon the nipple was mounted on the top of the barrel.

The design of the French pistols was to have a strong influence in America, for when the Revolutionary War broke out in 1775 the supply of weapons from Britain ended. An

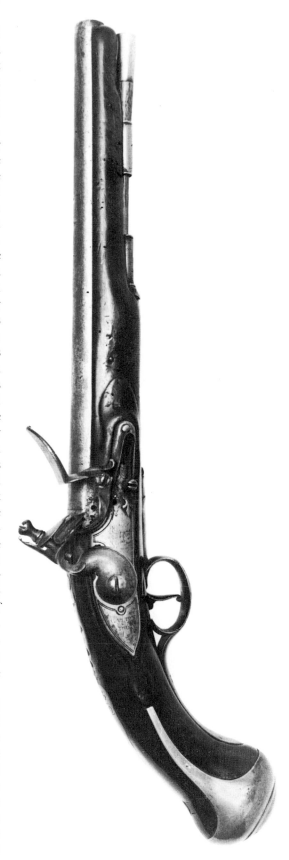

Flintlock pistol dated 1760 and made by Galton. The straps on the butt cap extend well up the butt. On the barrel is engraved 'Roy^L Drag^S', indicating that it was issued to a regiment of Royal Dragoons. G. Kellam, Broadstairs, Kent.

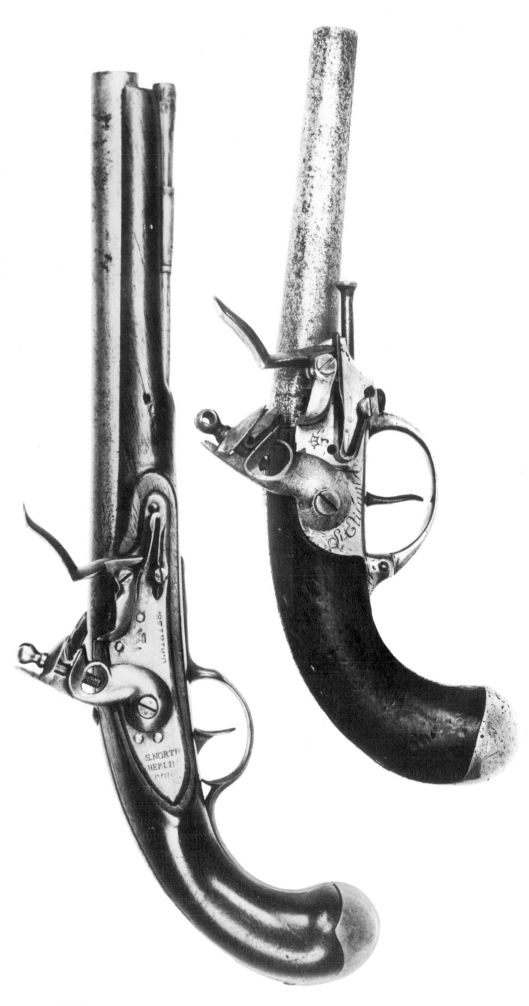

embargo had been placed on the supply of arms to American colonies before hostilities broke out, when the British Government realized how serious the situation was becoming. France came to the aid of the rebellious colonies and the weapons issued by the French were to affect the designs adopted by the United States in 1783.

When the British supply of arms ceased, local Committees of Safety were set up and one of their first tasks was to obtain pistols for the troops, and it is known that any stocks held by gunsmiths were purchased. The first native American-made pistols were those produced at the Rappahannock Forge, which had been set up by an act of the Assembly of Virginia in June 1775, near Fredericksburg. It was in operation only for some six years, for in May 1781 it had to be dismantled to avoid the attentions of a raiding party of British troops. When victory came in 1783, the United States of America decided, in the light of experience, to set up official government armouries. In 1794 Congress ordered that two Federal arsenals or armouries should be set up, one at Springfield in Massachusetts and the other at Harper's Ferry, Virginia, by the side of the Potomac River.

The output at Springfield was basically of long arms, but it was soon realized that pistols were in short supply, and in March 1799 a contract for 500 pistols was awarded to the gunmaker Simeon North of the town of Berlin, Connecticut. The weapons he produced were of such good quality that the order was increased. The pistols made by North were very similar to the French Model 1777, and the only obvious difference was

Left
French flintlock pistol Model 1777, made at St Etienne. This pistol has several unusual features: the frizzen spring is reversed and the ramrod is housed in an unusual place. G. Kellam, Broadstairs, Kent.

Far left
US military pistol by Simeon North. The lock plate carries the eagle symbol and 'U. States'. The US Navy in 1808 adopted this pattern, which is fitted with a belt hook. West Point Museum, New York.

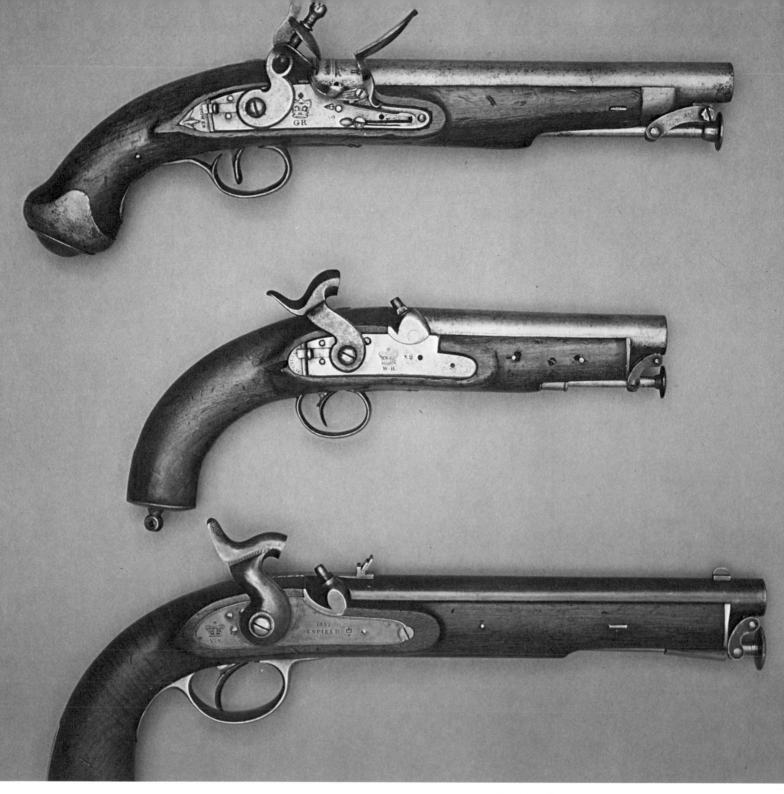

that the barrel was an inch longer at 8½ in (21 cm) over all. Most pistols carried on the barrel the letters 'U.S.', identifying them as government property. The version produced at Harper's Ferry, the Model of 1806, was, however, more in keeping with the British style of half stock, with long spurs extending upwards from the butt cap. The barrel bore the official US mark and the lock plate carried the spread eagle and the letters 'U.S.' with 'Harper's Ferry 1806'.

The United States government did not adopt the percussion cap system until 1842, and large numbers of flintlock weapons continued in use for some years after this. It was not until 1848 that the weapons held in the government armouries were inspected and orders given for their conversion to the new percussion system. The conversions used were the same as those adopted by most European countries. The first step consisted of removing the pan and frizzen and blocking up the touch-

British military pistols of the nineteenth century.
Top British cavalry flintlock pistol of *c* 1800 with swivel ramrod and ring-necked cock. The lock has a sliding-bolt safety catch and is marked 'GR' and 'Tower'.
Centre William IV flintlock pistol converted to the percussion system. The lock carries this monarch's royal cypher and is marked 'Enfield'.
Bottom Rifled percussion pistol made at Enfield during the period 1855–60. It has leaf back-sights and the lock has the cypher 'V.R.'.
Pattern Room, Royal Small Arms Factory, Enfield.

Below
Simeon North pistol, Model of 1813, used by the US Army and Navy. It has a French-type muzzle band. West Point Museum, New York.

Right
British military flintlock pistol of William IV (1830–7). The butt cap had by this time become very plain without any trace of the side arms found on earlier models. G. Kellam, Broadstairs, Kent.

hole, screwing a nipple into the barrel and substituting a solid-nosed hammer for the old flintlock cock. Later alterations consisted of screwing a lug and nipple into the touch-hole, and later still a plug was brazed on to the barrel.

Like the United States, Britain learnt as a result of war that her methods of firearms supply and production were really inadequate for the modern world. The Crimean War (1853–56) highlighted so many faults of the British Army's supply system that urgent action was required. The problem was not a new one and had been highlighted during the long period of the Napoleonic Wars (1793–1815). The heavy demands made by the armed forces of Britain and her allies during these wars, plus the strain of supplying the large number of volunteer units which had been formed to resist an anticipated invasion by Napoleon, had convinced the Board of Ordnance that their arrangements needed overhauling.

Officers were sent to Liège in Belgium to explore the possibility of procuring weapons from this source, but with little success. Attention also focused on a small armoury which had been set up in 1804 at Lewisham, to the south of London, and the armed forces were scoured for men with any skill in arms production. They were offered a rate of pay in addition to what they received from their service to work at Lewisham. From these small beginnings the factory at Lewisham increased in size and efficiency, but it was found to have limitations, particularly those imposed by the site itself. It was argued, quite rightly, that a new site should be sought which had an adequate supply of water power and was also readily accessible to all forms of transport. After much discussion it was decided that a place to the north of London, known as Enfield Lock, would be very suitable. Not only were adequate water facilities available but not far away was the gunpowder works at Waltham Abbey. Furthermore, if a new canal were built, it would be possible to transport the completed weapons from Enfield directly by boat to the Tower of London where they could be in-

Left
British percussion pistol, its lock bearing the royal cypher and the date '1845'. Pistols were generally withdrawn from British cavalry in 1838 except for the Lancers, and Sergeant Majors and Trumpeters in other cavalry regiments. The chain holds a leather-topped nipple protector which could be used for practice firing on an empty pistol. G. Kellam, Broadstairs, Kent.

Below
The lock and butt plate of the 1845 pistol; stamp marks identify it as belonging to the 16th Lancers. G. Kellam, Broadstairs, Kent.

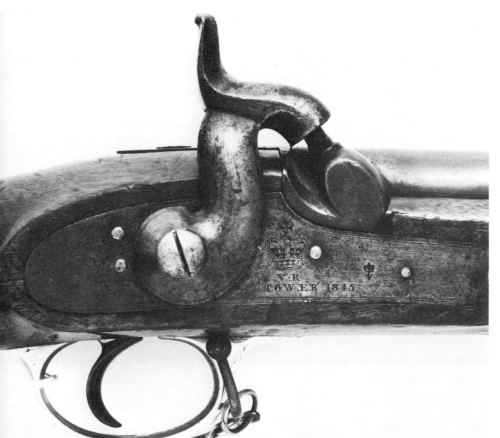

The Crimean War (1853–6) was one of the first major wars in which the revolver saw active service. Many British officers armed themselves with Colt or Adams percussion revolvers. In the episode depicted, Cornet Handley killed three of his four Cossack attackers with his revolver.

SWORD HARDENING FURNACES

PRINCIPAL BOILER HOUSE

THE GRINDERY

ANNEALING FURNA

CASTING SMALL BRASS W

LARGE ROOM

THE FORGES

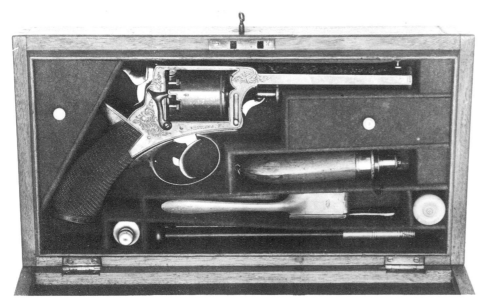

Above
Cased Tranter percussion revolver, its barrel engraved 'W.A.Wynter 33rd Regmt.'. This British weapon belonged to an ensign who during the Abyssinian War of 1867-8 helped to carry the flag into the stronghold of the king.

Top
This engraving shows various aspects of the Royal Small Arms Factory at Enfield Lock in the 1890s. Much of the machinery is driven by belts from a common power source.

spected. Land was acquired in the area, and in 1812 a Royal Engineer was despatched to begin the building of the Royal Armoury at Enfield Lock. Waterwheels were set up, and they were to provide the main source of power for the armouries for many years; steam power was introduced in 1861. Houses for the workers were built, and in 1816 the site was ready for occupation; in 1818 all facilities and work from Lewisham were transferred to Enfield. The factory for some time remained on a comparatively small scale: in 1834 it employed only 43 workmen, one storeman, a clerk and a superintendent.

At Enfield, barrels, locks and stocks were made, and a few swords. The heavy demands of the Crimean War, the first major conflict in which Britain had been engaged since 1815, showed up Enfield's limitations. Although the factory supplied some weapons, a large proportion of those required were still produced by

British military percussion pistol with rifled barrel. The stock is stamped 'Enfield' and the lock carries the royal cypher and the date '1858' over the word 'Tower'. The holster is a very rare item. G. Kellam, Broadstairs, Kent.

Above
The American Civil War (1861–5) has been described as the first modern war. This engraving is of the attack on Knoxville, Tennessee. The town was captured by Union forces in September 1863 and was besieged by Confederate troops from 16 November until 4 December.

Right
Heavy percussion pistol made for British colonial troops in 1871, long after metal cartridge weapons were in general use in most armies. It was made in Birmingham.

independent and commercial gunmakers; consequently it was decided that production at Enfield had to be stepped up.

Three army officers and the ordnance inspector of machinery went to America to examine the arms industry and its methods of production. They purchased milling machinery, woodworking machines and secured the services of Mr Burton, Master Armourer at Harper's Ferry. He came to Enfield to design new tools and to install the machinery; three Americans from the Springfield factory were also employed as foremen to teach the British workmen how to use the new machines. New buildings were set up at Enfield, and in 1857 a very new and modern small-arms factory became operational; in 1858 over 120 men were employed there. Some of the workmen had previously been employed at Colonel Colt's London factory.

The British Army flintlock pistol was to remain basically unaltered throughout its long life except in minor details. For example, the 1759 pattern with a 9-in (23-cm) barrel, introduced for the Light Dragoons, was simple with a plain butt cap, small lock and a wooden ramrod with a brass head. In 1796 it was recommended by the Board of Ordnance that the Heavy Cavalry should have only one pistol, also with a 9-in (23-cm) barrel, and, very sensibly, that the carbine and pistol should be of the same calibre. This new pistol was unusual in two respects. Firstly, it had no ramrod, it being the intention to carry this in the holster; secondly, most of them were fitted with a special lock designed by the London gunmaker Henry Nock, which had no

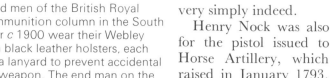

Above right
These proud men of the British Royal Artillery Ammunition column in the South African War c 1900 wear their Webley revolvers in black leather holsters, each fitted with a lanyard to prevent accidental loss of the weapon. The end man on the right wears his holster on the left; those of the others are worn on the right.

Below
This pencil sketch of a Union cavalryman by Edwin Forbes, made in September 1863, shows the characteristic position of the revolver. Since a cavalryman needed his right hand to hold the reins, the revolver was positioned to facilitate drawing with the left hand.

Below right
Cased Webley revolver, one of the most widely used of military weapons. It broke open by pressing the catch seen next to the hammer.

screws at all and could be dismantled very simply indeed.

Henry Nock was also responsible for the pistol issued to the Royal Horse Artillery, which had been raised in January 1793. They were issued with a double-barrelled pistol. One of the 18-in (45.7-cm) barrels was rifled and the pistol was fitted with a detachable stock so that, in theory, it could serve both as pistol and carbine. There were two triggers and the left-hand barrel, the rifled one, was fired with the rear trigger.

During the early part of the nineteenth century many pistols were fitted with a lock incorporating a safety catch. This was a bolt which pushed forward to engage with a slot in the rear of the cock. These pistols had a swivel ramrod which was secured permanently to the pistol. It was ingeniously designed so that the ramrod continued to be housed beneath the barrel but could be swung forward on a link to ram home the bullet and then be replaced in its housing. In 1838 the pistol was officially abolished as a cavalry weapon in the British Army, although the Lancers were allowed to keep one each and cavalry regiments retained an issue of 13 pistols for the use of various non-commissioned officers and trumpeters. These pistols were fitted with a percussion lock and were fully stocked, with a plain brass butt cap.

The introduction of the metal, centre-fire cartridge forced upon all military authorities the need to rethink their use of the pistol and revolver. In the 1860s and '70s virtually every nation set about arming its officers, some NCOs and most of its cavalry with a cartridge-loading centre-fire revolver. The Adams patent centre-fire, breech-loading revolver was adopted by the British in 1868, and many of the earlier percussion-type revolvers were converted to the centre-fire system. In 1869, 7,000 are recorded as being available for conversion, at a price of one guinea each.

The Mark I service revolver had a side-rod ejector, rather like the Colt system. In 1872 Adams claimed a patent for a swivelled ramrod which differed in that, when not required, it

was pushed home in a recess in the pin holding the cylinder in place. In 1880 the British Army changed to the revolver developed at the Small Arms Factory at Enfield. The new Enfield revolver was a .476-in (12.1-mm) centre-fire, six-chambered weapon with a $5\frac{7}{8}$-in (12.8-cm) barrel. The revolver was a self-extracting type, and when it was broken, *i.e.* unlocked at the top and the barrel assembly pushed down, the cylinder moved forward leaving the empty cases to fall out. It was a rather ugly weapon and was not popular. In July 1887 the War Department commissioned P. Webley & Son to supply 10,000 self-ejecting revolvers. These had a short, 4-in (10.2-cm) barrel and were of .442-in (11.2-mm) calibre.

According to the official *Textbook for Small Arms*, the Webley Mk I was officially adopted in August 1890, although it was not until 1892 that the Webley was officially described as supplanting the Enfield revolvers. However, this did not mean that British officers were all armed with the Webley, for Army Regulations specified that an officer might use any type of pistol he chose so long as it accepted the standard Army ammunition. The Webley revolver went through a number of models and

Top
In this picture of an encounter between a lone cowboy and a band of Indians, the artist Charles Schreyvogel clearly shows the 1873 Colt Single Action Army revolver.

Above
Revolver team of the 8th (AC) Company Royal Tank Corps. The photograph was probably taken in the 1920s or early '30s. The men are all armed with the standard British Army Webley revolver.

Right
Although the US Government Model 1911 and 1911A1 are probably the best-known of Colt's automatics, the firm has produced a range of other models.
Top Pocket Model introduced in 1903, and notable for its concealed hammer. It was .32-in (8·1-mm) calibre and held eight shots.
Bottom Smaller Pocket Model introduced in 1908 of .25-in (6.35-mm) calibre with a six-shot magazine.

Over the top! Brandishing his revolver, a British officer in World War I leads his men, who wear gas masks, to the attack. The men's attitudes suggest that the picture was specially posed.

remained in service throughout World War II. Following the trend in most countries, the British then decided to abandon the revolver and the Browning ´Hipower 9-mm self-loading pistol was adopted.

In the United States, not surprisingly, a Colt revolver became the official arm. It was the Colt Army Revolver Model of 1873, which was .45 calibre with a 7½-in (19-cm) barrel; an artillery version with a 5½-in (13.9-cm) barrel was also used. In 1911 the United States forces adopted the famous .45 Colt automatic.

On the Continent of Europe the range of revolvers was considerable although, in fact, most of them were based on two or three designs. The Austro-Hungarian Empire armed its cavalrymen with a large Gasser revolver, a rather ugly weapon with a spindly side ejector fitted beneath the barrel. Belgium and France preferred a Chamelot Delvigne (Models 1871 and 1873) as did the Italians and Swiss (Model 1872).

The big rival of Colt in America was, of course, Smith and Wesson. One of their revolvers, Model 1882, was adopted by the Turkish Army, whilst their Russian opponents in the War of 1877–78 used the Model 1878

Top
Japanese Nambu 8-mm automatic pistol;
originally adopted in 1925, it was first
issued with the large trigger guard in
1939. The grip is of mahogany.

Centre
German Dreyse eight-shot .32 automatic
first introduced in 1907. The catch at the
back is operated to free the barrel for
maintenance.

Bottom
British Webley and Scott self-loading
.455 automatic pistol adopted by the
Royal Navy in 1913 but not popular.

The Luger 1908 pistol was adopted by the German Army and several models were used. It was also available as a commercial weapon.
Top Carbine with shoulder stock and special hand grip beneath the barrel.
Bottom Artillery model with a barrel of 8 in (20.3 cm), attachable shoulder stock and snail-drum magazine.
Pattern Room, Royal Small Arms Factory, Enfield.

German Walther P38 adopted by Germany in 1939 to replace the Luger pistol. A fine, rugged, double-action weapon, it proved popular and effective.

and some Schofield, Smith and Wesson revolvers. Their Models 1874 and 1875 saw limited service with the US Army.

The pre-requisites of all service weapons were reliability, accuracy and rugged construction, and certainly most of the revolvers had a good claim to these qualities. However, during this century there has been a gradual conversion from revolvers to automatics. Germany favoured the Luger in World War I, and in 1938 it abandoned it to adopt the Walther P38. This trend has continued until the present, and today the vast majority of armies equip their appropriate personnel with automatic pistols. Probably the most common is the

Browning Hipower which is used by, among others, the armed forces of Argentina, Australia, Bangladesh, Belgium, Canada, Chile, India, Ireland, Jamaica, Malawi, Malaysia, Netherlands, New Zealand, Oman, Panama, Singapore, Taiwan, United Kingdom and Venezuela.

Those countries which do not favour the Hipower generally accept that 9 mm is the optimum calibre, although the United States and one or two of the countries largely supplied by her retain their faith in the Colt 1911 A1 with its heavy .45-calibre bullet. The Czechs and the Poles have taken firepower one step further, and both use their machine pistol to arm their troops.

Despite many changes in weapons technology, the British Army retained the revolver for its officers and some senior NCOs. Here men of the Leicestershire Regiment, the old 17th Foot, attack German paratroops landing in Crete in May 1941.

Above
Browning Hipower 9-mm automatic. This model is fitted with adjustable sights although the majority of military weapons have fixed sights. It has a large magazine with a capacity of 13 rounds.

Below
Walther PPK 9-mm pistol with Nazi and Third Reich butt decoration incorporating the swastika and eagle. This double-action automatic was carried by numbers of Nazi officers.

Far right, above
Although the Walther P38 was officially adopted as the standard German Army pistol, the 1908 Luger continued to be used by many troops. This photograph from the German propaganda magazine *Signal* shows a Luger being used on the Eastern Front in July 1942.

Far right, below
It has been common policy in the past to arm officers with pistols and revolvers rather than rifles. Here the leader of a German group waits for the order to attack on the Eastern Front, his pistol raised and ready.

Although this is not strictly a military use, the police forces of many countries are being forced, often reluctantly, to consider the question of arming their members. It is interesting to note that they, in contrast to the armies, feel that the revolver will give them better results. Most American and British police forces arm their men with revolvers. There is much discussion as to the optimum calibre for police work, and most use the .38 Special cartridge whose bullet is actually .357 in (9.1 mm) in diameter. In countries such as Britain, where concealment of the weapon is considered desirable, the tendency is to use short-barrelled weapons, mainly 2 in (50.8 mm), although this inevitably leads to a lowering of standards of accurate shooting. Some American forces do favour the automatic and there is a growing demand by some forces for the reintroduction of heavy-calibre weapons such as the Colt .45 1911 A1.

Despite the impression given by films and television, it is very difficult to shoot a handgun with any degree of accuracy, and there is mounting support for the abandonment of revolvers and automatics. Some military thinkers favour the use of machine pistols, whilst others feel that the arming of officers with a handgun is outdated, and that they should carry the same weapons as their men.

INDEX

Figures in italics refer to illustrations.